MAT
POWER
PRACTICE

MAT
POWER
PRACTICE

COMPLETE
PREPARATION FOR
THE MILLER
ANALOGIES TEST

LEARNINGEXPRESS®

NEW YORK

Library of Congress Cataloging-in-Publication Data
MAT power practice. — 1st ed.
    p. cm.
 ISBN-13: 978-1-57685-774-8 (pbk. : alk. paper)
 ISBN-10: 1-57685-774-3 (pbk. : alk. paper)
 1. Miller analogies test—Study guides. I. LearningExpress (Organization)
 LB2367.6.M39 2011
 378.1'662—dc21
                        2010034696

Printed in the United States of America

9 8 7 6 5 4 3 2 1

First Edition

ISBN-13: 978-1-57685-774-8
ISBN-10: 1-57685-774-3

For more information or to place an order, contact LearningExpress at:
    2 Rector Street
    26th Floor
    New York, NY 10006

Or visit us at:
    www.learnatest.com

Editor: Marco A. Annunziata
Production Editor: Eric Titner
Editorial Assistant: Miranda Pennington

CONTENTS ▶

About *MAT: Power Practice*..1

CHAPTER 1:   MAT Overview 3

CHAPTER 2:   The LearningExpress Test Preparation System 9

CHAPTER 3:   MAT Practice Test 1 27

CHAPTER 4:   MAT Practice Test 2 47

CHAPTER 5:   MAT Practice Test 3 67

CHAPTER 6:   MAT Practice Test 4 87

CHAPTER 7:   MAT Practice Test 5 107

CHAPTER 8:   MAT Practice Test 6 127

CHAPTER 9:   MAT Practice Test 7 147

CHAPTER 10: MAT Practice Test 8 167

CHAPTER 11: MAT Practice Test 9 187

CHAPTER 12: MAT Practice Test 10 207

CHAPTER 13: MAT Practice Test 11 227

CONTRIBUTORS ▶

Felice Primeau Devine is a freelance writer and editor who specializes in content development for test preparation and career development books. She began her career working in editorial services for a college textbook publisher, and later held marketing and editorial positions for several different publishers. She has a BA in English Literature from Clark University in Worcester, MA.

Judith Hicks was a classroom teacher in Compton, California, and has been a teacher and educator in the U.S. and abroad for nine years. She holds a Reading Specialist credential, and has contributed to a variety of textbook and curriculum projects. She is currently pursuing a PhD in Education at Stanford University.

Kathryn Lavelle, MA, is a Professor of Mathematics at Westchester Community College in Valhalla, New York. She has an MA in Mathematics Education from Lehman College, and has taught mathematics for 30 years.

Stephen A. Reiss, MBA, is the founder and owner of the Math Magician and the Reiss SAT Seminars, test preparation centers in San Diego. Reiss has authored and co-authored several test preparation books, and is a member of Mensa.

Mike Segretto has been an assessment writer for ten years, while also creating a wide assortment of informational and entertainment material for various websites and print publications. He holds a degree in film and English from Hofstra University.

ABOUT MAT: POWER PRACTICE ▶

LearningExpress understands the importance of achieving a top score on your Miller Analogies Test (MAT) and we strive to publish the most authentic and comprehensive MAT test preparation materials available today. Practice does indeed make perfect, and that's why we've created this book, composed of 11 full-length MAT practice exams complete with detailed answer explanations—it offers you all the extra practice you need to get a great score. Whether used on its own or as a powerful companion to other MAT preparation titles, *MAT Power Practice* is the key to a top score and a brighter future!

1 ▶ MAT Overview

This chapter is designed to give you a solid overview of the Miller Analogies Test—including tips for earning a great score!

What is the MAT?

The Miller Analogies Test, or MAT, is a 60-minute test consisting of 120 analogy questions that is required for entrance into many graduate school programs. You've probably answered analogy questions on tests you've taken in the past. An analogy question tests your ability to recognize relationships between sets of items. For example:

Wood : Carve :: Clay : Mold

This analogy shows the relationship between a material and the way it is shaped. A sculptor shapes *wood* by *carving* it and shapes *clay* by *molding* it.

There are several different content areas tested on the MAT, including math, history, science, literature, vocabulary, fine arts, general knowledge, and anagrams. The following pages will explain what is covered in each content area, the best strategies for solving MAT analogies, how the test is scored, and when and where to take it. Taking a test can be stressful, but the MAT is a lot like taking a trivia challenge or solving a puzzle. By the time you finish *MAT: Power Practice*, you may decide that taking the MAT is actually fun!

What Content Areas are Tested on the MAT?

The content areas on the MAT range from subjects you probably studied in high school to subjects that might seem more like they were pulled from a trivia game. The content areas are discussed in a bit more depth here:

General Knowledge

General knowledge includes questions about culture, the business world, work, and basic life experiences. Here's a sample general knowledge question:

> Carpenter : Wrench :: Baker : (**a.** Saw **b.** Spatula **c.** Plate **d.** Chef)

The answer is **b.** A wrench is a tool used by a carpenter. A spatula is a tool used by a baker.

Humanities

Humanities includes questions about world history, fine art, literature, philosophy, religion, and music. Here's a sample humanities question:

> Aesop : Grimm :: (**a.** Fable **b.** Legend **c.** Myth **d.** Parable) : Fairy Tale

The answer is **a.** Aesop is a famous writer of fables. The Brothers Grimm were famous writers of fairy tales.

Mathematics

Mathematics includes questions about numbers, computation, and quantities. Here's a sample mathematics question:

> Inch : Foot :: Dozen : (**a.** 12 **b.** Yard **c.** 36 **d.** Gross)

The answer is **d.** There are 12 inches in 1 foot and there are 12 dozen in 1 gross

Language

Language includes questions about vocabulary, word meanings, grammar, and usage. Here's a sample language question:

> Massive : (**a.** Large **b.** Miniscule **c.** Size **d.** Short) :: Huge : Tiny

The answer is **b.** Massive is a synonym of huge and miniscule is a synonym of tiny.

Natural Sciences

Natural Sciences includes questions about biology, chemistry, physics, and ecology. Here's a sample natural sciences question:

> Botanists : Plants :: Ichthyologist : (**a.** Metals **b.** Fish **c.** Detritus **d.** Viruses)

The answer is **b.** A botanist studies plants; an ichthyologist studies fish.

Social Sciences

Social Sciences includes questions about psychology, sociology, economics, political science, and anthropology. Here's a sample social sciences question:

> Cent : Dollar :: (**a.** Pound **b.** Franc **c.** Cent **d.** Mark) : Euro

The answer is **c.** In currency, a cent is $\frac{1}{100}$th of both a dollar and a euro.

What Kind of Relationship Types are on the MAT?

Within each content area, you will also encounter the following four relationship types.

Semantic Relationships

Semantic relationships test your ability to recognize meaning, definition, synonyms, antonyms, contrast, degree, intensity, word parts, and expressions. Here's a sample semantic question from the humanities content area:

(**a.** Discord **b.** Rhythm **c.** Melodious **d.** Harmony) : Melody :: Overtone : Tune

The answer is **d.** Harmony and overtone are synonyms for musical tones that are higher in frequency than the fundamental tone. Melody and tune are synonyms for the fundamental tones of a musical piece.

Classification Relationships

Classification relationships test your ability to recognize hierarchy, category, membership, and whole/part relationships. Here's a sample classification question from the natural sciences content area:

Wombat : Marsupial :: (**a.** Platypus **b.** Kangaroo **c.** Ostrich **d.** Turtle) : Monotreme

The answer is **a.** A wombat is classified as a marsupial—a mammal with a pouch and a yolk sac. A platypus is a monotreme—a mammal that lays eggs.

Association Relationships

Association relationships test your ability to recognize object/characteristic relationships, order, sequence, transformation, agent/object relationships, creator/creation relationships, function, and purpose. Here's a sample association question from the general knowledge content area.

Cable car : (**a.** Taxi **b.** Subway **c.** Monorail **d.** Gondola) :: San Francisco : Venice

The answer is **d.** Cable cars are forms of public transportation associated with San Francisco, California. Gondolas are forms of public transformation associated with Venice, Italy.

Logical/Mathematical Relationships

Logical/Mathematical relationships test your ability to recognize mathematical equivalence, multiples, negation, and letter or sound patterns. Here's a sample association question from the mathematics content area:

XII : LX :: CC : (**a.** D **b.** DC **c.** M **d.** MM)

The answer is **c.** In Roman Numerals, LX (60) is five times > XII (12) and M (1,000) is five times > CC (200).

How Can I Conquer the MAT?

The MAT may seem unusual, but there are some pretty simple strategies for conquering it. One thing you should know is that the test gets harder as it continues. The 120 questions are organized in three similarly sized levels of difficulty. That means the first 40 or so questions are the easiest ones, the next 40 are medium difficulty, and the final 40 are the hardest. But don't be intimidated by those final 40. Some of them may be perfectly suited to your personal knowledge. You may know nothing about philosophy, so those questions might be particularly challenging, but you might be a math whiz, so you'll gain points by mastering these analogies.

You should also be aware that the questions are structured in two ways. The first structure is:

A : A :: B : B

For A : A :: B : B questions, the relationship exists between the first two items and the second two items in the analogy.

For example:

Watch : (**a.** Face **b.** Hand **c.** Appliance **d.** Program) :: Television : Screen

The answer to this question is **a.** The face is the part of the watch that displays its information. The screen is the part of a television that displays its information. So the relationships are between the two items in the first half of the analogy (Watch and Face) and the two items in the second half (Television and Screen). The other structure is:

A : B :: A : B

For A : B :: A : B questions, the relationship exists between the first items in both halves of the analogy and the second items in both halves of the analogy. For example:

Clinton : Eisenhower :: Gore : (**a.** Truman **b.** Agnew **c.** Goldwater **d.** Nixon)

The answer to this question is **d.** Al Gore was Vice President under Bill Clinton and Richard Nixon was Vice President under Dwight Eisenhower. So the relationships exist between the first items in both halves of the analogy (Clinton and Gore) and the second items in both halves of the analogy (Eisenhower and Nixon).

Five Tips for Mastering the MAT

Now that you know how the MAT analogies are organized, let's take a look at five tips that will help you choose your answers wisely and make the most of the 60 minutes you have to answer them.

Faster is Better

Answering 120 questions in 60 minutes means you have roughly 30 seconds to figure out each answer. That isn't much time. So, if you're having trouble with a question, move on. When you finish the easiest questions, return to the harder ones. You don't want to waste your time trying to figure out a question you may or may not get right when there are a bunch of easier ones waiting for you.

Process of Elimination

A key to performing well on any multiple-choice test is using the process of elimination. Some answer choices may be obviously incorrect. Cross those out and concentrate on the ones that are more plausible. The MAT doesn't penalize you for incorrect answers, so narrowing down your choices increases your odds of answering correctly and earning credit for the question.

Spot the Relationship

Before selecting your answer, be sure you understand the structural relationship of each question. Are you dealing with an A : A :: B : B question, or is an A : B :: A : B one on the agenda? Understanding the relationship in the question will help you figure out the correct answer.

Make an Assumption

Even before you examine the answer choices, think of the word you'd choose to complete the analogy. Then check the answer choices for the one that best matches your assumption. If you can't find such an answer choice, rethink the relationship in the analogy and try again.

Be Prepared

We're not just talking about bringing a pencil here. Your preparation should, of course, include a good deal of studying, but you should also come to the test center well rested and comfortably dressed. Even though you may have butterflies in your stomach before taking the test, be sure to eat a good breakfast first. It will keep you fueled mentally and physically.

How About Some Samples?

Now that you have a basic understanding of the MAT test and how to answer its 120 questions, try answering the following 12 samples. Then check your answers on the following page.

1. Prime : (**a.** 8 **b.** 9 **c.** 11 **d.** 12) :: Composite : 10

2. (**a.** Flat **b.** Interesting **c.** Simplistic **d.** Instructions) : Complex :: Basic : Intricate

3. Mare : Stallion :: Doe : (**a.** Bull **b.** Buck **c.** Male **d.** Jack)

4. Bond : Debt :: Stock : (**a.** Option **b.** Equity **c.** Class **d.** Leverage)

5. Global Warming : Flooding :: Low Pressure Systems : (**a.** Clear Skies **b.** Calm **c.** Cyclones **d.** Earthquakes)

6. Brackets : (**a.** Comma **b.** Period **c.** Em dash **d.** Word) :: Parentheses : Question Mark

7. Neurosurgeon : Cobbler :: Operation : (**a.** Apple **b.** Shoe **c.** Repair **d.** Instruct)

8. *Player Piano* : Vonnegut :: *Seize the Day* : (**a.** Heller **b.** Herzog **c.** Burgess **d.** Bellow)

9. Blood : Circulatory :: (**a.** Bones **b.** Liver **c.** Skin **d.** Carpuscles) : Integumentary

10. LX : XC :: C : (**a.** CX **b.** CL **c.** CC **d.** CM)

11. Rappaccini's Daughter : Samson :: (**a.** Operetta **b.** Elegy **c.** Libretto **d.** Opera) : Oratorio

12. Lorenz : Geese :: Goodall : (**a.** Chimps **b.** Antelopes **c.** Peacocks **d.** Meerkats)

1. The answer is **c.** 11 is a prime number, the only divisors are 1 and 11; 10 is a composite number and has more divisors than 1 and 10.

2. The answer is **c.** Simplistic and basic are synonyms; complex and intricate are synonyms.

3. The answer is **b.** A mare is a female horse; a stallion is a male horse. A doe is a female deer; a buck is a male deer.

4. The answer is **b.** Both bonds and stocks are certificates issued by institutions – Bonds are debt certificates and stocks are equity certificates.

5. The answer is **c.** Global warming can cause coastal flooding; low pressure systems can cause cyclones.

6. The answer is **b.** Brackets and parentheses are both used to enclose additional information included within a sentence. A period and a question mark are used to conclude a sentence.

7. The answer is **c.** A neurosurgeon performs operations. A cobbler performs repairs.

8. The answer is **d.** *Player Piano* is a 1952 novel by writer Kurt Vonnegut. *Seize the Day* is a 1956 novel by Saul Bellow.

9. The answer is **c.** The circulatory system is mostly comprised of blood; the integumentary system is mostly comprised of skin.

10. The answer is **b.** LX (60) times $1\frac{1}{2}$ equals XC (90); C (100) times $1\frac{1}{2}$ equals CL (150)

11. The answer is **d.** *Rappaccini's Daughter* is an opera by Mexican composer Daniel Catán. *Samson* is an oratorio by German composer George Handel.

12. The answer is **a.** Konrad Lorenz studied geese; Jane Goodall studied chimps.

How is the MAT Scored?

Within a couple of weeks after you take the MAT you will receive your score report in the mail. This score report will include a scaled score between 200 and 600, your percentile rank in your intended graduate school major, and your percentile rank among everyone else who has taken the MAT. Both percentile ranks range from 1 to 99. Remember that your score is based on the number of questions you answered correctly. You are *not* penalized for incorrect answers. Furthermore, your percentile rank among all test takers won't affect you. The numbers that matter are your percentile rank in your intended graduate school major and your percentile rank compared to others applying to the same school and program as you. You can find out the latter score, as well as how much the MAT will affect your admission, by calling the admissions office of the school to which you are applying.

What is the Non-Score Option?

After you take the MAT you may choose the "non score" option. This means your test will not be scored, you won't receive a score report, and you may take the test again for free.

Where and When Can I Take the MAT?

The MAT is administered all year long at more than 500 Controlled Test Centers (CTCs) throughout the United States, Canada, and overseas. Depending on your CTC, you may be administered a written or computer-based test. Most locations only offer one or the other, though a few offer a choice. You can find the locations and phone numbers of each CTC on the official MAT website, **www.MillerAnalogies.com**, by clicking on the "Find a MAT Testing Center" link. The site also contains details about fees, disability accommodations, optional services, scoring information, frequently asked questions, and other essential information for test takers, including an official Study Guide and candidate bulletin.

The LearningExpress Test Preparation System

CHAPTER OVERVIEW

Taking any written exam, including the MAT, can be tough. It demands a lot of preparation if you want to achieve a top score. The LearningExpress Test Preparation System, developed exclusively for LearningExpress by leading test experts, gives you the discipline you need to be successful!

The LearningExpress Test Preparation System

Your future academic career may depend on you getting a high score on this test, and there are all sorts of pitfalls that can keep you from doing your best. Here are some of the obstacles that can stand in the way of your success:

- being unfamiliar with the format of the exam
- being paralyzed by test anxiety
- leaving your preparation to the last minute, or not preparing at all
- not knowing vital test-taking skills: how to pace yourself through the exam, how to use the process of elimination, and when to guess
- not being in top mental and physical shape
- messing up on exam day by having to work on an empty stomach or shivering through the exam because the room is cold

What's the common denominator in all these test-taking pitfalls? One word: *control*. Who's in control, you or the exam? The LearningExpress Test Preparation System puts you in control. In just nine easy-to-follow steps, you will learn everything you need to know to make sure that you are in charge of your preparation and your performance on the exam. Other test takers may let the exam get the better of them; other test takers may be unprepared or out of shape, but not you. After completing this chapter, you will have taken all the steps you need to get a high score on the MAT.

Here's how the LearningExpress Test Preparation System works: nine easy steps lead you through everything you need to know and do to get ready for this exam. Each of the steps listed below, and on the following pages, includes both reading about the step and one or more activities. It's important that you do the activities along with the reading, or you won't be getting the full benefit of the system. Each step tells you approximately how much time that step will take you to complete.

Step 1. Get Information (30 minutes)

Step 2. Conquer Test Anxiety (20 minutes)

Step 3. Make a Plan (50 minutes)

Step 4. Learn to Manage Your Time (10 minutes)

Step 5. Learn to Use the Process of Elimination (20 minutes)

Step 6. Know When to Guess (20 minutes)

Step 7. Reach Your Peak Performance Zone (10 minutes)

Step 8. Get Your Act Together (10 minutes)

Step 9. Do It! (10 minutes)

Total time for complete system (180 minutes—3 hours)

We estimate that working through the entire system will take you approximately three hours. It's perfectly okay if you work at a faster or slower pace. If you can take a whole afternoon or evening, you can work through the entire LearningExpress Test Preparation System in one sitting. Otherwise, you can break it up, and do just one or two steps a day over the next several days. It's up to you—remember, you are in control.

Step 1: Get Information

Time to complete: 30 minutes

Activities: Research the MAT exam

Knowledge is power. The first step in the LearningExpress Test Preparation System is finding out everything you can about the MAT. The more details you can find out about the exam, the more efficiently you will be able to study. Here's a list of some things you might want to find out about your exam:

- What skills are tested?
- How many sections are on the exam?

- How many questions are in each section?
- Are the questions ordered from easy to hard, or is the sequence random?
- How much time is allotted for each section?
- Are there breaks between sections?
- What is the passing score, and how many questions do you have to answer right in order to get that score?
- Does a higher score give you any advantages?
- How is the exam scored, and is there a penalty for wrong answers?
- Are you permitted to go back to a prior section or move on to the next section if you finish early?
- Can you write in the exam booklet, or will you be given scratch paper?
- What should you bring with you on exam day?

Step 2: Conquer Test Anxiety

Time to complete: 20 minutes
Activity: Take the Test Anxiety Quiz (page 13)
Having complete information about the exam is the first step in getting control of it. Next, you have to overcome one of the biggest obstacles to test success: test anxiety. Test anxiety can not only impair your performance on the exam itself, but it can even prevent you from preparing properly. In Step 2, you will learn stress management techniques that will help you succeed on your exam. Learn these strategies now, and practice them as you work through the questions in this book, so they'll be second nature to you by exam day.

Combating Test Anxiety

The first thing you need to know is that a little test anxiety is a good thing. Everyone gets nervous before a big exam—and if that nervousness motivates you to prepare thoroughly, so much the better. On page 13 is the Test Anxiety Quiz. Stop here and answer the questions on that page to find out whether your level of test anxiety is something you should worry about.

Stress Management before the Exam

If you feel your level of anxiety is getting the best of you in the weeks before the exam, here is what you need to do to bring the level down again:

- Get prepared. There's nothing like knowing what to expect and being prepared for it to put you in control of test anxiety. That's why you're reading this book. Use it faithfully, and remind yourself that you're better prepared than most of the people taking the exam.
- Practice self-confidence. A positive attitude is a great way to combat test anxiety. This is no time to be humble or shy. Stand in front of the mirror and say to your reflection, "I'm prepared. I'm full of self-confidence. I'm going to ace this exam. I know I can do it." Say it into a recorder, and play it back once a day. If you hear it often enough, you will believe it.
- Fight negative messages. Every time someone starts telling you how hard the exam is or how it's almost

impossible to get a high score, start telling them your self-confidence messages mentioned previously. If the someone with the negative messages is you—telling yourself you don't do well on exams, that you just can't do this—don't listen. Turn on your recorder and listen to your self-confidence messages.

■ Visualize. Imagine yourself reporting for duty on your first day of dental assisting. Think of yourself wearing your uniform with pride and learning skills you will use for the rest of your life. Visualizing success can help make it happen—and it reminds you of why you're doing all this work to prepare for the exam.

■ Exercise. Physical activity helps calm down your body and focus your mind. Besides, being in good physical shape can actually help you do well on the exam. Go for a run, lift weights, go swimming—and do it regularly.

Stress Management on Exam Day

There are several ways you can bring down your level of test stress and anxiety on exam day. They'll work best if you practice them in the weeks before the exam, so you know which ones work best for you.

■ Deep breathing. Take a deep breath while you count to five. Hold it for a count of one, and then let it out on a count of five. Repeat several times.

■ Move your body. Try rolling your head in a circle. Rotate your shoulders. Shake your hands from the wrist. Many people find these movements very relaxing.

■ Visualize again. Think of the place where you are most relaxed: lying on the beach in the sun, walking through the park, or whatever relaxes you. Now, close your eyes and imagine you're actually there. If you practice in advance, you will find that you need only a few seconds of this exercise to experience a significant increase in your sense of well-being.

Stress Management during the Exam

When anxiety threatens to overwhelm you during the exam, there are still things you can do to manage your stress level:

■ Repeat your self-confidence messages. You should have them memorized by now. Say them quietly to yourself, and believe them!

■ Visualize one more time. This time, visualize yourself moving smoothly and quickly through the exam, answering every question correctly and finishing just before time is up. Like most visualization techniques, this one works best if you've practiced it ahead of time.

■ Find an easy question. Skim over the test until you find an easy question, and answer it. Getting even one circle filled in gets you into the test-taking groove.

■ Take a mental break. Everyone loses concentration once in a while during a long exam. It's normal, so you shouldn't worry about it. Instead, accept what has happened. Say to yourself, "Hey, I lost it there for a minute. My brain is taking a break." Put down your pencil, close your eyes, and do some deep breathing for a few seconds. Then, you're ready to go back to work. Try these techniques ahead of time, and see if they work for you!

Test Anxiety Quiz

You need to worry about test anxiety only if it is extreme enough to impair your performance. The following questionnaire will provide a diagnosis of your level of test anxiety. In the blank before each statement, write the number that most accurately describes your experience.

0 = Never
1 = Once or twice
2 = Sometimes
3 = Often

___ I have gotten so nervous before an exam that I simply put down the books and didn't study for it.

___ I have experienced disabling physical symptoms such as vomiting and severe headaches because I was nervous about an exam.

___ I have simply not showed up for an exam because I was scared to take it.

___ I have experienced dizziness and disorientation while taking an exam.

___ I have had trouble filling in the little circles because my hands were shaking too hard.

___ I have failed an exam because I was too nervous to complete it.

___ **Total: add up the numbers in the blanks above.**

Understanding Your Test Stress Scores

Here are the steps you should take, depending on your score.

- **Below 3:** Your level of test anxiety is nothing to worry about. It's probably just enough to give you that little extra edge.
- **Between 3 and 6:** Your test anxiety may be enough to impair your performance, and you should practice the stress-management techniques listed in this section to try to bring your test anxiety down to manageable levels.
- **Above 6:** Your level of test anxiety is a serious concern. In addition to practicing the stress-management techniques listed in this section, you may want to seek additional, personal help. Call your local high school or community college and ask for the academic counselor. Tell the counselor that you have a level of test anxiety that sometimes keeps you from being able to take the exam. The counselor may be willing to help you or may suggest someone else who you should talk to.

Step 3: Make a Plan

Time to complete: 50 minutes

Activity: Construct a study plan

Many people perform poorly on exams because they forget to make a study schedule. The most important thing you can do to better prepare yourself for the MAT is to create a study plan or schedule. Spending hours the day before the exam poring over sample test questions not only raises your level of anxiety, but it is also not a substitute for careful preparation and practice over time.

Even more important than making a plan is making a commitment. You can't review everything in one night. You have to set aside some time every day for study and practice. Try to set aside at least 20 minutes a day. Twenty minutes daily will do you more good than two hours crammed into a Saturday.

If you have months before the exam, you're lucky. Don't put off your study until the week before the exam. Start now. Even ten minutes a day, with half an hour or more on weekends, can make a big difference in your score.

Step 4: Learn to Manage Your Time

Time to complete: 10 minutes to read, many hours of practice

Activities: Practice these strategies as you take the sample exams

Once you are familiar and comfortable with the format of the MAT, you can work on managing your time on the exam. Keep the following things in mind:

- Listen carefully to directions. By the time you get to the exam, you should know how the test works, but listen just in case something has changed.
- Pace yourself. Glance at your watch every few minutes, and compare the time to how far you've gotten in the section. Leave some extra time for review, so that when one-quarter of the time has elapsed, you should be more than a quarter of the way through the section, and so on. If you're falling behind, pick up the pace.
- Keep moving. Don't spend too much time on one question. If you don't know the answer, skip the question and move on. Circle the number of the question in your test booklet in case you have time to come back to it later.
- Keep track of your place on the answer sheet. If you skip a question, make sure you skip on the answer sheet, too. Check yourself every five to ten questions to make sure that the question number and the answer sheet number match.
- Don't rush. You should keep moving, although rushing won't help. Try to keep calm and work methodically and quickly.

Step 5: Learn to Use the Process of Elimination

Time to complete: 20 minutes

Activity: Complete worksheet on Using the Process of Elimination (pages 24–25)

After time management, the next most important tool for taking control of your exam is using the process of elimination wisely. It's standard test-taking wisdom that you should always read all of the answer choices before you choose your answer. This helps you find the right answer by eliminating wrong answer choices. And, sure enough, that standard wisdom applies to this exam, too.

Let's say you're facing a question that goes like this:

13. "Biology uses a *binomial* system of classification." In this sentence, the word *binomial* most nearly means
   a. understanding the law.
   b. having two names.
   c. scientifically sound.
   d. having a double meaning.

If you happen to know what *binomial* means, you don't need to use the process of elimination, but let's assume that you don't. So, you look at the answer choices. "Understanding the law" sure doesn't sound very likely for something having to do with biology. So, you eliminate choice **a**—and now you only have three answer choices to deal with. Mark an **X** next to choice **a** so you never have to read it again.

Move on to the other answer choices.

If you know that the prefix *bi* - means *two*, as in *bicycle*, you will flag answer **b** as a possible answer. Make a check mark beside it, meaning "good answer, I might use this one."

Choice **c**, "scientifically sound," is a possibility. At least it's about science, not law. It could work here, though, when you think about it, having a "scientifically sound" classification system in a scientific field is kind of redundant.

You remember the *bi-* in *binomial*, and probably continue to like answer **b** better. But you're not sure, so you put a question mark next to **c**, meaning "well, maybe." Now, look at choice **d**, "having a double meaning." You're still keeping in mind that *bi* - means *two*, so this one looks possible at first. But then you look again at the sentence the word belongs in, and you think, "Why would biology want a system of classification that has two meanings? That wouldn't work very well!" If you're really taken with the idea that *bi-* means *two*, you might put a question mark here. But if you're feeling a little more confident, you will put an **X**. You've already got a better answer picked out.

Now, your question looks like this:

13. "Biology uses a *binomial* system of classification." In this sentence, the word *binomial* most nearly means
   ✗ **a.** understanding the law.
   ✓ **b.** having two names.
   ? **c.** scientifically sound.
   ? **d.** having a double meaning.

You have only one check mark, for a good answer. If you're pressed for time, you should simply mark answer **b** on your answer sheet. If you've got the time to be extra careful, you could compare your check mark answer to your question mark answers to make sure that it's better. (It is: the *binomial* system in biology is the one that gives a two-part genus and species name like homo sapiens.)

It's good to have a system for marking good, bad, and maybe answers. We recommend using this one:

   ✗ = bad
   ✓ = good
   ? = maybe

If you don't like these marks, devise your own system. Just make sure you do it long before exam day—while you're working through the practice exams in this book—so you won't have to worry about it during the exam. Even when you think you're absolutely clueless about a question, you can often use the process of elimination to get rid of at least one answer choice. If so, you're better prepared to make an educated guess, as you will see in Step 6.

More often, the process of elimination allows you to get down to only two possibly right answers. Then you're in a strong position to guess. And sometimes, even though you don't know the right answer, you find it simply by getting rid of the wrong ones, as you did in the example above.

Try using your process of elimination on the questions in the worksheet Using the Process of Elimination beginning on the next page. The answer explanations there show one possible way you might use the process to arrive at the right answer. The process of elimination is your tool for the next step, which is knowing when to guess.

Using the Process of Elimination

Use the process of elimination to answer the following questions.

1. Ilsa is as old as Meghan will be in five years. The difference between Ed's age and Meghan's age is twice the difference between Ilsa's age and Meghan's age. Ed is 29. How old is Ilsa?
- a. 4
- b. 10
- c. 19
- d. 24

2. "All drivers of commercial vehicles must carry a valid commercial driver's license whenever operating a commercial vehicle." According to this sentence, which of the following people need **NOT** carry a commercial driver's license?
- a. a truck driver idling his engine while waiting to be directed to a loading dock
- b. a bus operator backing her bus out of the way of another bus in the bus lot
- c. a taxi driver driving his personal car to the grocery store
- d. a limousine driver taking the limousine to her home after dropping off her last passenger of the evening

3. What has smoking been linked to?

    a. increased risk of stroke and heart attack

    b. all forms of respiratory disease

    c. increasing mortality rates over the past ten years

    d. juvenile delinquency

4. Which of the following words is spelled correctly?

    a. incorrigible

    b. outragous

    c. domestickated

    d. understandible

Answers

Here are the answers, as well as some suggestions as to how you might have used the process of elimination to find them.

1. d. You should have eliminated answer **a** right off the bat. Ilsa can't be four years old if Meghan is going to be Ilsa's age in five years. The best way to eliminate other answer choices is to try plugging them in to the information given in the problem.

    For instance, for answer **b**, if Ilsa is 10, then Meghan must be 5. The difference in their ages is 5. The difference between Ed's age, 29, and Meghan's age, 5, is 24. Is 24 two times 5? No. Then answer **b** is wrong. You could eliminate answer **c** in the same way and be left with answer **d**.

2. c. Note the word not in the question, and go through the answers one by one. Is the truck driver in choice **a** "operating a commercial vehicle"? Yes, idling counts as "operating," so he needs to have a commercial driver's license. Likewise, the bus operator in answer **b** is operating a commercial vehicle; the question doesn't say the operator has to be on the street. The limo driver in **d** is operating a commercial vehicle, even if it doesn't have a passenger in it. However, the cabbie in answer **c** is not operating a commercial vehicle, but his own private car.

3. a. You could eliminate answer **b** simply because of the presence of the word "all." Such absolutes hardly ever appear in correct answer choices. Choice **c** looks attractive until you think a little about what you know—aren't fewer people smoking these days, rather than more? So how could smoking be responsible for a higher mortality rate? (If you didn't know that mortality rate means the rate at which people die, you might keep this choice as a possibility, but you'd still be able to eliminate two answers and have only two to choose from.) And choice **d** is plain silly, so you could eliminate that one, too. And you're left with the correct choice, **a**.

4. a. How you used the process of elimination here depends on which words you recognized as being spelled incorrectly. If you knew that the correct spellings were outrageous, domesticated, and understandable, then you were home free. Surely you knew that at least one of those words was misspelled!

Step 6: Know When to Guess

Time to complete: 20 minutes
Activity: Complete Worksheet on Your Guessing Ability (page 19)
Armed with the process of elimination, you're ready to take control of one of the big questions in test-taking: Should I guess? The first and main answer is yes. Unless the exam has a so-called "guessing penalty," you have nothing to lose and everything to gain from guessing. The more complicated answer depends both on the exam and on you—your personality and your "guessing intuition."

How the Guessing Penalty Works

A guessing penalty really only works against random guessing—filling in the little circles to make a nice pattern on your answer sheet. If you can eliminate one or more answer choices, as outlined above, you're better off taking a guess than leaving the answer blank, even on the sections that have a penalty.

Depending on the number of answer choices in a given exam, some proportion of the number of questions you get wrong is subtracted from the total number of questions you got right. For instance, if there are four answer choices, typically the guessing penalty is one-third of your wrong answers. Suppose you took an exam of 100 questions. You answered 88 of them right and 12 wrong. If there's no guessing penalty, your score is simply 88. But if there's a one-third point guessing penalty, the scorers take your 12 wrong answers and divide by three to come up with four. Then they subtract that four from your correct answer score of 88 to leave you with a score of 84. Thus, you would have been better off if you had simply not answered those 12 questions. Then your total score would still be 88 because there wouldn't be anything to subtract.

When There Is No Guessing Penalty

When there is guessing penalty, there are still two things you need to know about yourself before you go into the exam:

- Are you a risk-taker?
- Are you a good guesser?

Your risk-taking temperament matters most on exams with a guessing penalty. Without a guessing penalty, even if you're a play-it-safe person, guessing is perfectly safe. Overcome your anxieties, and go ahead and mark an answer.

But what if you're not much of a risk-taker, and you think of yourself as the world's worst guesser? Complete the worksheet Your Guessing Ability on the next two pages to get an idea of how good your intuition is.

Your Guessing Ability

The following are ten really hard questions. You're not supposed to know the answers. Rather, this is an assessment of your ability to guess when you don't have a clue. Read each question carefully, as if you were expected to answer it. If you have any knowledge at all of the subject of the question, use that knowledge to help you eliminate wrong answer choices. Use this answer grid to fill in your answers to the questions.

1.	ⓐ	ⓑ	ⓒ	ⓓ		6.	ⓐ	ⓑ	ⓒ	ⓓ
2.	ⓐ	ⓑ	ⓒ	ⓓ		7.	ⓐ	ⓑ	ⓒ	ⓓ
3.	ⓐ	ⓑ	ⓒ	ⓓ		8.	ⓐ	ⓑ	ⓒ	ⓓ
4.	ⓐ	ⓑ	ⓒ	ⓓ		9.	ⓐ	ⓑ	ⓒ	ⓓ
5.	ⓐ	ⓑ	ⓒ	ⓓ		10.	ⓐ	ⓑ	ⓒ	ⓓ

1. September 7 is Independence Day in:
   a. India.
   b. Costa Rica.
   c. Brazil.
   d. Australia.

2. Which of the following is the formula for determining the momentum of an object?
   a. $p = mv$
   b. $F = ma$
   c. $P = IV$
   d. $E = mc2$

3. Because of the expansion of the universe, the stars and other celestial bodies are all moving away from each other. This phenomenon is known as:
   a. Newton's first law.
   b. the big bang.
   c. gravitational collapse.
   d. Hubble flow.

4. American author Gertrude Stein was born in:
   a. 1713.
   b. 1830.
   c. 1874.
   d. 1901.

5. Which of the following is NOT one of the Five Classics attributed to Confucius?
   a. the *I Ching*
   b. the *Book of Holiness*
   c. the *Spring and Autumn Annals*
   d. the *Book of History*

6. The religious and philosophical doctrine that holds that the universe is constantly in a struggle between good and evil is known as:
   a. Pelagianism.
   b. Manichaeanism.
   c. neo - Hegelianism.
   d. Epicureanism.

7. The third Chief Justice of the U.S. Supreme Court was:
   a. John Blair.
   b. William Cushing.
   c. James Wilson.
   d. John Jay.

8. Which of the following is the poisonous portion of a daffodil?
   a. the bulb
   b. the leaves
   c. the stem
   d. the flowers

9. The winner of the Masters golf tournament in 1953 was:

    a. Sam Snead.

    b. Cary Middlecoff.

    c. Arnold Palmer.

    d. Ben Hogan.

10. The state with the highest per capita personal income in 1980 was:

    a. Alaska.

    b. Connecticut.

    c. New York.

    d. Texas.

Answers

Check your answers against the correct answers below.

1. c.

2. a.

3. d.

4. c.

5. b.

6. b.

7. b.

8. a.

9. d.

10. a.

How Did You Do?

You may have simply gotten lucky and actually known the answer to one or two questions. In addition, your guessing was probably more successful if you were able to use the process of elimination on any of the questions.

Maybe you didn't know who the third Chief Justice was (question 7), but you knew that John Jay was the first. In that case, you would have eliminated answer **d** and, therefore, improved your odds of guessing correctly from one in four to one in three.

According to probability, you should get two and a half answers correct, so getting either two or three right would be average. If you got four or more right, you may be a really terrific guesser. If you got one or none right, you may be a really poor guesser.

Keep in mind, though, that this is only a small sample. You should continue to keep track of your guessing ability as you work through the sample questions in this book. Circle the number of questions you guessed on as you make your guesses; or, if you don't have time while you take the practice tests, go back afterward and try to remember which questions you guessed on. Remember, on a test with four answer choices, your chances of getting a right answer is one in four. So keep a separate "guessing" score for each exam. How many questions did you guess on? How many did you get right? If the number you got right is at least one-fourth of the number of questions you guessed on, you are at least an average guesser, maybe better—and you should always go ahead and guess on the real exam. If the number you got right is significantly lower than one-fourth of the number you guessed on, you need to improve your guessing skills.

Step 7: Reach Your Peak Performance Zone

Time to complete: 10 minutes to read; weeks to complete!

Activity: Complete the Physical Preparation Checklist (page 31)

To get ready for a challenge like a big exam, you also have to take control of your physical and mental state. Exercise, proper diet, and rest will ensure that your body works with, rather than against, your mind on test day, as well as during your preparation.

Exercise

If you don't already have a regular exercise program, the time during which you're preparing for an exam is actually an excellent time to start one. And if you're already keeping fit—or trying to get fit—don't let the pressure of preparing for an exam fool you into quitting now. Exercise helps reduce stress by pumping good-feeling hormones called endorphins into your system. It also increases the oxygen supply throughout your body, including your brain, so you will be at peak performance on exam day.

A half-hour of vigorous activity—enough to raise a sweat—every day should be your aim. If you're really pressed for time, every other day is OK. Choose an activity you like and get out there and do it. Jogging with a friend always makes the time go faster, as does running with a radio.

But don't overdo it. You don't want to exhaust yourself. Moderation is the key.

Diet

First of all, cut out the junk. Go easy on caffeine, and try to eliminate alcohol and nicotine for at least two weeks before the exam.

What your body needs for peak performance is a balanced diet. Eat plenty of fruits and vegetables, along with protein and carbohydrates. Foods that are high in lecithin (an amino acid), such as fish and beans, are especially good "brain foods."

The night before the exam, you might "carbo-load" the way athletes do before a contest. Eat a big plate of spaghetti, rice and beans, or whatever your favorite carbohydrate is.

Rest

You probably know how much sleep you need every night to be at your best, even if you don't always get it. Make sure you do get that much sleep, though, for at least a week before the exam. Moderation is important here, too. Too much sleep will just make you groggy. If you're not a morning person and your exam will be given in the morning, you should reset your internal clock so that your body doesn't think you're taking an exam at 3 a.m. You have to start this process well before the exam. The way it works is to get up half an hour earlier each morning, and then go to bed half an hour earlier that night. Don't try it the other way around; you will just toss and turn if you go to bed early without having gotten up early. The next morning, get up another half an hour earlier, and so on. How long you will have to do this depends on how late you're used to getting up. Use the Physical Preparation Checklist on the next page to make sure you're in tip-top form.

Physical Preparation Checklist

For the week before the exam, write down 1) what physical exercise you engaged in and for how long and 2) what you ate for each meal. Remember, you're trying for at least half an hour of exercise every other day (preferably every day) and a balanced diet that's light on junk food.

Exam minus 7 days

Exercise: _____ for _____ minutes

Breakfast:_____

Lunch: _____

Dinner: _____

Snacks:_____

Exam minus 6 days

Exercise: _____ for _____ minutes

Breakfast:_____

Lunch: _____

Dinner: _____

Snacks:_____

Exam minus 5 days

Exercise: _____ for _____ minutes

Breakfast:_____

Lunch: _____

Dinner: _____

Snacks:_____

Exam minus 4 days

Exercise: _____ for _____ minutes

Breakfast:_____

Lunch: _____

Dinner: _____

Snacks:_____

Exam minus 3 days

Exercise: _____ for _____ minutes

Breakfast:_____

Lunch: _____

Dinner: _____

Snacks:_____

Exam minus 2 days

Exercise: _____ for _____ minutes

Breakfast:_____

Lunch: _____

Dinner: _____

Snacks:_____

Exam minus 1 day

Exercise: _____ for _____ minutes

Breakfast:_____

Lunch: _____

Dinner: _____

Snacks:_____

Step 8: Get Your Act Together

Time to complete: 10 minutes to read; time to complete will vary
Activity: Complete Final Preparations worksheet (page 24)
You're in control of your mind and body; you're in charge of test anxiety, your preparation, and your test-taking strategies. Now, it's time to take charge of external factors, like the exam site and the materials you need to take the exam.

Find Out Where the Exam Is and Make a Trial Run

The testing agency or your dental assisting instructor will notify you when and where your exam is being held. Do you know how to get to the exam site? Do you know how long it will take to get there? If not, make a trial run, preferably on the same day of the week at the same time of day. Make note on the Final Preparations worksheet of the amount of time it will take you to get to the exam site. Plan on arriving 10–15 minutes early, so you can get the lay of the land, use the bathroom, and calm down. Then, figure out how early you will have to get up that morning, and make sure you get up that early every day for a week before the exam.

Gather Your Materials

The night before the exam, lay out the clothes you will wear and the materials you will need to bring with you to the exam. Plan on dressing in layers; you won't have any control over the temperature of the examination room. Have a sweater or jacket you can take off if it's too warm. Use the checklist on the worksheet Final Preparations on the next page to help you pull together what you will need.

Don't Skip Breakfast

Even if you don't usually eat breakfast, do so on exam morning. A cup of coffee doesn't count. Don't do doughnuts or other sweet foods, either. A sugar high will leave you with a sugar low in the middle of the exam. A mix of protein and carbohydrates is best. Cereal with milk and just a little sugar or eggs with toast will do your body a world of good.

Getting to the Exam Site

Location of exam site: _____

Date: _____

Departure time: _____

Do I know how to get to the exam site? Yes _____ No _____   If no, make a trial run.

Time it will take to get to exam site: _____

Things to Lay Out the Night Before

Clothes I will wear _____

Sweater/jacket _____

Watch _____

Photo ID _____

No. 2 pencils _____ .

Other Things to Bring/Remember

_____   _____

_____   _____

_____   _____

_____   _____

Step 9: Do It!

Time to complete: 10 minutes, plus test - taking time

Activity: Ace the dental assisting exam!

Fast forward to exam day. You're ready. You made a study plan and followed through. You practiced your test-taking strategies while working through this book. You're in control of your physical, mental, and emotional state. You know when and where to show up and what to bring with you. In other words, you're better prepared than most of the other people taking the MAT exam with you. You're psyched!

Just one more thing. When you're done with the exam, you will have earned a reward. Plan a celebration. Call up your friends and plan a party, or have a nice dinner for two, or pick out a movie to see—whatever your heart desires. Give yourself something to look forward to. And then do it. Go into the exam, full of confidence, armed with test-taking strategies you've practiced until they've become second nature. You're in control of yourself, your environment, and your performance on the exam. You're ready to succeed. So do it. Go in there and ace the exam!

C H A P T E R

3 ▶ MAT Practice Test 1

CHAPTER SUMMARY

This is the first of eleven MAT practice tests in this book. These practice tests are based on the actual MAT—use them to see how you would do if you took the exam today and to determine your strengths and weaknesses as you plan your study schedule.

The MAT consists of 120 analogies to be answered in 60 minutes. It is recommended that you take the test in as relaxed a manner as you can, using the answer sheet on page 29. After you take the test, use the detailed answer explanations and chart that follows to review each question and diagnose your strengths and weaknesses.

MAT Practice Test 1

1.	ⓐ	ⓑ	ⓒ	ⓓ
2.	ⓐ	ⓑ	ⓒ	ⓓ
3.	ⓐ	ⓑ	ⓒ	ⓓ
4.	ⓐ	ⓑ	ⓒ	ⓓ
5.	ⓐ	ⓑ	ⓒ	ⓓ
6.	ⓐ	ⓑ	ⓒ	ⓓ
7.	ⓐ	ⓑ	ⓒ	ⓓ
8.	ⓐ	ⓑ	ⓒ	ⓓ
9.	ⓐ	ⓑ	ⓒ	ⓓ
10.	ⓐ	ⓑ	ⓒ	ⓓ
11.	ⓐ	ⓑ	ⓒ	ⓓ
12.	ⓐ	ⓑ	ⓒ	ⓓ
13.	ⓐ	ⓑ	ⓒ	ⓓ
14.	ⓐ	ⓑ	ⓒ	ⓓ
15.	ⓐ	ⓑ	ⓒ	ⓓ
16.	ⓐ	ⓑ	ⓒ	ⓓ
17.	ⓐ	ⓑ	ⓒ	ⓓ
18.	ⓐ	ⓑ	ⓒ	ⓓ
19.	ⓐ	ⓑ	ⓒ	ⓓ
20.	ⓐ	ⓑ	ⓒ	ⓓ
21.	ⓐ	ⓑ	ⓒ	ⓓ
22.	ⓐ	ⓑ	ⓒ	ⓓ
23.	ⓐ	ⓑ	ⓒ	ⓓ
24.	ⓐ	ⓑ	ⓒ	ⓓ
25.	ⓐ	ⓑ	ⓒ	ⓓ
26.	ⓐ	ⓑ	ⓒ	ⓓ
27.	ⓐ	ⓑ	ⓒ	ⓓ
28.	ⓐ	ⓑ	ⓒ	ⓓ
29.	ⓐ	ⓑ	ⓒ	ⓓ
30.	ⓐ	ⓑ	ⓒ	ⓓ
31.	ⓐ	ⓑ	ⓒ	ⓓ
32.	ⓐ	ⓑ	ⓒ	ⓓ
33.	ⓐ	ⓑ	ⓒ	ⓓ
34.	ⓐ	ⓑ	ⓒ	ⓓ
35.	ⓐ	ⓑ	ⓒ	ⓓ
36.	ⓐ	ⓑ	ⓒ	ⓓ
37.	ⓐ	ⓑ	ⓒ	ⓓ
38.	ⓐ	ⓑ	ⓒ	ⓓ
39.	ⓐ	ⓑ	ⓒ	ⓓ
40.	ⓐ	ⓑ	ⓒ	ⓓ
41.	ⓐ	ⓑ	ⓒ	ⓓ
42.	ⓐ	ⓑ	ⓒ	ⓓ
43.	ⓐ	ⓑ	ⓒ	ⓓ
44.	ⓐ	ⓑ	ⓒ	ⓓ
45.	ⓐ	ⓑ	ⓒ	ⓓ

46.	ⓐ	ⓑ	ⓒ	ⓓ
47.	ⓐ	ⓑ	ⓒ	ⓓ
48.	ⓐ	ⓑ	ⓒ	ⓓ
49.	ⓐ	ⓑ	ⓒ	ⓓ
50.	ⓐ	ⓑ	ⓒ	ⓓ
51.	ⓐ	ⓑ	ⓒ	ⓓ
52.	ⓐ	ⓑ	ⓒ	ⓓ
53.	ⓐ	ⓑ	ⓒ	ⓓ
54.	ⓐ	ⓑ	ⓒ	ⓓ
55.	ⓐ	ⓑ	ⓒ	ⓓ
56.	ⓐ	ⓑ	ⓒ	ⓓ
57.	ⓐ	ⓑ	ⓒ	ⓓ
58.	ⓐ	ⓑ	ⓒ	ⓓ
59.	ⓐ	ⓑ	ⓒ	ⓓ
60.	ⓐ	ⓑ	ⓒ	ⓓ
61.	ⓐ	ⓑ	ⓒ	ⓓ
62.	ⓐ	ⓑ	ⓒ	ⓓ
63.	ⓐ	ⓑ	ⓒ	ⓓ
64.	ⓐ	ⓑ	ⓒ	ⓓ
65.	ⓐ	ⓑ	ⓒ	ⓓ
66.	ⓐ	ⓑ	ⓒ	ⓓ
67.	ⓐ	ⓑ	ⓒ	ⓓ
68.	ⓐ	ⓑ	ⓒ	ⓓ
69.	ⓐ	ⓑ	ⓒ	ⓓ
70.	ⓐ	ⓑ	ⓒ	ⓓ
71.	ⓐ	ⓑ	ⓒ	ⓓ
72.	ⓐ	ⓑ	ⓒ	ⓓ
73.	ⓐ	ⓑ	ⓒ	ⓓ
74.	ⓐ	ⓑ	ⓒ	ⓓ
75.	ⓐ	ⓑ	ⓒ	ⓓ
76.	ⓐ	ⓑ	ⓒ	ⓓ
77.	ⓐ	ⓑ	ⓒ	ⓓ
78.	ⓐ	ⓑ	ⓒ	ⓓ
79.	ⓐ	ⓑ	ⓒ	ⓓ
80.	ⓐ	ⓑ	ⓒ	ⓓ
81.	ⓐ	ⓑ	ⓒ	ⓓ
82.	ⓐ	ⓑ	ⓒ	ⓓ
83.	ⓐ	ⓑ	ⓒ	ⓓ
84.	ⓐ	ⓑ	ⓒ	ⓓ
85.	ⓐ	ⓑ	ⓒ	ⓓ
86.	ⓐ	ⓑ	ⓒ	ⓓ
87.	ⓐ	ⓑ	ⓒ	ⓓ
88.	ⓐ	ⓑ	ⓒ	ⓓ
89.	ⓐ	ⓑ	ⓒ	ⓓ
90.	ⓐ	ⓑ	ⓒ	ⓓ

91.	ⓐ	ⓑ	ⓒ	ⓓ
92.	ⓐ	ⓑ	ⓒ	ⓓ
93.	ⓐ	ⓑ	ⓒ	ⓓ
94.	ⓐ	ⓑ	ⓒ	ⓓ
95.	ⓐ	ⓑ	ⓒ	ⓓ
96.	ⓐ	ⓑ	ⓒ	ⓓ
97.	ⓐ	ⓑ	ⓒ	ⓓ
98.	ⓐ	ⓑ	ⓒ	ⓓ
99.	ⓐ	ⓑ	ⓒ	ⓓ
100.	ⓐ	ⓑ	ⓒ	ⓓ
101.	ⓐ	ⓑ	ⓒ	ⓓ
102.	ⓐ	ⓑ	ⓒ	ⓓ
103.	ⓐ	ⓑ	ⓒ	ⓓ
104.	ⓐ	ⓑ	ⓒ	ⓓ
105.	ⓐ	ⓑ	ⓒ	ⓓ
106.	ⓐ	ⓑ	ⓒ	ⓓ
107.	ⓐ	ⓑ	ⓒ	ⓓ
108.	ⓐ	ⓑ	ⓒ	ⓓ
109.	ⓐ	ⓑ	ⓒ	ⓓ
110.	ⓐ	ⓑ	ⓒ	ⓓ
111.	ⓐ	ⓑ	ⓒ	ⓓ
112.	ⓐ	ⓑ	ⓒ	ⓓ
113.	ⓐ	ⓑ	ⓒ	ⓓ
114.	ⓐ	ⓑ	ⓒ	ⓓ
115.	ⓐ	ⓑ	ⓒ	ⓓ
116.	ⓐ	ⓑ	ⓒ	ⓓ
117.	ⓐ	ⓑ	ⓒ	ⓓ
118.	ⓐ	ⓑ	ⓒ	ⓓ
119.	ⓐ	ⓑ	ⓒ	ⓓ
120.	ⓐ	ⓑ	ⓒ	ⓓ

Directions: For each question, select the answer in the parentheses that best completes the analogy.

1. Flute : (**a.** Copper **b.** Woodwind **c.** String **d.** Scale) :: Trumpet : Brass

2. Cent : Dollar :: (**a.** Pound **b.** Franc **c.** Cent **d.** Mark) : Euro

3. (**a.** Apex **b.** Heaven **c.** Heights **d.** Nadir) : Zenith :: Fear : Composure

4. Pill : Bore :: Core : (**a.** Center **b.** Mug **c.** Bar **d.** Placebo)

5. Boiling : Freezing :: 100° : (**a.** Fahrenheit, **b.** Celsius **c.** 0°, **d.** 212°)

6. Aesop : Grimm :: (**a.** Fable **b.** Legend **c.** Myth **d.** Parable) : Fairy Tale

7. Pilfer : Steal :: (**a.** Return **b.** Damage **c.** Exercise **d.** Furnish) : Equip

8. Native : Aboriginal :: Naive : (**a.** Learned **b.** Arid **c.** Unsophisticated **d.** Tribe)

9. (**a.** Compact Disc **b.** Cassette **c.** Record Album **d.** Movie) : Film Strip :: Vinyl : Celluloid

10. Mother : Father :: May : (**a.** January **b.** March **c.** June **d.** November)

11. 28° : Celsius :: (**a.** 48°, **b.** 64°, **c.** 73°, **d.** 82°) : Fahrenheit

12. (**a.** Tension **b.** Soiree **c.** Eulogy **d.** Sari) : Festive :: Funeral : Somber

13. Taoism : Buddhism :: (**a.** China **b.** Mexico **c.** Canada **d.** Italy) : India

14. Soldier : Employee :: (**a.** Fire **b.** Discharge **c.** Hire **d.** Promote) : Lay Off

15. Fetish : Fixation :: Slight : (**a.** Flirt **b.** Sloth **c.** Insult **d.** Confuse)

16. IX : 9 :: XL : (**a.** 15 **b.** 25 **c.** 40 **d.** 50)

17. Cellist : Set Designer :: (**a.** Musician **b.** Conductor **c.** Cello **d.** Orchestra) : Film crew

18. (**a.** Script **b.** Playwright **c.** Stage **d.** Actor) : Play :: Musician : Concert

19. (**a.** Liberal **b.** Democrat **c.** Conservative **d.** Party) : Republican :: Labour : Tory

20. Capricorn : (**a.** Mermaid **b.** Virgo **c.** Princess **d.** Sagittarius) :: Goat : Woman

21. Hovel : Dirty :: Hub : (**a.** Unseen **b.** Prideful **c.** Busy **d.** Shovel)

22. Femur : Tarsals :: Humerus : (**a.** Phlanges **b.** Ulna **c.** Sternum **d.** Carpals)

23. Espana : Spain :: (**a.** Germania **b.** Deutschland **c.** Berlin **d.** Deutschen) : Germany

24. Wombat : Marsupial :: (**a.** Platypus **b.** Kangaroo **c.** Ostrich **d.** Turtle) : Monotreme

25. Exports : Trade Deficit :: Revenue : (**a.** Federal Deficit **b.** Gross Domestic Product **c.** Federal Deficit **d.** Federal Surplus)

26. Clinton : Eisenhower :: Gore : (**a.** Truman **b.** Agnew **c.** Goldwater **d.** Nixon)

27. Prime : (**a.** 8 **b.** 9 **c.** 11 **d.** 12) :: Composite : 10

28. Bog : (**a.** Dream **b.** Foray **c.** Marsh **d.** Night) :: Slumber : Sleep

29. (**a.** Subway **b.** Church **c.** Transition **d.** Line) : Segue :: Throng : Mass

30. Italy : (**a.** Europe **b.** Switzerland **c.** Rome **d.** Sweden) :: Canada : United States

31. Yacht : Sail :: Canoe : (**a.** Boat **b.** Motor **c.** Row **d.** Stern)

32. Sea : River :: (**a.** Ocean **b.** Coast **c.** Delta **d.** Crag) : Bank

33. Botanist : Plants :: Ichthyologist : (**a.** Metals **b.** Fish **c.** Detritus **d.** Viruses)

34. Egg : Albumin :: Cell : (**a.** Mitochondria **b.** Cytoplasm **c.** Membrane **d.** Nucleus)

35. Watch : Television :: (**a.** Face **b.** Hand **c.** Appliance **d.** Program) : Screen

36. 2 : Venus :: (**a.** 4 **b.** 7 **c.** 11 **d.** 3) : Uranus

37. Sleeve : Shirt :: (**a.** Arm **b.** Waist **c.** Belt **d.** Leg) : Slacks

38. Bread : Fabric :: (**a.** Baker **b.** Oven **c.** Wheat **d.** Knead) : Loom

39. XII : LX :: CC : (**a.** D **b.** DC **c.** M **d.** MM)

40. West Side Story : (**a.** Sound of Music **b.** Kiss Me Kate **c.** Into the Woods **d.** Sweeney Todd) :: Romeo and Juliet : Taming of the Shrew

41. Ginsberg : (**a.** Kerouac **b.** Plath **c.** Larkin **d.** Marlowe) :: Longfellow : Bryant

42. Ledger : Accounts :: (**a.** Pundit **b.** Weather **c.** Astrology **d.** Diary) : Observations

43. (**a.** Stream **b.** Swim **c.** Artery **d.** Plasma) : Blood :: Viaduct : Water

44. Kick : (**a.** Bucket **b.** Can **c.** Ball **d.** Heel) :: Buy : Farm

45. *The Iliad* : (**a.** *Lady Chatterley's Lover* **b.** *Sons and Lovers* **c.** *The Rainbow* **d.** *Homer*) :: *The Odyssey* : *Women in Love*

46. Auckland : Mumbai :: (**a.** New Zealand **b.** Vancouver **c.** Australia **d.** Wales) : India

47. Short : Long :: Gamma Waves : (**a.** Ultraviolet Waves **b.** X-Rays **c.** Radio Waves **d.** Infrared Waves)

48. Warhol : Braque :: (**a.** Soup can **b.** Surrealism **c.** Impressionism **d.** Pop Art) : Cubism

49. Mt. Elbrus : Europe : : Mt. McKinley : (**a.** United States **b.** Canada **c.** Australia **d.** North America)

50. Wesley : Methodists :: (**a.** Calvin **b.** Smith **c.** Knox **d.** Lee) : Shakers

51. Pilgrim : Journey :: Recluse : (**a.** Ocean **b.** Home **c.** Space **d.** Thanksgiving)

52. Vestibule : Building :: (**a.** Foyer **b.** Veranda **c.** Porch **d.** Yard) : House

53. *Dr. Strangelove* : Sellers :: (**a.** *The Manchurian Candidate* **b.** *Moonstruck* **c.** *The Shining* **d.** *The Party*) : Nicholson

54. Herd : Buffalo :: (**a.** Skulk **b.** Gang **c.** Sounder **d.** Team) : Foxes

55. 1919 : (**a.** 1947 **b.** 1945 **c.** 1949 **d.** 1938) :: Treaty of Versailles : Paris Peace Treaties

56. President : Prime Minister :: (**a.** Vote **b.** Shah **c.** Vice President **d.** Congress) : Diet

57. Jest : Earnest :: Esteem : (**a.** Just **b.** Honor **c.** Disgrace **d.** Mettle)

58. Confederate : (**a.** North **b.** Partner **c.** History **d.** Teacher) :: Narrator : Chronicler

59. $\frac{4}{5}$: $1\frac{2}{5}$ :: 2 : (**a.** $2\frac{1}{5}$ **b.** $2\frac{2}{5}$ **c.** $2\frac{3}{5}$ **d.** $2\frac{4}{5}$)

60. Logic : Metaphysics :: Ethics : (**a.** Physics **b.** Aesthetics **c.** Mathematics **d.** Morality)

61. Quartzite : Granite :: Metamorphic : (**a.** Sedimentary **b.** Lava **c.** Volcanic **d.** Igneous)

62. Basic : Acidic :: Bleach : (**a.** Lemon Juice **b.** Lye **c.** Pure Water **d.** Baking Soda)

63. (**a.** Jarrett **b.** Chalkias **c.** Perlman **d.** Suzuki) : Violin :: Ma : Cello

64. Testosterone : Testes :: (**a.** Human Growth Hormone **b.** Insulin **c.** Epinephrine **d.** Dopamine) : Pancreas

65. Sodium : Mercury :: Na : (**a.** Ra **b.** Pb **c.** Hg **d.** W)

66. Inca : Aztec :: Peru : (**a.** Brazil **b.** Mexico **c.** Guatemala **d.** Spain)

67. Mendel : Peas :: Morgan : (**a.** Fruit Flies **b.** Cocklebur **c.** Mice **d.** Trypanosoma)

68. Outlaw : (**a.** Chase **b.** Police **c.** Crime **d.** Forbid) :: Offend : Affront

69. Endure : Continue :: Entreat : (**a.** Plea **b.** Segue **c.** Purchase **d.** Surrender)

70. Vespa : Porsche :: (**a.** 1 **b.** 2 **c.** 5. **d.** 6) : 4

71. Boxing Day : (**a.** St. Andrew's Day **b.** Bonfire Night **c.** Swan Upping **d.** Thanksgiving) :: Late Summer Bank Holiday : Martin Luther King, Jr. Day

72. *Homo Sapiens* : Human :: *Musca Domestica* : (**a.** House Cat **b.** House Fly **c.** Field Mouse **d.** Barn Owl)

73. (**a.** Braise **b.** Fry **c.** Barbecue **d.** Roast) : Boil :: Sear : Broil

74. Armstrong : (**a.** Astronaut **b.** Fly **c.** Apollo 11 **d.** NASA) :: Ride : Challenger

75. Groening : Cartoon :: Schulz : (**a.** Comic Book **b.** Joke **c.** Peanuts **d.** Comic Strip)

76. (**a.** *Death of a Salesman* **b.** *Waiting for Godot* **c.** *Pygmalion* **d.** *Streetcar Named Desire*) : *Cat on a Hot Tin Roof* :: *Pillars of Society* : *A Doll's House*

77. Babe Ruth : Hank Aaron :: (**a.** New York **b.** Yankees **c.** Mets **d.** Baseball) : Braves

78. Sales clerk : Meteorologist :: (**a.** Cash register **b.** Pressure **c.** Supermarket **d.** Grocery) : Barometer

79. 60 : (**a.** 20 **b.** 30 **c.** 60 **d.** 160) :: 248 : 124

80. mm : cm :: 1 : (**a.** 1 **b.** 10 **c.** 100 **d.** 1000)

81. Rick Blaine : Michael Curtiz :: (**a.** Luca Brasi **b.** Mario Puzo **c.** Al Pacino **d.** Michael Corleone) : Francis Ford Coppola

82. (**a.** Mornay **b.** Samjang **c.** Chutney **d.** Bordelaise) : Béchamel :: Relish : Sauce

83. Eudora Welty : (**a.** Herman Melville **b.** Kenneth Grahame **c.** Emily Dickinson **d.** Agatha Christie) :: Tennessee Williams : John Updike

84. 17 : 19 :: (**a.** 33 **b.** 31 **c.** 29 **d.** 27) : 37

85. *Heart of Darkness* : *Oil!* :: (**a.** *The Secret Sharer* **b.** *Apocalypse Now* **c.** *Magnolia* : **d.** *Full Metal Jacket*) : *There Will Be Blood*

86. Pierce : (**a.** Civil War **b.** World War II **c.** Korean War **d.** Mexican War) :: Truman : World War I

87. Abandon : Reclaim :: Abate : (**a.** Abolish **b.** Debate **c.** Rise **d.** Level)

88. Pithecanthropus Erectus : Time Out :: (**a.** The Modern Jazz Quartet **b.** Thelonius Monk **c.** Charles Mingus **d.** Ornette Coleman) : The Dave Brubeck Quartet

89. Béla Viktor János Bartók : Igor Stravinsky :: Richard Wagner : (**a.** Hector Berlioz **b.** Benjamin Britten **c.** William Walton **d.** Sergei Prokofiev)

90. Curb : Spur :: Revere : (**a.** Flout **b.** Pout **c.** Tout **d.** Shout)

91. LX : XC :: C : (**a.** CX **b.** CL **c.** CC **d.** CM)

92. Thyroid : Kidney :: Calcitonin : (**a.** Renin **b.** Glucagon **c.** Insulin **d.** Estrogen)

93. Shallot : (**a.** Eggplant **b.** Okra **c.** Pineapple **d.** Leek) :: Artichoke : Cauliflower

94. Shoat : Piglet :: (**a.** Kitten **b.** Pup **c.** Kid **d.** Cub) : Bunny

95. Vienna : Minsk :: Austria : (**a.** Croatia **b.** Moldova **c.** Belarus **d.** Romania)

96. Monaco : Spain :: (**a.** Governor **b.** Prince **c.** President **d.** Prime Minister) : King

97. Fillmore : New York :: Hayes : (**a.** Ohio **b.** New York **c.** Pennsylvania **d.** Oregon)

98. Vervet : (**a.** Tamarin **b.** Bonobo **c.** Lorises **d.** Tarsier) :: Monkey : Ape

99. Klineberg : Levi-Strauss :: Anthropology : (**a.** Structuralism **b.** Behaviorism **c.** Pragmatism **d.** Functionalism)

100. Placental : (**a.** Mammal **b.** Reptile **c.** Eutheria **d.** Heterotroph) :: Monotreme : Protheria

101. Vixen : Todd :: (**a.** Jenny **b.** Jill **c.** Doe **d.** Ewe) : Jack

102. Enfeeble : Fortify :: Concede : (**a.** Dispute **b.** Close **c.** Expect **d.** Surrender)

103. Slack : (**a.** Tight **b.** Silent **c.** Negligent **d.** Cowardly) :: Plucky : Courageous

104. Single Reed : Double Reed :: Clarinet : (**a.** Saxophone **b.** Octavin **c.** Bassoon **d.** Trombone)

105. (**a.** Prickle **b.** Sounder **c.** Herd **d.** Bevy) : Porcupine :: Skulk : Fox

106. Plume : Feather :: Flume : (**a.** Duck **b.** Gorge **c.** Nest **d.** Laughter)

107. Morlock : Aggressive :: (**a.** Eloi **b.** Moreau **c.** Martian **d.** Griffin) : Passive

108. Frick : (**a.** Figge **b.** Hood **c.** Ponce **d.** Anacostia Community) :: Whitney : High Desert

109. Feet : Turkey :: (**a.** Sleep **b.** Down **c.** Shoulder **d.** Wake) : Dream

110. Bona Fide : Deceit :: Languid : (**a.** Action **b.** Weakness **c.** Truthful **d.** Bon Mot)

111. Durham : (**a.** Oxford **b.** Stanford **c.** Cornell **d.** Duke) :: Providence : Brown

112. Burgess Shale : (**a.** British Columbia **b.** Ireland **c.** Utah **d.** Eritrea) :: La Brea : California

113. At Loggerheads : (**a.** Forest **b.** Awe **c.** Disagreement **d.** Agreement) :: Dumbstruck : Amazement

114. Canonize : Unshroud :: Ignore : (**a.** Gape **b.** Jibe **c.** Bunk **d.** Slag)

115. Developmental Stages : Piaget :: (**a.** Education **b.** Linguistic Stages **c.** Generative grammar **d.** Anarchy) : Chomsky

116. Sheath : Bolero :: Shift : (**a.** Doublet **b.** Tent **c.** Jumper **d.** Breeks)

117. Cooperative : (**a.** Merchandise **b.** Partnership **c.** Raw Materials **d.** Business) :: Tangible : Intangible

118. (**a.** Melville **b.** Ahab **c.** Billy Budd **d.** Redburn) : Moby Dick :: Javert : Jean Valjean

119. Rational : $\sqrt{36}$ :: Irrational : (**a.** $\sqrt{1}$ **b.** $\sqrt{25}$ **c.** $\sqrt{10}$ **d.** $\sqrt{49}$)

120. Common Log : 10 :: Natural Log : (**a.** i **b.** e **c.** $\sqrt{-1}$ **d.** 0)

Answers

1. Flute : **Woodwind** :: Trumpet : Brass

   The answer is **b.** The flute is a woodwind instrument. The trumpet is a type of brass instrument.

2. Cent : Dollar :: **Cent** : Euro

   The answer is **c.** In currency, a cent is $\frac{1}{100}$th of both a dollar and a euro.

3. **Nadir** : Zenith :: Fear : Composure

   The answer is **d.** Nadir is the opposite of zenith and fear is the opposite of composure.

4. Pill : Bore :: Core : **Center**

   The answer is **a.** A pill is another word for a bore and a core is another word for a center.

5. Boiling : Freezing :: 100 : **0**

   The answer is **c.** 100 degrees Celsius is the boiling point for water; 0 degrees Celsius is the freezing point for water.

6. Aesop : Grimm :: **Fable** : Fairy Tale

   The answer is **a.** Aesop is a famous writer of fables. The Brothers Grimm were famous writers of fairy tales.

7. Pilfer : Steal :: **Furnish** : Equip

   The answer is **d.** To pilfer means to steal and to furnish means to equip.

8. Native : Aboriginal :: Naive : **Unsophisticated**

   The answer is **c.** Native is a synonym for aboriginal and naive is a synonym for unsophisticated.

9. **Record Album** : Film Strip :: Vinyl : Celluloid

   The answer is **c.** A record album is made of vinyl; a film strip is made of celluloid.

10. Mother : Father :: May : **June**

    The answer is **c.** In the United States, Mother's Day is celebrated on the second Sunday in May and Father's Day is celebrated on the third Sunday in June.

11. 28 : Celsius :: **82** : Fahrenheit

    The answer is **d.** The conversion from Celsius to Fahrenheit is: degrees F = [degrees C] $\frac{9}{5}$ + 32; therefore, 28 $\frac{9}{5}$ + 32 = 82.4.

12. **Soiree** : Festive :: Funeral : Somber

    The answer is **b.** A soiree is described as festive and a funeral is described as somber.

13. Taoism : Buddhism :: **China** : India

    The answer is **a.** The philosophical tradition of Taoism was founded in China. The philosophical tradition of Buddhism was founded in India.

14. Soldier : Employee :: **Discharge** : Lay Off

    The answer is **b.** Discharge means to dismiss a soldier from duty. To lay off means to dismiss an employee from his or her job.

15. Fetish : Fixation :: Slight : **Insult**

The answer is **c.** A fetish is a synonym for a fixation and a slight is a synonym for an insult.

16. IX : 9 :: XL : **40**

The answer is **c.** IX is the Roman numeral for 9 and XL is the Roman numeral for 40.

17. Cellist : Set Designer :: **Orchestra** : Film crew

The answer is **d.** A cellist is a member of an orchestra. A set designer is a member of a film crew.

18. **Actor** : Play :: Musician : Concert

The answer is **d.** An actor is the performer who appears in a play. A musician is the person who performs in a concert.

19. **Democrat** : Republican :: Labour : Tory

The answer is **b.** Democrat and Republican are the major political parties in the United States, just as Labour and Tory are the major parties in Great Britain.

20. Capricorn : **Mermaid** :: Goat : Woman

The answer is **a.** Capricorn is an astrological creature that has the front half of a goat and the hind half of a fish. A mermaid is a mythological creature that has the top half of a woman and the bottom half of a fish.

21. Hovel : Dirty :: Hub : **Busy**

The answer is **c.** A hovel is described as dirty, and a hub is described as busy.

22. Femur : Tarsals :: Humerus : **Carpals**

The answer is **d.** The femur is the thigh bone; the tarsals are foot bones. The humerus is the upper arm bone; the carpals are hand bones.

23. Espana : Spain :: **Deutschland** : Germany

The answer is **b.** Espana is the domestic name of Spain.

24. Wombat : Marsupial :: **Platypus** : Monotreme

The answer is **a.** A wombat is a marsupial—a mammal with a pouch and a yolk sac. A platypus is a monotreme—a mammal that lays eggs.

25. Exports : Trade Deficit :: Revenue : **Federal Deficit**

The answer is **c.** A trade deficit exists when exports lag behind imports. A federal deficit exists when revenue lags behind spending.

26. Clinton : Eisenhower :: Gore : **Nixon**

The answer is **d.** Al Gore was Vice President under Bill Clinton and Richard Nixon was Vice President under Dwight Eisenhower.

27. Prime : **11** :: Composite: 10

The answer is **c.** 11 is a prime number, the only divisors are 1 and 11; 10 is a composite number and has more divisors than just 1 and 10.

28. Bog : **Marsh** :: Slumber : Sleep

The answer is **c.** A bog is a synonym for a marsh, and slumber is a synonym for sleep.

29. Transition : Segue :: Throng : Mass

The answer is **c.** A transition is a synonym for a segue, and a throng is a synonym for a mass.

30. Italy : **Switzerland** :: Canada : United States

The answer is **b.** Canada and the United States both share a common border, as do Italy and Switzerland.

31. Yacht : Sail :: Canoe : **Row**

The answer is **c.** A yacht is a type of sail boat and a canoe is a type of row boat.

32. Sea : River :: **Coast** : Bank

The answer is **b.** The land that borders a river is called a bank and the land that borders a sea is called the coast.

33. Botanist : Plants :: Ichthyologist : **Fish**

The answer is **b.** A botanist studies plants; an ichthyologist studies fish.

34. Egg : Albumin :: Cell : **Cytoplasm**

The answer is **b.** Albumin is the white of an egg—everything between the shell and the yolk; the cytoplasm is everything between the cell membrane and the nucleus.

35. Watch : Television :: **Face** : Screen

The answer is **a.** The face is the part of the watch that displays its information. The screen is the part of a television that displays its information.

36. 2 : Venus :: 7 : Uranus

The answer is **b.** Venus is the second planet from the sun in our solar system; Uranus is the seventh.

37. Sleeve : Shirt :: **Leg** : Slacks

The answer is **d.** One's limb is covered by a sleeve when wearing a shirt. One's limb is covered by a leg when wearing slacks.

38. Bread : Fabric :: **Oven** : Loom

The answer is **b.** Bread is made in an appliance called an oven. Fabric is made on an apparatus called a loom.

39. XII : LX :: CC : **M**

The answer is **c.** In Roman Numerals, LX (60) is five times XII (12) and M (1000) is five times CC (200).

40. West Side Story : **Kiss Me Kate** :: Romeo and Juliet : Taming of the Shrew

The answer is **b.** West Side Story is a musical based on William Shakespeare's play Romeo and Juliet; Kiss Me Kate is a musical based on Shakespeare's Taming of the Shrew.

41. Ginsberg : **Kerouac** :: Longfellow : Bryant

The answer is **a.** Allen Ginsberg and Jack Kerouac were both beat writers. Henry Wadsworth Longfellow and William Cullen Bryant were considered fireside poets.

42. Ledger : Accounts :: **Diary** : Observations

The answer is **d.** A ledger is a book that contains accounts, and a diary is a book that contains observations.

43. **Artery** : Blood :: Viaduct : Water

The answer is **c.** An artery carries blood and a viaduct carries water.

44. Kick : **Bucket** :: Buy : Farm

The answer is **a.** "Kick the bucket" and "buy the farm" are both euphemisms for dying.

45. *The Iliad* : **The Rainbow** :: *The Odyssey* : *Women in Love*

The answer is **c.** Homer's epic poem *The Odyssey* is a sequel to his earlier poem *The Iliad*. D.K. Lawrence's novel *Women in Love* is a sequel to his earlier novel *The Rainbow*.

46. Auckland : Mumbai :: **New Zealand** : India

The answer is **a.** Auckland is a city in New Zealand and Mumbai is a city in India.

47. Short : Long :: Gamma Waves : **Radio Waves**

The answer is **c.** Gamma waves are the shortest waves on the electromagnetic spectrum; radio waves are the longest.

48. Warhol : Braque :: **Pop Art** : Cubism

The answer is **d.** Andy Warhol was an artist in the pop art movement. Georges Braque was an artist in the cubist movement.

49. Mt. Elbrus : Europe :: Mt. McKinley : **United States**

The answer is **a.** Mt. Elbrus is the highest peak in Europe and Mt. McKinley is the highest peak in North America.

50. Wesley : Methodists :: **Lee** : Shakers

The answer is **d.** John Wesley founded the Methodist church and (Mother) Ann Lee founded the United Society of Believers in Christ's Second Appearing, commonly known as the Shakers.

51. Pilgrim : Journey :: Recluse : **Home**

The answer is **b.** A pilgrim can be found on a journey, and a recluse can be found at home.

52. Vestibule : Building :: **Foyer** : House

The answer is **a.** A vestibule is the entrance to a building, and a foyer is the entrance to a home.

53. Dr. Strangelove : Sellers :: **The Shining** : Nicholson

The answer is **c.** Dr. Strangelove is a film by Stanley Kubrick starring Peter Sellers. The Shining is a Kubrick film starring Jack Nicholson.

54. Herd : Buffalo :: **Skulk** : Foxes

The answer is **a.** A group of buffalo is called a herd; a group of foxes is called a skulk.

55. 1919 : **1947** :: Treaty of Versailles : Paris Peace Treaties

The answer is **a.** The Treaty of Versailles was signed in 1919 to formally end World War I and the Paris Peace Treaties were signed in 1947 to formally end World War II.

56. President : Prime Minister :: **Congress** : Diet

The answer is **d.** A president and a prime minister are both executive officials of government and a congress and a diet are both legislative bodies of government.

57. Jest : Earnest :: Esteem : **Disgrace**

The answer is **c.** Jest is an antonym for earnest, and esteem is an antonym for disgrace.

58. Confederate : **Partner** :: Narrator : Chronicler

The answer is **b.** A confederate is a synonym for a partner, and a narrator is a synonym for a chronicler.

59. $\frac{4}{5} : 1\frac{2}{5} :: 2 : 2\frac{3}{5}$

The answer is **c.** $2\frac{3}{5}$ $1\frac{2}{5}$ is $\frac{3}{5}$ more than $\frac{4}{5}$. $2\frac{3}{5}$ is $\frac{3}{5}$ more than 2.

60. Logic : Metaphysics :: Ethics : **Aesthetics**

The answer is **b.** Logic, metaphysics, ethics, and aesthetics all relate to branches of philosophy.

61. Quartzite : Granite :: Metamorphic : **Igneous**

The answer is **d.** Quartzite is a metamorphic rock; granite is an igneous rock.

62. Basic : Acidic :: Bleach : **Lemon Juice**

The answer is **a.** Bleach is highly basic. Lemon juice is the only choice that is acidic.

63. **Perlman** : Violin :: Ma : Cello

The answer is **c.** Itzhak Perlman is a famous violinist and Yo-Yo Ma is a famous cellist.

64. Testosterone : Testes :: **Human Growth Hormone** : Pancreas

The answer is **a.** Testosterone is a hormone produced by the testes; insulin is produced by the pancreas.

65. Sodium : Mercury :: Na : **Hg**

The answer is **c.** Na is the chemical symbol for sodium; Hg is the chemical symbol for mercury.

66. Inca : Aztec :: Peru : **Mexico**

The answer is **b.** The Incans lived in what is now Peru and the Aztecs lived in what is now Mexico.

67. Mendel : Peas :: Morgan : **Fruit Flies**

The answer is **a.** Gregor Mendel explored genetic variety with peas; Thomas Hunt Morgan explored genetic variety with fruit flies (*Drosophila melanogaster*).

68. Outlaw : **Forbid** :: Offend : Affront

The answer is **d.** To outlaw means to forbid, and to offend means to affront.

69. Endure : Continue :: Entreat : **Plea**

The answer is **a.** To endure means to continue, and to entreat means to plead.

70. Vespa : Porsche :: **2** : 4

The answer is **b.** A Vespa is a two-wheeled motor scooter. A Porsche is a four-wheeled automobile.

71. Boxing Day : **Thanksgiving** :: Late Summer Bank Holiday : Easter Sunday

The answer is **d.** Boxing Day and Late Summer Bank Holiday are both English holidays. Thanksgiving and Martin Luther King, Jr. Day are American holidays.

72. *Homo Sapiens* : Human :: *Musca Domestica* : **House Fly**

The answer is **b.** *Homo sapiens* is the genus and species for humans; *musca domestica* is the genus and species for house flies.

73. **Braise** : Boil :: Sear : Broil

The answer is **a.** Braising and boiling are two cooking methods that require water; searing and broiling are two cooking methods that do not.

74. Armstrong : **Apollo 11** :: Ride : Challenger

The answer is **c.** Astronaut Neil Armstrong flew to the moon in the Apollo 11 rocket. Astronaut Sally Ride flew on the Space Shuttle Challenger.

75. Groening : Cartoon :: Schulz : **Comic Strip**

The answer is **d.** Matt Groening is the creator of "The Simpsons" cartoon and Charles M. Schulz is the creator of the comic strip "Peanuts."

76. *Streetcar Named Desire* : *Cat on a Hot Tin Roof* :: *Pillars of Society* : *A Doll's House*

The answer is **d.** *Streetcar Named Desire* and *Cat on a Hot Tin Roof* are plays written by Tennessee Williams. *Pillars of Society* and *A Doll's House* are plays written by Henrik Ibsen.

77. Babe Ruth : Hank Aaron :: **Yankees** : Braves

The answer is **b.** Babe Ruth played baseball for the New York Yankees. Hank Aaron played for the Atlanta Braves.

78. Sales clerk : Meteorologist :: **Cash register** : Barometer

The answer is **a.** A cash register is a piece of equipment used by a sales clerk. A barometer is a piece of equipment used by a meteorologist.

79. 60 : **30** :: 248 : 124

The answer is **b.** $\frac{1}{2}$ of 248 is 124. $\frac{1}{2}$ of 60 is 30.

80. mm : cm :: 1 : **10**

The answer is **b.** 10 millimeters (mm) is equal to 1 centimeter (cm). The ratio is 10 to 1.

81. Rick Blaine : Michael Curtiz :: **Michael Corleone** : Francis Ford Coppola

The answer is **d.** Rick Blaine is the main character in Michael Curtiz's film Casablanca. Michael Corleone is the main character in Francis Ford Coppola's film The Godfather.

82. **Chutney** : Béchamel :: Relish : Sauce

The answer is **c.** Chutney is a type of Indian relish. Béchamel is a type of French sauce.

83. Eudora Welty : **Emily Dickinson** :: Tennessee Williams : John Updike

The answer is **c.** Eudora Welty and Tennessee Williams are both writers from Mississippi. Emily Dickinson and John Updike are both writers from Massachusetts.

84. 17 : 19 :: **31** : 37

The answer is **b.** 17 and 19 are prime numbers in sequence and 31 and 37 are prime numbers in sequence.

85. *Heart of Darkness* : *Oil!* :: **Apocalypse Now** : *There Will Be Blood*

The answer is **b.** Francis Ford Coppola's 1979 film *Apocalypse Now* is a loose adaptation of Joseph Conrad's 1899 novel *Heart of Darkness*. Paul Thomas Anderson's 2007 film *There Will Be Blood* is a loose adaptation of Upton Sinclair's 1927 novel *Oil!*

86. Pierce : **Mexican War** :: Truman : World War I

The answer is **d.** Both presidents served in wars before their presidencies: Pierce served in the Mexican War, Truman served in World War I.

87. Abandon : Reclaim :: Abate : **Rise**

The answer is **c.** To abandon is an antonym of to reclaim, and to abate is an antonym of to rise.

88. Pithecanthropus Erectus : Time Out :: **Charles Mingus** : The Dave Brubeck Quartet

The answer is **c.** Pithecanthropus Erectus is a 1956 jazz album by Charles Mingus. Time Out is a 1959 jazz album by The Dave Brubeck Quartet.

89. Béla Viktor János Bartók : Igor Stravinsky :: Richard Wagner : **Hector Berlioz**

The answer is **a.** Béla Viktor János Bartók and Igor Stravinsky are both 20th century composers. Richard Wagner and Hector Berlioz are 19th century composers.

90. Curb : Spur :: Revere : **Flout**

The answer is **a.** To curb is an antonym of to spur, and to revere is an antonym of to flout.

91. LX : XC :: C : **CL**

The answer is **b.** LX (60) times 1.5 equals XC (90). C (100) times 1.5 equals CL (150).

92. Thyroid : Kidney :: Calcitonin : **Renin**

The answer is **a.** The thyroid secretes Calcitonin; the kidney secretes Renin.

93. Shallot : **Leek** :: Artichoke : Cauliflower

The answer is **d.** The shallot and the leek are both kinds of bulb vegetables. The artichoke and cauliflower are inflorescent vegetables.

94. Shoat : Piglet :: **Kitten** : Bunny

The answer is **a.** Shoat is another word for piglet; kitten is another word for bunny.

95. Vienna : Minsk :: Austria : **Belarus**

The answer is **c.** Vienna is the capital of Austria and Minsk is the capital of Belarus.

96. Monaco : Spain :: **Prince** : King

The answer is **b.** Monaco is a principality, with prince as its head of state. Spain's head of state is a king.

97. Fillmore : New York :: Hayes : **Ohio**

The answer is **a.** Millard Fillmore was born in New York and Rutherford **B.** Hayes was born in Ohio.

98. Vervet : **Bonobo** :: Monkey : Ape

The answer is **b.** A vervet is a monkey; a bonobo is an ape.

99. Klineberg : Levi-Strauss :: Anthropology : **Structuralism**

The answer is **a.** Klineberg was an anthropologist and Levi-Strauss was a structuralist.

100. Placental : **Eutheria** :: Monotreme : Protheria

The answer is **c.** Protheria is another word for monotreme, an egg-laying mammal. Eutheria is another word for placental, a subclass of mammals that uses a placenta in the bearing of live young.

101. Vixen : Todd :: **Jenny** : Jack

The answer is **a.** A vixen is a female fox; a todd is a male fox. A jenny is a female donkey; a jack is a male donkey.

102. Enfeeble : Fortify :: Concede : **Dispute**

The answer is **a.** To enfeeble is an antonym of to fortify, and to concede is an antonym of to dispute.

103. Slack : **Negligent** :: Plucky : Courageous

The answer is **c.** Slack is a synonym for negligent, and plucky is a synonym for courageous.

104. Single Reed : Double Reed :: Clarinet : **Bassoon**

The answer is **c.** The clarinet is an instrument that only uses a single reed in its mouthpiece. The bassoon, however, requires a double reed.

105. **Prickle** : Porcupine :: Skulk : Fox

The answer is **a.** A prickle is a group of porcupines; a skulk is a group of foxes.

106. Plume : Feather :: Flume : **Gorge**

The answer is **b.** A plume is a feather, and a flume is a gorge.

107. Morlock : Aggressive :: **Eloi** : Passive

The answer is **a.** In the novel *The Time Machine* by H.G. Wells, the Morlocks are an aggressive race of creatures while the Eloi are a passive race.

108. Frick : **Anacostia Community** :: Whitney : High Desert

The answer is **d.** The Frick and the Whitney are both art museums. The Anacostia Community Museum and the High Desert Museum are natural history museums.

109. Feet : Turkey :: **Down** : Dream

The answer is **b.** The words *feet* and *turkey* both complete common expressions that begin with the word *cold.* To have "cold feet" is to be wary or frightened and to go "cold turkey" is to quit something suddenly. The words *down* and *dream* both complete common expressions that begin with the word *pipe.* To "pipe down" is to be quiet. A "pipe dream" is an unrealistic wish or goal.

110. Bona Fide : Deceit :: Languid : **Action**

The answer is **a.** Bona fide is characterized by a lack of deceit, and languid is characterized by a lack of action.

111. Durham : **Duke** :: Providence : Brown

The answer is **d.** Duke University is located in Durham, North Carolina. Brown University is located in Providence, Rhode Island.

112. Burgess Shale : **British Columbia** :: La Brea : California

The answer is **a.** The Burgess Shale has a wealth of fossils in British Columbia; the La Brea Tar Pits have a wealth of fossils in California.

113. At Loggerheads : **Disagreement** :: Dumbstruck : Amazement

The answer is **c.** At loggerheads means to be in disagreement, and dumbstruck means to be in amazement.

114. Canonize : Unshroud :: Ignore : **Gape**

The answer is **a.** Canonize is an antonym for unshroud, and ignore is an antonym for gape.

115. Developmental stages : Piaget :: **Generative grammar** : Chomsky

The answer is **c.** Psychologist Jean Piaget is known for his theory of developmental stages and linguist Noam Chomsky is known for his theory of generative grammar.

116. Sheath : Bolero :: Shift : **Doublet**

The answer is **a.** A sheath and a shift are two kinds of dresses. A bolero and a doublet are two kinds of jackets.

117. Cooperative : **Partnership** :: Tangible : Intangible

The answer is **b.** A cooperative and a partnership are two types of businesses. Tangible and intangible describe two types of products.

118. **Ahab** : Moby Dick :: Javert : Jean Valjean

The answer is **b.** In Herman Melville's 1851 novel *Moby Dick*, Captain Ahab pursues the white whale Moby Dick. In Victor Hugo's 1862 novel *Les Misérables*, Inspector Javert pursues the convict Jean Valjean.

119. Rational : $\sqrt{36}$ :: Irrational : $\sqrt{10}$

The answer is **c.** 36 is a perfect square, so the $\sqrt{36}$ is a rational number. 10 is not a perfect square so $\sqrt{10}$ is an irrational number.

120. Common Log : 10 :: Natural Log : **e**

The answer is **b.** A common log has a base of 10. A natural log has a base e.

Scoring Your MAT Practice Test

As mentioned in Chapter 1, when you receive your personal score report for the official MAT, you'll be provided with a scaled score and two percentile ranks, all of which are derived from the number of items you answered correctly—known as your raw score.

Because there are different forms and formats of the official MAT, and typically 20 of the 120 questions on the official MAT are experimental and do not count toward your official scaled score and percentile ranks, it is impossible to create an accurate raw score to scaled score or raw score to percentile chart for the practice tests in this book.

In the end, you are striving to correctly answer the highest number of questions as possible and familiarize yourself with the MAT format so you're fully prepared to do your best on test day. For now, what's much more important than your overall score is how you did on each of the content areas tested on the exam. You need to diagnose your strengths and weaknesses so that you can concentrate your efforts as you prepare. The question types are mixed in the practice exam, so in order to tell where your strengths and weaknesses lie, you'll need to compare your answer sheet with the following **MAT Practice Test 1 Review**, which shows which of the content areas each question falls into.

Use your performance here in conjunction with the LearningExpress Test Preparation System in Chapter 2 to help you devise a study plan. You should plan to spend more time studying areas that correspond to the questions you found hardest and less time on the content areas in which you did well. Once you have spent some time reviewing, take the next MAT Practice Test to see if you've improved.

MAT PRACTICE TEST 1	
CONTENT AREA	**QUESTION NUMBERS**
Language and Vocabulary	2, 3, 7, 8, 12, 15, 21, 28, 29, 42, 43, 51, 52, 57, 58, 68, 69, 87, 90, 102, 103, 106, 110, 113, 114
Humanities	1, 6 , 9, 13, 17, 18, 40, 41, 45, 48, 53, 63, 76, 81, 83, 85, 88, 89, 104, 107, 118
Social Science	2, 19, 23, 25, 26, 30, 32, 46, 49, 50, 55, 56, 60, 66, 86, 95, 96, 97, 99, 115
Natural Science	5, 11, 22, 24, 33, 34, 36, 47, 54, 61, 62, 64, 65, 67, 72, 92, 94, 98, 100, 101, 105, 112
General	10, 14, 20, 31, 35, 37, 38, 44, 70, 71, 73, 74, 75, 77, 78, 82, 93, 108, 109, 111, 116, 117
Mathematics	16, 27, 39, 59, 79, 80, 84, 91, 119, 120

MAT Practice Test 2

CHAPTER SUMMARY

Here's another sample MAT test for you to practice.

For this second practice test, simulate the actual test-taking experience as closely as you can. Find a quiet place to work where you won't be disturbed. If you own this book, use the answer sheet on the following pages and find some #2 pencils to fill in the circles. Use a timer or stopwatch to time yourself—you'll have 60 minutes to complete the official MAT. After you take the test, use the detailed answer explanations that follow to review.

MAT Practice Test 2

1.	ⓐ	ⓑ	ⓒ	ⓓ
2.	ⓐ	ⓑ	ⓒ	ⓓ
3.	ⓐ	ⓑ	ⓒ	ⓓ
4.	ⓐ	ⓑ	ⓒ	ⓓ
5.	ⓐ	ⓑ	ⓒ	ⓓ
6.	ⓐ	ⓑ	ⓒ	ⓓ
7.	ⓐ	ⓑ	ⓒ	ⓓ
8.	ⓐ	ⓑ	ⓒ	ⓓ
9.	ⓐ	ⓑ	ⓒ	ⓓ
10.	ⓐ	ⓑ	ⓒ	ⓓ
11.	ⓐ	ⓑ	ⓒ	ⓓ
12.	ⓐ	ⓑ	ⓒ	ⓓ
13.	ⓐ	ⓑ	ⓒ	ⓓ
14.	ⓐ	ⓑ	ⓒ	ⓓ
15.	ⓐ	ⓑ	ⓒ	ⓓ
16.	ⓐ	ⓑ	ⓒ	ⓓ
17.	ⓐ	ⓑ	ⓒ	ⓓ
18.	ⓐ	ⓑ	ⓒ	ⓓ
19.	ⓐ	ⓑ	ⓒ	ⓓ
20.	ⓐ	ⓑ	ⓒ	ⓓ
21.	ⓐ	ⓑ	ⓒ	ⓓ
22.	ⓐ	ⓑ	ⓒ	ⓓ
23.	ⓐ	ⓑ	ⓒ	ⓓ
24.	ⓐ	ⓑ	ⓒ	ⓓ
25.	ⓐ	ⓑ	ⓒ	ⓓ
26.	ⓐ	ⓑ	ⓒ	ⓓ
27.	ⓐ	ⓑ	ⓒ	ⓓ
28.	ⓐ	ⓑ	ⓒ	ⓓ
29.	ⓐ	ⓑ	ⓒ	ⓓ
30.	ⓐ	ⓑ	ⓒ	ⓓ
31.	ⓐ	ⓑ	ⓒ	ⓓ
32.	ⓐ	ⓑ	ⓒ	ⓓ
33.	ⓐ	ⓑ	ⓒ	ⓓ
34.	ⓐ	ⓑ	ⓒ	ⓓ
35.	ⓐ	ⓑ	ⓒ	ⓓ
36.	ⓐ	ⓑ	ⓒ	ⓓ
37.	ⓐ	ⓑ	ⓒ	ⓓ
38.	ⓐ	ⓑ	ⓒ	ⓓ
39.	ⓐ	ⓑ	ⓒ	ⓓ
40.	ⓐ	ⓑ	ⓒ	ⓓ
41.	ⓐ	ⓑ	ⓒ	ⓓ
42.	ⓐ	ⓑ	ⓒ	ⓓ
43.	ⓐ	ⓑ	ⓒ	ⓓ
44.	ⓐ	ⓑ	ⓒ	ⓓ
45.	ⓐ	ⓑ	ⓒ	ⓓ

46.	ⓐ	ⓑ	ⓒ	ⓓ
47.	ⓐ	ⓑ	ⓒ	ⓓ
48.	ⓐ	ⓑ	ⓒ	ⓓ
49.	ⓐ	ⓑ	ⓒ	ⓓ
50.	ⓐ	ⓑ	ⓒ	ⓓ
51.	ⓐ	ⓑ	ⓒ	ⓓ
52.	ⓐ	ⓑ	ⓒ	ⓓ
53.	ⓐ	ⓑ	ⓒ	ⓓ
54.	ⓐ	ⓑ	ⓒ	ⓓ
55.	ⓐ	ⓑ	ⓒ	ⓓ
56.	ⓐ	ⓑ	ⓒ	ⓓ
57.	ⓐ	ⓑ	ⓒ	ⓓ
58.	ⓐ	ⓑ	ⓒ	ⓓ
59.	ⓐ	ⓑ	ⓒ	ⓓ
60.	ⓐ	ⓑ	ⓒ	ⓓ
61.	ⓐ	ⓑ	ⓒ	ⓓ
62.	ⓐ	ⓑ	ⓒ	ⓓ
63.	ⓐ	ⓑ	ⓒ	ⓓ
64.	ⓐ	ⓑ	ⓒ	ⓓ
65.	ⓐ	ⓑ	ⓒ	ⓓ
66.	ⓐ	ⓑ	ⓒ	ⓓ
67.	ⓐ	ⓑ	ⓒ	ⓓ
68.	ⓐ	ⓑ	ⓒ	ⓓ
69.	ⓐ	ⓑ	ⓒ	ⓓ
70.	ⓐ	ⓑ	ⓒ	ⓓ
71.	ⓐ	ⓑ	ⓒ	ⓓ
72.	ⓐ	ⓑ	ⓒ	ⓓ
73.	ⓐ	ⓑ	ⓒ	ⓓ
74.	ⓐ	ⓑ	ⓒ	ⓓ
75.	ⓐ	ⓑ	ⓒ	ⓓ
76.	ⓐ	ⓑ	ⓒ	ⓓ
77.	ⓐ	ⓑ	ⓒ	ⓓ
78.	ⓐ	ⓑ	ⓒ	ⓓ
79.	ⓐ	ⓑ	ⓒ	ⓓ
80.	ⓐ	ⓑ	ⓒ	ⓓ
81.	ⓐ	ⓑ	ⓒ	ⓓ
82.	ⓐ	ⓑ	ⓒ	ⓓ
83.	ⓐ	ⓑ	ⓒ	ⓓ
84.	ⓐ	ⓑ	ⓒ	ⓓ
85.	ⓐ	ⓑ	ⓒ	ⓓ
86.	ⓐ	ⓑ	ⓒ	ⓓ
87.	ⓐ	ⓑ	ⓒ	ⓓ
88.	ⓐ	ⓑ	ⓒ	ⓓ
89.	ⓐ	ⓑ	ⓒ	ⓓ
90.	ⓐ	ⓑ	ⓒ	ⓓ

91.	ⓐ	ⓑ	ⓒ	ⓓ
92.	ⓐ	ⓑ	ⓒ	ⓓ
93.	ⓐ	ⓑ	ⓒ	ⓓ
94.	ⓐ	ⓑ	ⓒ	ⓓ
95.	ⓐ	ⓑ	ⓒ	ⓓ
96.	ⓐ	ⓑ	ⓒ	ⓓ
97.	ⓐ	ⓑ	ⓒ	ⓓ
98.	ⓐ	ⓑ	ⓒ	ⓓ
99.	ⓐ	ⓑ	ⓒ	ⓓ
100.	ⓐ	ⓑ	ⓒ	ⓓ
101.	ⓐ	ⓑ	ⓒ	ⓓ
102.	ⓐ	ⓑ	ⓒ	ⓓ
103.	ⓐ	ⓑ	ⓒ	ⓓ
104.	ⓐ	ⓑ	ⓒ	ⓓ
105.	ⓐ	ⓑ	ⓒ	ⓓ
106.	ⓐ	ⓑ	ⓒ	ⓓ
107.	ⓐ	ⓑ	ⓒ	ⓓ
108.	ⓐ	ⓑ	ⓒ	ⓓ
109.	ⓐ	ⓑ	ⓒ	ⓓ
110.	ⓐ	ⓑ	ⓒ	ⓓ
111.	ⓐ	ⓑ	ⓒ	ⓓ
112.	ⓐ	ⓑ	ⓒ	ⓓ
113.	ⓐ	ⓑ	ⓒ	ⓓ
114.	ⓐ	ⓑ	ⓒ	ⓓ
115.	ⓐ	ⓑ	ⓒ	ⓓ
116.	ⓐ	ⓑ	ⓒ	ⓓ
117.	ⓐ	ⓑ	ⓒ	ⓓ
118.	ⓐ	ⓑ	ⓒ	ⓓ
119.	ⓐ	ⓑ	ⓒ	ⓓ
120.	ⓐ	ⓑ	ⓒ	ⓓ

Directions: For each question, select the answer in the parentheses that best completes the analogy.

1. Mare : Stallion :: Doe : (**a.** Bull **b.** Buck **c.** Male **d.** Jack)

2. Lennon : Cobain :: Liverpool : (**a.** America **b.** Seattle **c.** Nirvana **d.** Guitar)

3. Blood : Lymph :: (**a.** Cardiovascular **b.** Digestive **c.** Respiratory **d.** Nervous) : Lymphatic

4. Miserly : Cheap :: Homogeneous : (**a.** Extravagant **b.** Unkind **c.** Alike **d.** Friendly)

5. Vapid : (**a.** Inspired **b.** Turgid **c.** Wet **d.** Insipid) :: Rapid : Swift

6. John Keats : (**a.** Lord Byron **b.** Ludwig van Beethoven **c.** Classical **d.** Poet) :: Camille Saint-Saëns : Wolfgang Amadeus Mozart

7. Slipper : Ballet :: (**a.** Tutu **b.** Dance **c.** Grass Skirt **d.** Shoe) : Hula

8. 52 : 33 :: 25 : (**a.** 6 **b.** 9 **c.** 23 **d.** 27)

9. Waffle : Hamburger :: Syrup : (**a.** Beef **b.** Bun **c.** Ketchup **d.** Salt)

10. Hank Williams : Robert Johnson :: Country : (**a.** Soul **b.** Blues **c.** Sing **d.** Record)

11. Radius : Diameter :: Pint : (**a.** Circle **b.** Circumference **c.** Quart **d.** Gallon)

12. Othello : (**a.** Hamlet **b.** Twelfth Night **c.** King Lear **d.** Henry V) :: Tragedy : Comedy

13. Quixotic : Pragmatic :: Murky : (**a.** Rapid **b.** Cloudy **c.** Clear **d.** Friendly)

14. Smear : Libel :: Heed : (**a.** Represent **b.** Doubt **c.** Consider **d.** Need)

15. France : Russia :: Louisiana Purchase : (**a.** Alaska **b.** Canada **c.** New York **d.** Westward Expansion)

16. Bond : Debt :: Stock : (**a.** Option **b.** Equity **c.** Class **d.** Leverage)

17. Pistil : Female :: (**a.** Testes **b.** Leaf **c.** Stamen **d.** Mortar) : Male

18. Id : Superego :: Desire : (**a.** Self **b.** Ethics **c.** Conscience **d.** Morality)

19. Obscene : Coarse :: Obtuse : (**a.** Subject **b.** Obstinate **c.** Obscure **d.** Stupid)

20. Michigan : Ontario :: (**a.** Great **b.** Charles **c.** Buffalo **d.** Huron) : Erie

21. Gander : (**a.** Worker **b.** Male **c.** Drone **d.** Tom) :: Gaggle : Hive

22. (**a.** Eagle **b.** Ocean **c.** Moon **d.** Freedom) : United States :: Sun : Japan

23. Jibe : Praise :: (**a.** Jib **b.** Delude **c.** Worship **d.** Wed) : Enlighten

24. Piercing : (**a.** Diamond **b.** Watch **c.** Siren **d.** Ears) :: Hushed : Whisper

25. (**a.** Cub **b.** Kid **c.** Calf **d.** Pup) : Joey :: Shark : Kangaroo

26. (a. Heart b. Hemoglobin c. Ventricle d. Artery) : Courier :: Oxygen : Package

27. Quebec : Alberta :: Victoria : (a. Melbourne b. Ontario c. Queensland d. New Zealand)

28. Crocus : Perennial :: Bean : (a. Plant b. Biennial c. Annual d. Triennial)

29. 144 : 12 :: (a. 150 b. 225 c. 275 d. 300) : 15

30. Nymph : (a. Maiden b. Sinner c. Candle d. Priest) :: Seraphim : Angel

31. Foreman : Teacher :: Construction Site : (a. Students b. Classroom c. Lesson d. Desk)

32. (a. Whitney b. Bell. c. Edison d. Wright) : Cotton Gin :: Deere : Steel Plow

33. Segregate : Unify :: Repair : (a. Approach b. Push c. Damage d. Outwit)

34. Lyric : (a. Text b. Music c. Dialogue d. Explanation) :: Song : Play

35. Saddle : (a. Leather b. Motor c. Seat d. Vehicle) :: Horse : Car

36. (a. Bran b. Burrito c. Mexican d. Corn) : Wheat :: Tortilla : Bun

37. (a. Mountain b. Lake c. River d. High) : Cliff :: Valley : Gorge

38. (a. Merlot b. Ale c. Liquor d. Whiskey) : Lager :: Wine : Beer

39. (a. Switch b. Bulb c. Shade d. Cord) : Ignition :: Lamp : Car

40. (a. Felix Mendelssohn b. Busby Berkeley c. George Gershwin d. Fred Astair) : Leonard Bernstein :: Bob Fosse : Leopold Stokowski

41. Queue : (a. Quiz b. Spy c. Line d. Surprise) :: Query : Question

42. (a. Furnace b. Smoke c. Water d. Cinder) : Ash :: Shard : Glass

43. Holst : Planets :: Grieg : (a. Morning Mood b. Peer Gynt c. In the Hall of the Mountain King d. Mars the Bringer of War)

44. Mozart : Bach :: Classical : (a. Romantic b. Renaissance c. Ballad d. Baroque)

45. Shadow : Trail :: (a. Litter b. Forest c. Hike d. Shame) : Disgrace

46. Kimono : Robe :: (a. Tabi b. Pagoda c. Obi d. Geta) : Sash

47. Oenophile : Bibliophile :: Wine : (a. Coffee b. Reading c. Libraries d. Books)

48. *Player Piano* : Vonnegut :: *Seize the Day* : (a. Heller b. Herzog c. Burgess d. Bellow)

49. Mammal : Dinosaur :: Cenozoic : (a. Cambrian b. Isopotic c. Geologic d. Cretaceous)

50. California : Massachusetts :: New Mexico : (a. South Dakota b. Florida c. Oregon d. Rhode Island)

51. Contract : Obligation :: Tort : (a. Equity b. Litigation c. Reform d. Entity)

52. (**a.** Marley's Ghost **b.** Scrooge Meets a Spirit **c.** Tiny Tim **d.** Charles Dickens) : Stubb Kills a Whale :: A Christmas Carol : Moby Dick

53. Roman Catholic : (**a.** Protestant **b.** Buddhist **c.** Lutheran **d.** Jewish) :: Shiite : Sunni

54. Reconcile : Fight :: (**a.** Hurry **b.** Stall **c.** Cover **d.** Shun) : Procrastinate

55. Babble : Language :: Static : (**a.** Sock **b.** Truce **c.** Word **d.** Transmission)

56. Apian : Ovine :: Bee : (**a.** Sheep **b.** Pig **c.** Cow **d.** Goose)

57. Bear : Ursine :: Pig : (**a.** Asinine **b.** Ursine **c.** Porcine **d.** Ovine)

58. (**a.** Wilson **b.** Polk **c.** Madison **d.** Tyler) : Taylor :: Coolidge : Hoover

59. Pacific : Atlantic :: Mariana Trench : (**a.** Java Trench **b.** South Sandwich Trench **c.** Puerto Rico Trench **d.** Panama Canal)

60. (**a.** Marconi **b.** Babbage **c.** Aiken **d.** Naismith) : Bain :: Telegraph : Fax

61. Shaft : Spear :: Neck : (**a.** Sleeve **b.** Guitar **c.** Sound **d.** Blood)

62. Lift : Elevator :: (**a.** Snack **b.** Eat **c.** Chip **d.** Potato) : French Fry

63. (**a.** Mongolia **b.** Constantinople **c.** Siam **d.** Nepal) : Persia :: Thailand : Iran

64. Soap : Lye :: (**a.** Glass **b.** Neon **c.** Halogen **d.** Alkali) : Silicate

65. Smart : Crazy :: (**a.** Wolf **b.** Whip **c.** Water **d.** Weasel) : Fox

66. Channel : Waterway :: (**a.** Polyester **b.** Zipper **c.** Cotton **d.** Stone) : Fabric

67. Formicary : Rabbit :: Warren : (**a.** Ants **b.** Cats **c.** Beetles **d.** Mice)

68. (**a.** Carnival **b.** Rifle **c.** Slide **d.** Cone) : Carousel :: Bullet : Cylinder

69. Giraffe : Herbivore :: Seal : (**a.** Monovore **b.** Carnivore **c.** Omnivore **d.** Piscivore)

70. Key : (**a.** Harpsichord **b.** Saxophone **c.** Marimba **d.** Lute) :: Fret : Mandolin

71. Crescent City : City of Lights :: (**a.** New Orleans **b.** New York City **c.** London **d.** Salzburg) : Paris

72. Blueprint : DNA :: (**a.** Architect **b.** RNA **c.** Cytisol **d.** Building) : Cell

73. (**a.** Haiku **b.** Aria **c.** Opera **d.** Lyric) : Song :: Tanka : Poem

74. Darwin : Lamarck :: Natural Selection : (**a.** Geology **b.** The Origin of Species **c.** Survival of the Fittest **d.** Use and Disuse)

75. Triangle : (**a.** Square **b.** Pentagon **c.** Hexagon **d.** Septagon) :: Rectangle : Octagon

76. XL : CC :: CCCXX : (**a.** CD **b.** DC **c.** MDC **d.** MCM)

77. Manicurist : Cuticle :: (**a.** Cosmetology **b.** Pedicurist **c.** Stylist **d.** Cosmetologist) : Skin

78. (a. Raise cain b. Put on ice c. Play Possum d. Green with envy) : Punch the clock :: Poker face : Bring home the bacon

79. $2.5 : \frac{5}{2}$ :: 2.25 : (a. $\frac{5}{4}$ b. $\frac{7}{2}$ c. $\frac{9}{4}$ d. $\frac{9}{2}$)

80. 1988 : Seoul :: 2008 : (a. Tokyo b. Beijing c. South Korea d. China)

81. Woolf : (a. Pound b. Eliot c. Faulkner d. Burroughs) :: Modernist : Postmodernist

82. (a. Drop b. Slip c. Ink d. Drink) : Sign :: Sink : Dip

83. Zembla : Nabokov :: Flatland : (a. Doyle b. Cervantes c. Baum d. Abbott)

84. Deconstruction : Derrida :: (a. Humanism b. Transcendental idealism c. Feminism d. Radical behaviorism) : Kant

85. Laius : Thebes :: Cisus : (a. Greece b. Rome c. Argos d. Sparta)

86. Rappaccini's Daughter : Samson :: (a. Operetta b. Elegy c. Libretto d. Opera) : Oratorio

87. Teeth : Fleam :: (a. Toe b. Gullet c. Claw d. Nail) : Peen

88. (a. Heathcliff b. Edgar Linton c. Isabella Linton d. Nelly Dean) : Wuthering Heights :: Nick Carraway : The Great Gatsby

89. Escher : Graphic :: (a. de Kooning b. Gorky c. Pollock d. Miró) : Abstract Expressionist

90. Vestige : (a. Artery b. Sacrament c. Clergy d. Footprint) :: Vestment : Garb

91. Supplicate : (a. Borrow b. Beg c. Steal d. Pinch) :: Replicate : Copy

92. (a. Stevenson b. Debs c. Johnson d. Carter) : Eisenhower :: McGovern : Nixon

93. 270 : 2 :: Dinosaurs : (a. Raptors b. Homo Sapiens c. Ferns d. Reptiles)

94. Limburger : Rodoric :: (a. Chimay b. Paneer c. Manouri d. Oaxaca) : Feta

95. Fricative : Stop :: F : (a. T b. Th c. V d. B)

96. Palatine : (a. Capitoline b. Florence c. Venice d. Vernal) :: Esquiline : Aventine

97. Perennial : (a. Continuous b. Occasional c. Tulip d. Garden) :: Annual : Yearly

98. 13 : Duodecimal :: (a. 10 b. 11 c. 12 d. 15) : Decimal

99. Skinner : Psychologist :: Bloomfield : (a. Psychiatrist b. Linguist c. Historian d. Physician)

100. Seneca : (a. Cayuga b. Pueblo c. Apache d. Seminole) :: Onondaga : Oneida

101. Chopard : Rolex :: (a. Hundai b. Chevrolet c. Cartier d. Opel) : Audi

102. Vinegar : Acetic Acid :: (a. Soda b. Silver c. Brine d. Air) : Sodium Chloride

103. Rancor : Enmity :: Languor : (a. Rank b. Language c. Sympathy d. Lethargy)

104. Diameter : Bucket :: Radius : (a. Circumference b. Peck c. Bushel d. Load)

105. Cat : (**a.** 3 **b.** 5. **c.** 7 **d.** 9) :: Tango : 2

106. Serbia : Croatia :: (**a.** Dinar **b.** Euro **c.** Rupee **d.** Zlotych) : Kuna

107. Forgo : (**a.** Go **b.** Begin **c.** Renounce **d.** Forget) :: Undo : Reverse

108. Crustacean : Arthropod :: Bryophyta : (**a.** Mosses **b.** Ferns **c.** Phylla **d.** Chloroplasts)

109. Uranium : Einsteinium :: Sugar : (**a.** Glucose **b.** Lactose **c.** Saccharine **d.** Fructose)

110. Quebec : Quebec City :: Saskatchewan : (**a.** Alberta **b.** Edmonton **c.** Regina **d.** Victoria)

111. Beaufort : Wind :: Saffir-Simpson : (**a.** Rain **b.** Heat **c.** Hurricanes **d.** Floods)

112. Pint : Peck :: (**a.** Cup **b.** Pint **c.** Quart **d.** Liter) : Gallon

113. Rapier : (**a.** Respite **b.** Sword **c.** Paper **d.** King) :: Despot : Ruler

114. Binary : Decimal :: 111 : (**a.** 3 **b.** 5 **c.** 7 **d.** 11)

115. Red : Sound :: Black : (**a.** Green **b.** Fury **c.** Sight **d.** Sensation)

116. Nylon : (**a.** Rayon **b.** Linen **c.** Acrylic **d.** Polyester) :: Petroleum : Cellulose

117. Lizards : Sea Lions :: Snakes : (**a.** Giraffes **b.** Marmots **c.** Monkeys **d.** Seals)

118. Decimal : Duodecimal :: 10 : (**a.** 12 **b.** 8 **c.** 2 **d.** 1)

119. (**a.** Privet **b.** Blackcurrant **c.** Daphne **d.** Pokeberry) : Gooseberry :: Holly : Elderberry

120. Impious : (**a.** Furious **b.** Irreverent **c.** Irksome **d.** Unfriendly) :: Indignant : Irked

Answers

1. Mare : Stallion :: Doe : **Buck**

The answer is **b.** A mare is a female horse; a stallion is a male horse. A doe is a female deer; a buck is a male deer.

2. Lennon : Cobain :: Liverpool : **Seattle**

The answer is **b.** John Lennon was a musician from the city of Liverpool in England. Kurt Cobain was a musician from the city of Seattle in the United States.

3. Blood : Lymph :: **Cardiovascular** : Lymphatic

The answer is **a.** The lymphatic system carries lymph; the cardiovascular system carries blood.

4. Miserly : Cheap :: Homogeneous : **Alike**

The answer is **c.** Miserly is another word for cheap, and homogeneous is another word for alike.

5. Vapid : **Insipid** :: Rapid : Swift

The answer is **d.** Vapid is another word for insipid, and rapid is another word for swift.

6. John Keats : **Lord Byron** :: Camille Saint-Saëns : Wolfgang Amadeus Mozart

The answer is **a.** John Keats and Lord Byron were both poets. Camille Saint-Saëns and Wolfgang Amadeus Mozart were both classical composers.

7. Slipper : Ballet :: **Grass Skirt** : Hula

The answer is **c.** A ballet slipper is worn by a ballet dancer and a grass skirt is worn by a hula dancer.

8. 52 : 33 :: 25 : **27**

The answer is **d.** 52 = 25 and 33 = 27.

9. Waffle : Hamburger :: Syrup : **Ketchup**

The answer is **c.** Syrup is the most popular condiment to use on waffles. Ketchup is the most popular condiment used on hamburgers.

10. Hank Williams : Robert Johnson :: Country : **Blues**

The answer is **b.** Hank Williams was a famous country musician and Robert Johnson was a famous blues musician.

11. Radius : Diameter :: Pint : **Quart**

The answer is **c.** The radius of a circle is $\frac{1}{2}$ of the diameter and a pint is $\frac{1}{2}$ of a quart.

12. Othello : **Twelfth Night** :: Tragedy : Comedy

The answer is **b.** William Shakespeare's play Othello is a tragedy; his play Twelfth Night is a comedy.

13. Quixotic : Pragmatic :: Murky : **Clear**

The answer is **c.** Quixotic is an antonym for pragmatic, and murky is an antonym for clear.

14. Smear : Libel :: Heed : **Consider**

The answer is **c.** To smear is a synonym of to libel, and to heed is a synonym of to consider.

15. France : Russia :: Louisiana Purchase : **Alaska**

The answer is **a.** The land referred to in the Louisiana Purchase was purchased from France and Alaska was purchased from Russia.

16. Bond : Debt :: Stock : **Equity**

The answer is **b.** Both bonds and stocks are certificates issued by institutions: Bonds are debt certificates and stocks are equity certificates.

17. Pistil : Female :: **Stamen** : Male

The answer is **c.** The pistil is the female reproductive organ of a plant; the stamen is the male reproductive organ of a plant.

18. Id : Superego :: Desire : **Conscience**

The answer is **c.** Id is a psychological term for desire and superego is a psychological term for conscience.

19. Obscene : Coarse :: Obtuse : **Stupid**

The answer is **d.** Obscene is a synonym for coarse, and obtuse is a synonym for stupid.

20. Michigan : Ontario :: **Huron** : Erie

The answer is **d.** Lakes Michigan, Ontario, Huron, and Erie are all Great Lakes.

21. Gander : **Drone** :: Gaggle : Hive

The answer is **c.** A gander is a male goose; a drone is a male bee. A gaggle is a group of geese; a hive is a group of bees.

22. **Eagle** : United States :: Sun : Japan

The answer is **a.** The rising sun is a symbol associated with Japan. An eagle is a symbol associated with the United States.

23. Jibe : Praise :: **Delude** : Enlighten

The answer is **b.** To jibe is an antonym of to praise, and to delude is an antonym of to enlighten.

24. Piercing : **Siren** :: Hushed : Whisper

The answer is **c.** A siren is described as piercing, and a whisper is described as hushed.

25. **Pup** : Joey :: Shark : Kangaroo

The answer is **d.** A pup is a baby shark; a joey is a baby kangaroo.

26. **Hemoglobin** : Courier :: Oxygen : Package

The answer is **b.** Hemoglobin carries and delivers oxygen as a mail courier carries and delivers packages.

27. Quebec : Alberta :: Victoria : **Queensland**

The answer is **c.** Quebec and Alberta are both Canadian provinces and Victoria and Queensland are both Australian provinces.

28. Crocus : Perennial :: Bean : **Annual**

The answer is **c.** A perennial plant has more than one growing cycle without being replanted. A crocus is an example of a perennial. Beans are an example of annual plants, which have to be replanted each year.

29. 144 : 12 :: **225** : 15

The answer is **b.** 144 is equal to 12 squared and 225 is equal to 15 squared.

30. Nymph : **Maiden** :: Seraphim : Angel

The answer is **a.** A nymph is a maiden, and a seraphim is an angel.

31. Foreman : Teacher :: Construction Site : **Classroom**

The answer is **b.** A foreman oversees workers on a construction site; a teacher oversees students in a classroom.

32. **Whitney** : Cotton Gin :: Deere : Steel Plow

The answer is **a.** Eli Whitney invented the cotton gin and John Deere invented the steel plow.

33. Segregate : Unify :: Repair : **Damage**

The answer is **c.** To segregate is an antonym of to unify, and to repair is an antonym of to damage.

34. Lyric : **Dialogue** :: Song : Play

The answer is **c.** The words in a song are called lyrics. The words in a play are called dialogue.

35. Saddle : **Seat** :: Horse : Car

The answer is **c.** When riding a horse, one sits on a saddle. When driving a car, one sits on a seat.

36. **Corn** : Wheat :: Tortilla : Bun

The answer is **d.** Corn is used to make a tortilla. Wheat is used to make a bun.

37. **Mountain** : Cliff :: Valley : Gorge

The answer is **a.** A gorge is a steep part of a valley and a cliff is a steep part of a mountain.

38. **Merlot** : Lager :: Wine : Beer

The answer is **a.** Merlot is a type of wine. Lager is a type of beer.

39. **Switch** : Ignition :: Lamp : Car

The answer is **a.** The switch is the part of the lamp used to turn it on. The ignition is the part of a car used to turn it on.

40. **Busby Berkeley** : Leonard Bernstein :: Bob Fosse : Leopold Stokowski

The answer is **b.** Busby Berkeley and Bob Fosse are both dance choreographers. Leonard Bernstein and Leopold Stokowski are both orchestra conductors.

41. Queue : **Line** :: Query : Question

The answer is **c.** A queue is another word for a line, and a query is another word for a question.

42. Cinder : Ash :: **Shard** : Glass

The answer is **d.** A cinder is a fragment of ash, and a shard is a fragment of glass.

43. Holst : Planets :: Grieg : **Peer Gynt**

The answer is **b.** "The Planets" is an orchestral suite by Gustav Holst. "Peer Gynt" is an orchestral suite by Edvard Grieg.

44. Mozart : Bach :: Classical : **Baroque**

The answer is **d.** Wolfgang Amadeus Mozart composed music in the classical form. Johann Sebastian Bach composed music in the baroque form.

45. Shadow : Trail :: **Shame** : Disgrace

The answer is **d.** To shadow is to trail someone, and to shame is to disgrace someone.

46. Kimono : Robe : **Obi** : Sash

The answer is **c.** A kimono is a type of Japanese robe. An obi is a type of Japanese sash.

47. Oenophile : Bibliophile :: Wine : **Books**

The answer is **d.** An oenophile is someone with a fine appreciation for wine. A bibliophile is a person with a fine appreciation for books.

48. *Player Piano* : Vonnegut :: *Seize the Day* : **Bellow**

The answer is **d.** *Player Piano* is a 1952 novel by writer Kurt Vonnegut. *Seize the Day* is a 1956 novel by Saul Bellow.

49. Mammal : Dinosaur :: Cenozoic : **Cretaceous**

The answer is **d.** Mammals have flourished in the Cenozoic Era; dinosaurs flourished in the Cretaceous Era.

50. California : Massachusetts :: New Mexico : **South Dakota**

The answer is **a.** Both California and Massachusetts are coastal states. New Mexico and South Dakota are both interior states that do not have borders touching sea coasts.

51. Contract : Obligation :: Tort : **Litigation**

The answer is **b.** A contract is an agreement involving an obligation and a tort is a wrong involving litigation.

52. Marley's Ghost : Stubb Kills a Whale :: A Christmas Carol : Moby Dick

The answer is **a.** Marley's Ghost is a chapter in Charles Dickens's novel *A Christmas Carol*. Stubbs Kills a Whale is a chapter in Herman Melville's novel *Moby Dick*.

53. Roman Catholic : **Protestant** :: Shiite : Sunni

The answer is **a.** Roman Catholic and Protestant represent two of the largest branches of Christianity. Shiite and Sunni represent two of the largest branches of Islam.

54. Reconcile : Fight :: **Hurry** : Procrastinate

The answer is **a.** Reconcile is an antonym of fight, and hurry is an antonym of procrastinate.

55. Babble : Language :: Static : **Transmission**

The answer is **d.** Babble is garbled language, and static is a garbled transmission.

56. Apian : Ovine :: Bee : **Sheep**

The answer is **a.** Apian describes bees; ovine describes sheep.

57. Bear : Ursine :: Pig : **Porcine**

The answer is **c.** Ursine means bear-like; porcine means pig-like.

58. Polk : Taylor :: Coolidge : Hoover

The answer is **b.** Polk preceded Taylor in the office of the U.S. President. Coolidge preceded Hoover.

59. Pacific : Atlantic :: Mariana Trench : **Puerto Rico Trench**

The answer is **c.** The deepest point of the Pacific Ocean is the Mariana Trench and the deepest point of the Atlantic Ocean is the Puerto Rico Trench.

60. Marconi : Bain :: Telegraph : Fax

The answer is **a.** Guglielmo Marconi invented the telegraph. Alexander Bain invented the fax machine.

61. Shaft : Spear :: Neck : **Guitar**

The answer is **b.** The shaft is part of a spear, and the neck is part of the guitar.

62. Lift : Elevator :: **Chip** : French fry

The answer is **c.** In England, an elevator is called a lift and a french fry is called a chip.

63. Siam : Persia :: Thailand : Iran

The answer is **c.** Thailand was formerly known as Siam; Iran was formerly known as Persia.

64. Soap : Lye :: **Glass** : Silicate

The answer is **a.** Soap contains lye; glass contains silicate.

65. Smart : Crazy :: **Whip** : Fox

The answer is **b.** "Smart as a whip" is a common simile and so is "crazy like a fox."

66. Channel : Waterway :: **Cotton** : Fabric

The answer is **c.** A channel is a natural waterway, and cotton is a natural fabric.

67. Formicary : Rabbit :: Warren : **Ants**

The answer is **a.** A formicary is an ant's nest; a warren is a rabbit's den.

68. Slide : Carousel :: Bullet : Cylinder

The answer is **c.** A slide (photographic transparency) goes into a carousel, and a bullet goes into a cylinder.

69. Giraffe : Herbivore :: Seal : **Piscivore**

The answer is **d.** Giraffes' diets are herbivorous—primarily comprised of leaves and grasses. Piscivores' diets are primarily comprised of fish; seals are piscivores.

70. Key : **Harpsichord** :: Fret : Mandolin

The answer is **a.** Notes are produced on a harpsichord by pressing its keys; notes are produced on a mandolin by pressing its frets.

71. Crescent City : City of Lights :: **New Orleans** : Paris

The answer is **a.** New Orleans is known as the Crescent City. Paris is known as the City of Lights.

72. Blueprint : DNA :: **Building** : Cell

The answer is **d.** Blueprints provide details on how, specifically, to construct a building; DNA provides details on how, specifically, to construct a cell.

73. **Aria** : Song :: Tanka : Poem

The answer is **b.** An aria is a kind of song and a tanka is a kind of poem.

74. Darwin : Lamarck :: Natural Selection : **Use and Disuse**

The answer is **d.** Lamarck's theory was the Principle of Use and Disuse. Darwin proved Lamarck wrong with his theory of natural selection.

75. Triangle : **Hexagon** :: Rectangle : Octagon

The answer is **c.** An octagon is a polygon that has 8 sides, twice as many sides as a rectangle. A hexagon is a polygon that has 6 sides, twice as many sides as a triangle.

76. XL : CC :: CCCXX : **MDC**

The answer is **c.** In Roman numerals, CCCXX (320) is eight times XL (40) MDC (1,600) is 8 times CC (200).

77. Manicurist : Cuticle :: **Cosmetologist** : Skin

The answer is **d.** A manicurist works on the appearance of cuticles. A cosmetologist works on the appearance of skin.

78. **Play Possum** : Punch the Clock :: Poker Face : Bring Home the Bacon

The answer is **c.** "Play possum" and "poker face" are both expressions that refer to pretending. "Make ends meet" and "bring home the bacon" are expressions that refer to money.

79. $2.5 : \frac{5}{2} :: 2.25 : \frac{9}{4}$

The answer is **c.** 2.5 equals $2\frac{5}{10}$, equivalent to the fraction $\frac{5}{2}$. 2.25 equals $2\frac{25}{100}$, equivalent to the fraction $\frac{9}{4}$.

80. 1988 : Seoul :: 2008 : **Beijing**

The answer is **b.** In 1988, the Olympic games were held in the South Korean city of Seoul. In 2008, they took place in Chinese city of Beijing.

81. Woolf : **Burroughs** :: Modernist : Postmodernist

The answer is **d.** Virginia Woolf was considered a master of modernist writing, while William S. Burroughs was a postmodernist.

82. **Ink** : Sign :: Sink : Dip

The answer is **c.** To ink means to sign, and to sink means to dip.

83. Zembla : Nabokov :: Flatland : **Abbott**

The answer is **d.** Zembla is a fictional land in Vladamir Nabokov's novel *Pale Fire*. Flatland is a fictional land in Edwin Abbott's novel *Flatland*.

84. Deconstruction : Derrida :: **Transcendental idealism** : Kant

The answer is **b.** Deconstruction is a philosophical term coined by Jacques Derrida. Transcendental idealism is a philosophical term coined by Immanuel Kant.

85. Laius : Thebes :: Cisus : **Argos**

The answer is **c.** In Greek mythology, Laius was king of Thebes and Cisus was king of Argos.

86. Rappaccini's Daughter : Samson :: **Opera** : Oratorio

The answer is **d.** Rappaccini's Daughter is an opera by Mexican composer Daniel Catán. Samson is an oratorio by German composer George Handel.

87. Teeth : Fleam :: **Claw** : Peen

The answer is **c.** Teeth and fleam are parts of a saw. Claw and peen are parts of a hammer.

88. **Nelly Dean** : Wuthering Heights :: Nick Carraway : The Great Gatsby

The answer is **d.** Nelly Dean is the narrator of Emily Brontë's 1847 novel *Wuthering Heights*. Nick Carraway is the narrator of F. Scott Fitzgerald's 1925 novel *The Great Gatsby*.

89. Escher : Graphic :: **de Kooning** : Abstract Expressionist

The answer is **a.** M.C. Escher was a 20th century Dutch graphic artist; Willem de Kooning was a 20th century Dutch abstract expressionist artist.

90. Vestige : **Footprint** :: Vestment : Garb

The answer is **d.** Vestige is another word for footprint, and vestment is another word for garb.

91. Supplicate : **Beg** :: Replicate : Copy

The answer is **b.** To supplicate is a synonym of to beg, and to replicate is a synonym of to copy.

92. **Stevenson** : Eisenhower :: McGovern : Nixon

The answer is **a.** Democratic candidate Adlai Stevenson ran for president against Eisenhower and lost. George McGovern was the unsuccessful Democratic candidate for president who lost to Nixon.

93. 270 : 2 :: Dinosaurs : **Homo Sapiens**

The answer is **b.** Dinosaurs first roamed the earth approximately 270 million years ago; homo sapiens first roamed the earth approximately 2 million years ago.

94. Limburger : Rodoric :: **Manouri** : Feta

The answer is **c.** Limburger and rodoric are both Belgian cheeses. Manouri and feta are Greek cheeses.

95. Fricative : Stop :: F : **T**

The answer is **a.** Referring to consonants, an f is a fricative sound and a t is a stop sound.

96. Palatine : **Capitoline** :: Esquiline : Aventine

The answer is **a.** Palatine, Capitoline, Esquiline and Aventine are four of the seven hills of Rome. The others are Quirinal, Viminal and Caelian.

97. Perennial : **Continuous** :: Annual : Yearly

The answer is **a.** A perennial event is a continuous occurrence, and an annual event is a yearly occurrence.

98. 13 : Duodecimal :: **15** : Decimal

The answer is **d.** The number 13 in duodecimal (base 12) is equal to the number 15 in decimal (base 10).

99. Skinner : Psychologist :: Bloomfield : **Linguist**

The answer is **b.** Skinner was a noted psychologist and Bloomfield was a noted linguist.

100. Seneca : **Cayuga** :: Onondaga : Oneida

The answer is **a.** Seneca, Cayuga, Onondaga, and Oneida are four of the original Five Nations of the Iroquois Confederacy. Mohawk is the fifth.

101. Chopard : Rolex :: **Opel** : Audi

The answer is **d.** Chopard and Rolex are both Swiss watch-making companies; Opel and Audi are both German car manufacturers.

102. Vinegar : Acetic Acid :: **Brine** : Sodium Chloride

The answer is **c.** Vinegar is a solution of acetic acid and water; brine is a solution of sodium chloride and water.

103. Rancor : Enmity :: Languor : **Lethargy**

The answer is **d.** Rancor is a synonym for enmity, and languor is a synonym for lethargy.

104. Diameter : Bucket :: Radius : **Peck**

The answer is **b.** The ratio of radius to diameter is 2:1. The ratio of peck to bucket is 2:1.

105. Cat : **9** :: Tango : 2

The answer is **d.** According to figurative expressions, a "cat has 9 lives" and "it takes 2 to tango."

106. Serbia : Croatia :: **Dinar** : Kuna

The answer is **a.** The dinar is the currency of Serbia. The kuna is the currency of Croatia.

107. Forgo : **Renounce** :: Undo : Reverse

The answer is **c.** "Forgo" is another word for "renounce", and "undo" is another word for "reverse".

108. Crustacean : Arthropod :: Bryophyta : **Mosses**

The answer is **a.** Crustaceans are examples of arthropods; mosses are examples of bryophyta.

109. Uranium : Einsteinium :: Sugar : **Saccharine**

The answer is **c.** Uranium is an element that occurs naturally; Einsteinium does not. Sugar is a sweetener that occurs in nature; Saccharine does not.

110. Quebec : Quebec City :: Saskatchewan : **Regina**

The answer is **c.** The capital of the Canadian province of Quebec is Quebec City and the capital of Saskatchewan is Regina.

111. Beaufort : Wind :: Saffir-Simpson : **Hurricanes**

The answer is **c.** The Beaufort scale measures the intensity of wind; the Saffir-Simpson scale measures the intensity of hurricanes.

112. Pint : Peck :: **Cup** : Gallon

The answer is **a.** There are 16 pints in one peck. There are 16 cups in one gallon.

113. Rapier : **Sword** :: Despot : Ruler

The answer is **b.** A rapier is a type of sword, and a despot is a type of ruler.

114. Binary : Decimal :: 111 : 7

The answer is **c.** The binary system uses 2 as its base. The number 111 in binary notation is equal to the number 7 in decimal notation.

115. Red : Sound :: Black : **Fury**

The answer is **b.** *The Red and the Black* is a novel by the writer Stendhal. *The Sound and the Fury* is a novel by the writer William Faulkner.

116. Nylon : **Rayon** :: Petroleum : Cellulose

The answer is **a.** Nylon is a fabric made from petroleum. Rayon is a fabric made from cellulose.

117. Lizards : Sea lions :: Snakes : **Seals**

The answer is **d.** Both lizards and sea lions have external ears; both snakes and seals do not.

118. Decimal : Duodecimal :: 10 : **12**

The answer is **a.** The decimal system uses 10 as its base. The duodecimal system uses 12 as its base.

119. **Blackcurrant** : Gooseberry :: Holly : Elderberry

The answer is **b.** The blackcurrant and the gooseberry are both edible berries. Holly and the elderberry are both poisonous berries.

120. Impious : **Irreverent** :: Indignant : Irked

The answer is **b.** Impious means irreverent, and indignant means irked.

Scoring Your MAT Practice Test

As mentioned in Chapter 1, when you receive your personal score report for the official MAT, you'll be provided with a scaled score and two percentile ranks, all of which are derived from the number of items you answered correctly—known as your raw score.

Because there are different forms and formats of the official MAT, and typically 20 of the 120 questions on the official MAT are experimental and do not count toward your official scaled score and percentile ranks, it is impossible to create an accurate raw score to scaled score or raw score to percentile chart for this and the other practice tests found in this book. In the end, you are striving to correctly answer the highest number of questions as possible and familiarize yourself with the MAT format—so you're fully prepared to do your best on test day. For now, what's much more important than your overall score is how you did on each of the content areas tested by the exam. You need to diagnose your strengths and weaknesses so that you can concentrate your efforts as you prepare. The question types are mixed in the practice exam, so in order to tell where your strengths and weaknesses lie, you'll need to compare your answer sheet with the following **MAT Practice Test 2 Review**, which shows which of the content areas each question falls into.

Use your performance here in conjunction with the LearningExpress Test Preparation System in Chapter 2 to help you devise a study plan. You should plan to spend more time studying areas that correspond to the questions you found hardest and less time on the content areas in which you did well. Once you have spent some time reviewing, take the next MAT Practice Test to see if you've improved.

CONTENT AREA	QUESTION NUMBERS
Language and Vocabulary	4, 5, 13, 14, 19, 23, 24, 30, 33, 41, 42, 45, 54, 55, 61, 66, 68, 82, 90, 91, 97, 103, 107, 113, 120
Humanities	2, 6, 7, 10, 12, 34, 40, 43, 44, 48, 52, 70, 73, 81, 83, 84, 85, 86, 88, 89, 115
Social Science	15, 16, 18, 20, 22, 27, 37, 50, 51, 53, 58, 59, 63, 71, 92, 95, 96, 99, 100, 110
Natural Science	1, 3, 17, 21, 25, 26, 28, 49, 56, 57, 64, 67, 69, 72, 74, 93, 102, 104, 108, 109, 111, 117
General	9, 31, 32, 35, 36, 38, 39, 46, 47, 60, 62, 65, 77, 78, 80, 87, 94, 101, 105, 106, 116, 119
Mathematics	8, 11, 29, 75, 76, 79, 98, 112, 114, 118

MAT Practice Test 3

CHAPTER SUMMARY

Here's another sample MAT test for you to practice with.

For this third practice test, simulate the actual test-taking experience as closely as you can. Find a quiet place to work where you won't be disturbed. If you own this book, use the answer sheet on the following pages and find some #2 pencils to fill in the circles with. Use a timer or stopwatch to time yourself—you'll have 60 minutes to complete the official MAT. After you take the test, use the detailed answer explanations that follow to review any questions you missed.

MAT Practice Test 3

1.	(a)	(b)	(c)	(d)
2.	(a)	(b)	(c)	(d)
3.	(a)	(b)	(c)	(d)
4.	(a)	(b)	(c)	(d)
5.	(a)	(b)	(c)	(d)
6.	(a)	(b)	(c)	(d)
7.	(a)	(b)	(c)	(d)
8.	(a)	(b)	(c)	(d)
9.	(a)	(b)	(c)	(d)
10.	(a)	(b)	(c)	(d)
11.	(a)	(b)	(c)	(d)
12.	(a)	(b)	(c)	(d)
13.	(a)	(b)	(c)	(d)
14.	(a)	(b)	(c)	(d)
15.	(a)	(b)	(c)	(d)
16.	(a)	(b)	(c)	(d)
17.	(a)	(b)	(c)	(d)
18.	(a)	(b)	(c)	(d)
19.	(a)	(b)	(c)	(d)
20.	(a)	(b)	(c)	(d)
21.	(a)	(b)	(c)	(d)
22.	(a)	(b)	(c)	(d)
23.	(a)	(b)	(c)	(d)
24.	(a)	(b)	(c)	(d)
25.	(a)	(b)	(c)	(d)
26.	(a)	(b)	(c)	(d)
27.	(a)	(b)	(c)	(d)
28.	(a)	(b)	(c)	(d)
29.	(a)	(b)	(c)	(d)
30.	(a)	(b)	(c)	(d)
31.	(a)	(b)	(c)	(d)
32.	(a)	(b)	(c)	(d)
33.	(a)	(b)	(c)	(d)
34.	(a)	(b)	(c)	(d)
35.	(a)	(b)	(c)	(d)
36.	(a)	(b)	(c)	(d)
37.	(a)	(b)	(c)	(d)
38.	(a)	(b)	(c)	(d)
39.	(a)	(b)	(c)	(d)
40.	(a)	(b)	(c)	(d)
41.	(a)	(b)	(c)	(d)
42.	(a)	(b)	(c)	(d)
43.	(a)	(b)	(c)	(d)
44.	(a)	(b)	(c)	(d)
45.	(a)	(b)	(c)	(d)

46.	(a)	(b)	(c)	(d)
47.	(a)	(b)	(c)	(d)
48.	(a)	(b)	(c)	(d)
49.	(a)	(b)	(c)	(d)
50.	(a)	(b)	(c)	(d)
51.	(a)	(b)	(c)	(d)
52.	(a)	(b)	(c)	(d)
53.	(a)	(b)	(c)	(d)
54.	(a)	(b)	(c)	(d)
55.	(a)	(b)	(c)	(d)
56.	(a)	(b)	(c)	(d)
57.	(a)	(b)	(c)	(d)
58.	(a)	(b)	(c)	(d)
59.	(a)	(b)	(c)	(d)
60.	(a)	(b)	(c)	(d)
61.	(a)	(b)	(c)	(d)
62.	(a)	(b)	(c)	(d)
63.	(a)	(b)	(c)	(d)
64.	(a)	(b)	(c)	(d)
65.	(a)	(b)	(c)	(d)
66.	(a)	(b)	(c)	(d)
67.	(a)	(b)	(c)	(d)
68.	(a)	(b)	(c)	(d)
69.	(a)	(b)	(c)	(d)
70.	(a)	(b)	(c)	(d)
71.	(a)	(b)	(c)	(d)
72.	(a)	(b)	(c)	(d)
73.	(a)	(b)	(c)	(d)
74.	(a)	(b)	(c)	(d)
75.	(a)	(b)	(c)	(d)
76.	(a)	(b)	(c)	(d)
77.	(a)	(b)	(c)	(d)
78.	(a)	(b)	(c)	(d)
79.	(a)	(b)	(c)	(d)
80.	(a)	(b)	(c)	(d)
81.	(a)	(b)	(c)	(d)
82.	(a)	(b)	(c)	(d)
83.	(a)	(b)	(c)	(d)
84.	(a)	(b)	(c)	(d)
85.	(a)	(b)	(c)	(d)
86.	(a)	(b)	(c)	(d)
87.	(a)	(b)	(c)	(d)
88.	(a)	(b)	(c)	(d)
89.	(a)	(b)	(c)	(d)
90.	(a)	(b)	(c)	(d)

91.	(a)	(b)	(c)	(d)
92.	(a)	(b)	(c)	(d)
93.	(a)	(b)	(c)	(d)
94.	(a)	(b)	(c)	(d)
95.	(a)	(b)	(c)	(d)
96.	(a)	(b)	(c)	(d)
97.	(a)	(b)	(c)	(d)
98.	(a)	(b)	(c)	(d)
99.	(a)	(b)	(c)	(d)
100.	(a)	(b)	(c)	(d)
101.	(a)	(b)	(c)	(d)
102.	(a)	(b)	(c)	(d)
103.	(a)	(b)	(c)	(d)
104.	(a)	(b)	(c)	(d)
105.	(a)	(b)	(c)	(d)
106.	(a)	(b)	(c)	(d)
107.	(a)	(b)	(c)	(d)
108.	(a)	(b)	(c)	(d)
109.	(a)	(b)	(c)	(d)
110.	(a)	(b)	(c)	(d)
111.	(a)	(b)	(c)	(d)
112.	(a)	(b)	(c)	(d)
113.	(a)	(b)	(c)	(d)
114.	(a)	(b)	(c)	(d)
115.	(a)	(b)	(c)	(d)
116.	(a)	(b)	(c)	(d)
117.	(a)	(b)	(c)	(d)
118.	(a)	(b)	(c)	(d)
119.	(a)	(b)	(c)	(d)
120.	(a)	(b)	(c)	(d)

Directions: For each question, select the answer in the parentheses that best completes the analogy.

1. Id : Ego :: Instinct : (**a.** Love **b.** Fear **c.** Logic **d.** Hunger)

2. 3D : Surround Sound :: Video : (**a.** Stereo **b.** Audio **c.** Movie **d.** Hear)

3. Conjugate : Pair :: Partition : (**a.** Divide **b.** Consecrate **c.** Parade **d.** Squelch)

4. (**a.** Object **b.** Prove **c.** Math **d.** Digress) : Subject :: Veer : Path

5. (**a.** Discord **b.** Rhythm **c.** Melodious **d.** Harmony) : Melody :: Overtone : Tune

6. Washington D.C. : (**a.** Nice **b.** Paris **c.** Lyon **d.** Versailles) :: United States : France

7. Rotation : Earth :: (**a.** Planet **b.** Spinning **c.** Sun **d.** Expanding) : Top

8. (**a.** Pick **b.** Guitar **c.** String **d.** Violin) : Plectrum :: Viola : Bow

9. (**a.** Exception **b.** Passage **c.** Routine **d.** Cause) : Excerpt :: Exercise : Maneuver

10. Implement : Rule :: (**a.** Propose **b.** Render **c.** Divide **d.** Teach) : Verdict

11. Essay : (**a.** Story **b.** Fairy Tale **c.** Journal **d.** Book) :: Fable : Novel

12. Fe : K :: Iron : (**a.** Potassium **b.** Sodium **c.** Calcium **d.** Zinc)

13. 4 : (**a.** 10 **b.** 12 **c.** 16 **d.** 18) :: 20 : 50

14. 1 : Hydrogen :: 3 : (**a.** Helium **b.** Lithium **c.** Carbon **d.** Plutonium)

15. Paste : Flour :: (**a.** Collage **b.** Art **c.** Application **d.** Magazine) : Papier-mâché

16. Two : (**a.** Two **b.** Six **c.** Four **d.** Five) :: Representative : Senator

17. Principle : Doctrine :: Living : (**a.** Will **b.** Dead **c.** Likelihood **d.** Livelihood)

18. Montana : Texas :: (**a.** Canada **b.** South Dakota **c.** Alaska **d.** England) : Mexico

19. Elementary : High :: (**a.** 3 **b.** 10 **c.** 15 **d.** 23) : 11

20. (**a.** Maslow **b.** Skinner **c.** Watson **d.** Rogers) : Freud :: Behaviorism : Psychoanalysis

21. Coffee : (**a.** Cup **b.** Milk **c.** Ounce **d.** Beans) :: Tea : Leaves

22. (**a.** Temperance **b.** Women's Suffrage **c.** Labor Laws **d.** Housing Equality) : Civil Rights :: Susan B. Anthony : Martin Luther King Jr.

23. (**a.** Ascent **b.** Absence **c.** Dollar **d.** Absorption) : Climb :: Recession : Withdrawal

24. Shallot : (**a.** Shark **b.** Muscle **c.** Dessert **d.** Onion) :: Scallop : Mollusk

25. Fulton : Steamboat :: Whitney : (**a.** Museum **b.** Television **c.** Fluorescent Light **d.** Cotton Gin)

26. Ethereal : Sky :: (**a.** Terrestrial **b.** Sidereal **c.** Oceanic **d.** Spiritual) : Earth

27. Hydrogen : Carbon :: (**a.** 1 **b.** 2 **c.** 4 **d.** 9) : 6

28. Civil War : 1861 :: Revolutionary War : (**a.** 1775 **b.** 1776 **c.** 1757 **d.** 1783)

29. (**a.** Equinox **b.** Fall **c.** Morning **d.** Winter) : Autumn :: Solstice : Summer

30. Diurnal : Day :: (**a.** Nexus **b.** Nocturnal **c.** Magnetic **d.** Celestial) : Night

31. Fit : Solid :: (**a.** Stone **b.** Fiddle **c.** Cave **d.** Shape) : Rock

32. Sombrero : Mexico :: (**a.** Fedora **b.** Fez **c.** Bonnet **d.** Boater) : Morocco

33. Congeal : Solidify :: (**a.** Conceal **b.** Singe **c.** Evaporate **d.** Charge) : Char

34. (**a.** Singer **b.** Wand **c.** King **d.** Rule) : Conductor :: Scepter : Baton

35. (**a.** Cool **b.** Annoying **c.** Tight **d.** Crazy) : Drum :: Cute : Button

36. Inch : Foot :: Dozen : (**a.** 12 **b.** Yard **c.** 36 **d.** Gross)

37. Cannellini : Fettuccini :: (**a.** Ravioli **b.** Cannoli **c.** Pinto **d.** Macaroni) : Rotini

38. Borealis : Australis :: North : (**a.** East **b.** Aurora **c.** South **d.** Hemisphere)

39. Radius : (**a.** Diameter **b.** Circumference **c.** Circle **d.** Chord) :: x : 2x

40. Franz Schubert : Romantic :: (**a.** Cage **b.** Schumann **c.** Dvorak **d.** Bizet) : Avant Garde

41. (**a.** Texas **b.** Accent **c.** London **d.** Dublin) : Brogue :: Austin : Drawl

42. Singing in the Rain : (**a.** Duck Soup **b.** The Quiet Man **c.** High Noon **d.** Easy Rider) :: Gold Diggers of 1933 : The Wild Bunch

43. (**a.** Absent **b.** Discharge **c.** Commendation **d.** AWOL) : Truant :: Military : School

44. Blank : Trochaic :: (**a.** Dactylic **b.** Free **c.** Caesurae **d.** Pentameter) : Iambic

45. Partisan : Biased :: (**a.** First **b.** Balanced **c.** Dogged **d.** Finite) : Limited

46. Deduce : Infer :: (**a.** Boast **b.** Infuriate **c.** Soar **d.** Reduce) : Crow

47. (**a.** Earnest **b.** The Wasteland **c.** Prufrock **d.** Love) : Eliot :: Gray : Wilde

48. (**a.** Holmes **b.** Watson **c.** Jones **d.** Squealer) : Moriarity :: Snowball : Napoleon

49. Polaris : Ursa Minor :: Rigel : (**a.** Pliedes **b.** Ursa Major **c.** Orion **d.** Taurus)

50. (**a.** Leg **b.** Sling **c.** Floor **d.** Wing) : Arm :: Column : Ceiling

51. Nerve : Adipose :: Impulses : (**a.** Clotting **b.** Secretion **c.** Cushioning **d.** Pumping)

52. Voluntary : Involuntary :: Skeletal : (**a.** Connective **b.** Nerve **c.** Smooth **d.** Bone)

53. Binary : Duodecimal :: 2 : (**a.** 6 **b.** 8 **c.** 10 **d.** 12)

54. Perseus : Heracles :: (**a.** Andromeda **b.** Zeus **c.** Medusa **d.** Cassiopeia) : Hydra of Lerna

55. Empire State Building : New York City :: Space Needle : (**a.** Chicago **b.** Toronto **c.** Seattle **d.** Boston)

56. (**a.** Pennsylvania **b.** South Carolina **c.** Maryland **d.** Tennessee) : Florida :: King Charles II : Ponce de Leon

57. Fair : Rough :: Square : (**a.** Circle **b.** Smooth **c.** Tumble **d.** Box)

58. Calvin : Eddy :: Presbyterian : (**a.** Christian Science **b.** Jehovah's Witness **c.** Unitarian **d.** Methodist)

59. (**a.** Crustacean **b.** Bone **c.** Spider **d.** Chitin) : Arthropod :: Calcium Carbonate : Mollusc

60. (**a.** Fire **b.** Forest **c.** Nourishment **d.** Hydrant) : Water :: Tree : Sap

61. Limp : Injury :: (**a.** Stumble **b.** Inflammation **c.** Rest **d.** Incarceration) : Conviction

62. Sahara : Painted :: Africa : (**a.** South America **b.** North America **c.** Europe **d.** Australia)

63. Beowulf : Aenid :: Rime of the Ancient Mariner : (**a.** Barbara Allen **b.** Virgil **c.** Epic **d.** Unknown)

64. Peter : Ivan :: Great : (**a.** Invincible **b.** Awful **c.** Terrible **d.** Invoker)

65. One : Several :: Monarchy : (**a.** Polyarchy **b.** Diarchy **c.** Oligarchy **d.** Shared kingdom)

66. 4 : (**a.** 6 **b.** 9 **c.** 12 **d.** 16) :: 64 : 216

67. Meteorite : Strikes :: Meteor : (**a.** Vaporizes **b.** Contacts **c.** Explodes **d.** Damages)

68. Brag : Garb :: Drab : (**a.** Mundane **b.** Actor **c.** Costume **d.** Bard)

69. Prim : (**a.** Timid **b.** Probable **c.** Neat **d.** Primary) :: Grim : Somber

70. Ostrich : Goose :: Kiwi : (**a.** Parrot **b.** Emu **c.** Cassowary **d.** Rhea)

71. Meiosis : (**a.** Reproduction **b.** Cells **c.** Binary Fission **d.** DNA) :: Eukaryotes : Bacteria

72. Scungilli : Conch :: (**a.** Macaroni **b.** Calamari **c.** Antipasto **d.** Scaloppini) : Squid

73. Gill : Liquid :: Furlong : (**a.** Speed **b.** Distance **c.** Radioativity **d.** Charge)

74. (**a.** Berserker **b.** Samurai **c.** Velite **d.** Cossack) : Norse :: Gladiator : Roman

75. Cable car : (**a.** Taxi **b.** Subway **c.** Monorail **d.** Gondola) :: San Francisco : Venice

76. Phenomenon : Phenomena :: Die : (**a.** Heaven **b.** Miracle **c.** Dice **d.** Phenomenal)

77. Turner : (**a.** HBO **b.** ABC **c.** CNN **d.** TMC) :: Murdoch : Fox

78. Insole : Shoe :: Tail : (**a.** Trousers **b.** Jacket **c.** Fashion **d.** Length)

79. Louvre : France :: (**a.** Prado **b.** Musee du Rodin **c.** Catalonia **d.** Andorra) : Spain

80. Complementary : Supplementary :: 90 : (**a.** 45 **b.** 180 **c.** 270 **d.** 360)

81. More : Utopia :: (**a.** Gulliver **b.** Swift **c.** Orwell **d.** Robinson) : Balnibarbi

82. Tractatus Logico-Philosophicus : (**a.** Wittgenstein **b.** Russell **c.** Frege **d.** Spinoza) :: Science of Logic : Hegel

83. Bernoulli : Bohr :: Fluid Dynamics : (**a.** Quantum Theory **b.** Environmentalism **c.** Immunity **d.** Probability)

84. Aristotle : (**a.** Euclid **b.** Foucault **c.** Plato **d.** DuMont) :: Mill : Bentham

85. (**a.** Semantic **b.** Extrovert **c.** Declarative **d.** Talkative) : Procedural :: Explicit : Implicit

86. Blue : (**a.** Rose **b.** African **c.** Surreal **d.** Cubism) :: Femme aux Bras Croisés : Garçon à la Pipe

87. (**a.** Concise **b.** Massive **c.** Elliptical **d.** Wordy) : Epigram :: Sweeping : Epic

88. Brew : (**a.** Drink **b.** Bar **c.** Wipe **d.** Contrive) :: Fret : Worry

89. Bergman : Buñuel :: (**a.** Citizen Kane **b.** The Wizard of Oz **c.** Cries and Whispers **d.** Virdiana) : The Discreet Charm of the Bourgeoisie

90. (**a.** Galileo **b.** Hutchinson **c.** Cooke **d.** Bacon) : Renaissance :: Locke : Enlightenment

91. 20 : 70 :: (**a.** 40 **b.** 60 **c.** 80 **d.** 90) : 140

92. Parrot : Mimic :: Dog : (**a.** Canine **b.** Talk **c.** Cat **d.** Hound)

93. *The Silver Chair* : (**a.** *Return of the King* **b.** *Harry Potter and the Sorcerer's Stone* **c.** *The Last Battle* **d.** *A Wrinkle in Time*) :: Harry Potter and the Goblet of Fire : The Two Towers

94. Vinaya Pitaka : (**a.** Islam **b.** Buddhism **c.** Mandaeanism **d.** Samaritanism) :: Kalpa Sūtra : Jainsim

95. (**a.** Salutation **b.** Company profile **c.** Competition **d.** Marketing research) : Mission statement :: Letterhead : Key projections

96. Precambrian : 85 :: Cenozoic : (**a.** 1 **b.** 10 **c.** 25 **d.** 50)

97. Prime : 11 :: Perfect : (**a.** 15 **b.** 22 **c.** 23 **d.** 28)

98. Triassic : (**a.** Paleozoic **b.** Jurassic **c.** Triassic **d.** Quaternary) :: Mesosoic : Cenozoic

99. Barber license : (**a.** Appraiser license **b.** Broadcast license **c.** Cosmetologist license **d.** Private investigator license) :: Accountant license : Drug manufacturing license

100. (**a.** Scalia **b.** Stevens **c.** Kennedy **d.** Powell) : Ford :: Souter : Bush

101. Adore : Abhor :: Censure : (**a.** Complain **b.** Count **c.** Extol **d.** Question)

102. Yeomanly : (**a.** Awkward **b.** Disloyal **c.** True **d.** Seaworthy) :: Perilous : Safe

103. Brooklyn : (**a.** Paris **b.** Mitte **c.** Germany **d.** Dresden) :: New York City : Berlin

104. Beaufort : Wind :: Saffir-Simpson : (**a.** Rain **b.** Heat **c.** Hurricanes **d.** Floods)

105. Chayefsky : Emerson :: Scene : (**a.** Setting **b.** Stanza **c.** Poem **d.** Script)

106. $\frac{3}{5} : \frac{1}{5} :: \frac{6}{7} : ($**a.** $\frac{2}{3}$ **b.** $\frac{1}{6}$ **c.** $\frac{1}{7}$ **d.** $\frac{2}{7})$

107. (**a.** Flagon **b.** Pint **c.** Quart **d.** Stone) : Half Gallon :: Peck : $\frac{1}{4}$B ushel

108. Honshu : Japan :: Sumatra : (**a.** Vietnam **b.** Philippines **c.** Indonesia **d.** India)

109. Hutton : Geology :: Dalton : (**a.** Atomic Theory **b.** Astronomy **c.** Organic Chemistry **d.** Quantum Mechanics)

110. Folded : Fault-Block :: (**a.** Blue **b.** Yellow **c.** Black **d.** White) : Red

111. Alabama : (**a.** Camelia **b.** Purple **c.** Rose **d.** Cactus) :: Illinois : Violet

112. Mythologize : Debunk :: Exile : (**a.** Stranger **b.** Welcome **c.** Push **d.** Exit)

113. Abate : Reduce :: Beat : (**a.** Surpass **b.** Rebate **c.** Deduce **d.** Encompass)

114. Bachelor : (**a.** Groom **b.** Police department **c.** Fire Engine **d.** Fire hall) :: Studio : Fire house

115. Corporate : Career :: (**a.** Liberal **b.** Community **c.** International **d.** Technical) : Junior

116. Moldavia : (**a.** Turkey **b.** Belarus **c.** Bulgaria **d.** Yugoslavia) :: Romania : Bessarabia

117. Rosh Hashanah : (**a.** Purim **b.** Sukkot **c.** Yom Hashoah **d.** Shavout) :: Yom Kippur : Passover

118. Spanakopita : Spinach :: Taramosalata : (**a.** Eggplant **b.** Caviar **c.** Cheese **d.** Zucchini)

119. 41 : 42 :: 21 : (**a.** 20 **b.** 21 **c.** 32 **d.** 23)

120. Infuse : Permeate :: Kindle : (**a.** Light **b.** Grow **c.** Steep **d.** Pound)

Answers

1. Id : Ego :: Instinct : **Logic**

The answer is **c.** According to psychologists, the id is the part of the self that operates according to instinct and the ego is the part that operates according to logic.

2. 3D : Surround Sound :: Video : **Audio**

The answer is **b.** 3D is an enhancing effect used in video. Surround sound is an enhancing effect used in audio.

3. Conjugate : Pair :: Partition : **Divide**

The answer is **a.** To conjugate means to pair, and to partition means to divide.

4. **Digress** : Subject :: Veer : Path

The answer is **d.** One digresses from a subject, and one veers from a path.

5. Harmony : Melody :: Overtone : Tune

The answer is **d.** Harmony and overtone are both musical tones that are higher in frequency than the fundamental tone. Melody and tune are both the fundamental tones of a musical piece.

6. Washington D.C. : **Paris** :: United States : France

The answer is **b.** Washington D.C. is the capital of the United States and Paris is the capital of France.

7. Rotation : Earth :: **Spinning** : Top

The answer is **b.** Rotation is the movement of the earth and spinning is the movement of a top.

8. Guitar : Plectrum :: Viola : Bow

The answer is **b.** One picks the strings of a guitar with a plectrum. One plays a viola with a bow.

9. Passage : Excerpt :: Exercise : Maneuver

The answer is **b.** A passage is another word for an excerpt, and an exercise is another word for a maneuver.

10. Implement : Rule :: **Render** : Verdict

The answer is **b.** A rule is implemented, and a verdict is rendered.

11. Essay : **Journal** :: Fable : Novel

The answer is **c.** Essays and journals are non-fiction forms of writing. Fables and novels are fiction.

12. Fe : K :: Iron : **Potassium**

The answer is **a.** Fe is the symbol for iron; K is the symbol for potassium.

13. 4 : **10** :: 20 : 50

The answer is **a.** 5 times 4 is 20 and 5 times 10 is 50.

14. 1 : Hydrogen :: 3 : **Lithium**

The answer is **b.** The atomic number for hydrogen is 1; the atomic number for Lithium is 3.

15. Paste : Flour :: **Collage** : Papier-mâché

The answer is **a.** Paste is used in the art of collage. Flour is used in the art of papier-mâché.

16. Two : **Six** :: Representative : Senator

The answer is **b.** United States Senators are elected for six year terms and United States Representatives are elected for two year terms.

17. Principle : Doctrine :: Living : **Livelihood**

The answer is **d.** "Principle" is another word for "doctrine", and "living" is another word for "livelihood".

18. Montana : Texas :: **Canada** : Mexico

The answer is **a.** Montana borders Canada and Texas borders Mexico.

19. Elementary : High : **3** : 11

The answer is **a.** 3rd grade is a stage of elementary school. 11th grade is a stage of high school.

20. **Skinner** : Freud :: Behaviorism : Psychoanalysis

The answer is **b.** The psychologist B.F. Skinner is associated with behaviorism; psychologist Sigmund Freud is associated with psychoanalysis.

21. Coffee : **Beans** :: Tea : Leaves

The answer is **d.** Coffee is made from beans and tea is made from leaves.

22. **Women's Suffrage** : Civil Rights :: Susan B. Anthony : Martin Luther King, Jr.

The answer is **b.** Susan B. Anthony was a leader of the women's suffrage movement and Martin Luther King, Jr. was a leader in the civil rights movement.

23. **Ascent** : Climb :: Recession : Withdrawal

The answer is **a.** An ascent is a climb, and a recession is a withdrawal.

24. Shallot : Onion :: Scallop : Mollusk

The answer is **d.** A shallot is a type of onion, and a scallop is a type of mollusk.

25. Fulton : Steamboat :: Whitney : **Cotton Gin**

The answer is **d.** Robert Fulton invented the steamboat and Eli Whitney invented the cotton gin.

26. Ethereal : Sky :: **Terrestrial** : Earth

The answer is **a.** Ethereal has to do with the sky; terrestrial has to do with the earth.

27. Hydrogen : Carbon :: **1** : 6

The answer is **a.** Hydrogen's atomic number is 1, carbon's atomic number is 6.

28. Civil War : 1861 :: Revolutionary War : **1775**

The answer is **a.** The Civil War began in 1861. The Revolutionary War began in 1775.

29. **Equinox** : Autumn :: Solstice : Summer

The answer is **a.** The autumnal equinox is the first day of autumn; the summer solstice is the first day of summer.

30. Diurnal : Day :: **Nocturnal** : Night

The answer is **b.** Diurnal describes the day; nocturnal describes the night.

31. Fit : Solid :: **Fiddle** : Rock

The answer is **b.** "Fit as a fiddle" is a common simile, and so is "solid as a rock."

32. Sombrero : Mexico :: **Fez** : Morocco

The answer is **b.** A sombrero is a hat associated with Mexico, and a fez is a hat associated with Morocco.

33. Congeal : Solidify :: **Singe** : Char

The answer is **b.** To congeal means to solidify, and to singe means to char.

34. **King** : Conductor :: Scepter : Baton

The answer is **c.** A king holds an ornamental rod called a scepter. A conductor leads a band with a rod called a baton.

35. **Tight** : Drum :: Cute : Button

The answer is **c.** The phrases "tight as a drum" and "cute as a button" are both common similes.

36. Inch : Foot :: Dozen : **Gross**

The answer is **d.** There are 12 inches in 1 foot and there are 12 dozen in 1 gross.

37. Cannellini : Fettuccini :: **Pinto** : Rotini

The answer is **d.** Cannellini and pintos are kinds of beans. Fettuccini and rotini are kinds of pasta.

38. Borealis : Australis :: North : **South**

The answer is **c.** Aurora Borealis is seen in the Northern Hemisphere; Aurora Australis is seen in the Southern Hemisphere.

39. Radius : **Diameter** :: x : $2x$

The answer is **a.** The diameter of a circle is equal to twice the radius. If x is the length of the radius of a circle, $2x$ is the length of the diameter of the circle.

40. Franz Schubert : Romantic :: **Cage** : Avant garde

The answer is **a.** Franz Schubert was a Romantic composer. John Cage was an avant-garde music composer.

41. **Dublin** : Brogue :: Austin : Drawl

The answer is **d.** The accent of a person from Dublin, Ireland is called a brogue. The accent of a person from Austin, Texas is called a drawl.

42. Singing in the Rain : **High Noon** :: Gold Diggers of 1933 : The Wild Bunch

The answer is **c.** The 1952 film Singing in the Rain and the 1933 film Gold Diggers of 1933 are both musicals. The 1952 film High Noon and the 1969 film The Wild Bunch are both westerns.

43. **AWOL** : Truant :: Military : School

The answer is **d.** Unofficial absence from the military is known as being AWOL, an acronym for "absent without leave." To be unofficially absent from school is to be truant.

44. Blank : Trochaic :: **Free** : Iambic

The answer is **b.** Blank and free are types of poetic verse. Trochaic and iambic are poetic meters.

45. Partisan : Biased :: **Finite** : Limited

The answer is **d.** Partisan is a synonym for biased, and finite is a synonym for limited.

46. Deduce : Infer :: **Boast** : Crow

The answer is **a.** Deduce is a synonym of infer, and boast is a synonym of crow.

47. **Prufrock** : Eliot :: Gray : Wilde

The answer is **c.** Poet T.S. Eliot wrote a poem about a character named Prufrock called "The Love Song of J. Alfred Prufrock." Oscar Wilde wrote a novel about a character named Gray called *The Picture of Dorian Gray.*

48. **Holmes** : Moriarty :: Snowball : Napoleon

The answer is **a.** The literary character Moriarty, who appeared in a series of books by Sir Arthur Conan Doyle, is the arch enemy of hero Sherlock Holmes. The literary character Napoleon is the enemy of Snowball in the novel Animal Farm by George Orwell.

49. Polaris : Ursa Minor :: Rigel : **Orion**

The answer is **c.** Polaris is the brightest star in the constellation Ursa Minor (the little dipper); Rigel is the brightest star in the constellation Orion.

50. **Sling** : Arm :: Column : Ceiling

The answer is **b.** A sling is used to support an arm, and a column is used to support a ceiling.

51. Nerve : Adipose :: Impulses : **Cushioning**

The answer is **c.** Nerve tissue controls impulses; adipose tissue provides cushioning.

52. Voluntary : Involuntary :: Skeletal : **Smooth**

The answer is **c.** Skeletal muscle is voluntary; smooth muscle is involuntary.

53. Binary : Duodecimal :: 2 : **12**

The answer is **d.** The binary system uses a base of 2. The duodecimal system uses a base of 12.

54. Perseus : Heracles :: **Medusa** : Hydra of Lerna

The answer is **c.** In Greek mythology, Perseus and Hercules were heroes, while Medusa and the Hydra of Lerna were the monsters they slew, respectively.

55. Empire State Building : New York City :: Space Needle : **Seattle**

The answer is **c.** The Empire State Building is a famous New York City landmark, and the Space Needle is a famous landmark in Seattle.

56. **South Carolina** : Florida :: King Charles II : Ponce de Leon

The answer is **b.** King Charles II named South Carolina and Ponce de Leon named Florida.

57. Fair : Rough :: Square : **Tumble**

The answer is **c.** "Fair and square" is a common expression meaning honest and straightforward. "Rough and tumble" is a common expression meaning tough and hearty.

58. Calvin : Eddy :: Presbyterian : **Christian Science**

The answer is **a.** John Calvin founded the Presbyterian church and Mary Baker Eddy founded the Christian Science church.

59. Chitin : Arthropod :: Calcium Carbonate : Mollusk

The answer is **d.** An arthropod's skeleton is made of chitin; a mollusk's shell is made of calcium carbonate.

60. Hydrant : Water :: Tree : Sap

The answer is **d.** A hydrant is a source of water, and a tree is a source of sap.

61. Limp : Injury :: **Incarceration** : Conviction

The answer is **d.** A limp is the result of an injury, and incarceration is the result of a conviction.

62. Sahara : Painted :: Africa : **North America**

The answer is **b.** The Sahara is a desert in Africa; the Painted Desert is in North America.

63. Beowulf : Aenid :: Rime of the Ancient Mariner : **Barbara Allen**

The answer is **a.** Beowulf and Virgil's Aenid are both epic poems. Samuel Taylor Coleridge's "Rime of the Ancient Mariner" and "Barbara Allen" are ballads.

64. Peter : Ivan :: Great : **Terrible**

The answer is **c.** Both rulers of Russia, they were known as Peter the Great and Ivan the Terrible.

65. One : Several :: Monarchy : **Oligarchy**

The answer is **c.** In a monarchy there is one ruler. In an oligarchy there are several rulers.

66. 4 : 6 :: 64 : 216

The answer is **a.** 43 equals 64 and 63 equals 216.

67. Meteorite : Strikes :: Meteor : **Vaporizes**

The answer is **a.** By definition, a meteorite strikes the earth, and a meteor vaporizes before striking the earth.

68. Brag : Garb :: Drab : **Bard**

The answer is **d.** Brag is the palindrome of garb, and drab is the palindrome of bard.

69. Prim : **Neat** :: Grim : Somber

The answer is **c.** Prim is a synonym for neat, and grim is a synonym for somber.

70. Ostrich : Goose :: Kiwi : **Parrot**

The answer is **a.** Both ostriches and kiwis are flightless birds. Both geese and parrots can fly.

71. Meiosis : **Binary Fission** :: Eukaryotes : Bacteria

The answer is **c.** Meiosis occurs in sexual reproduction in eukaryotes; binary fission occurs in asexual reproduction in bacteria.

72. Scungilli : Conch :: **Calamari** : Squid

The answer is **b.** When conch is served in an Italian dish, it is called scungilli; when squid is served in an Italian dish it is called calamari.

73. Gill : Liquid :: **Furlong** : Distance

The answer is **b.** A gill is a measure of liquid; a furlong is a measure of distance.

74. **Berserker** : Norse :: Gladiator : Roman

The answer is **a.** The berserkers were Norse warriors and gladiators were Roman warriors.

75. Cable car : **Gondola** :: San Francisco : Venice

The answer is **d.** San Francisco, California, is well known for its cable car public transportation system. The Italian city of Venice is famous for the gondolas that transport tourists through the Grand Canal.

76. Phenomenon : Phenomena :: Die : **Dice**

The answer is **c.** Phenomenon is the singular of phenomena, and die is the singular of dice.

77. Turner : **CNN** :: Murdoch : Fox

The answer is **c.** Ted Turner founded the CNN news channel and Rupert Murdoch founded the Fox news channel.

78. Insole : Shoe :: Tail : **Jacket**

The answer is **b.** An insole is part of a shoe. A tail is part of a jacket.

79. Louvre : France :: **Prado** : Spain

The answer is **a.** The Louvre is a famous museum in France and the Prado is a famous museum in Spain.

80. Complementary : Supplementary :: 90 : **180**

The answer is **b.** The sum of two complementary angles is 90 degrees. The sum of two supplementary angles is 180 degrees.

81. More : Utopia :: **Swift** : Balnibarbi

The answer is **b.** English writer Sir Thomas More created the fictional paradise of Utopia in his book *Utopia*. Balnibarbi is a fictional land in Jonathan Swift's novel *Gulliver's Travels*.

82. Tractatus Logico-Philosophicus : **Wittgenstein** :: Science of Logic : Hegel

The answer is **a.** *Tractatus Logico-Philosophicus* is a book by Austrian-British philosopher Ludwig Wittgenstein. *Science of Logic* is a book by German philosopher Georg Hegel.

83. Bernoulli : Bohr :: Fluid Dynamics : **Quantum Theory**

The answer is **a.** Daniel Bernoulli was the father of fluid dynamics; Neils Bohr was the father of quantum theory.

84. Aristotle : **Plato** :: Mill : Bentham

The answer is **c.** Greek philosopher Aristotle was a student of the philosopher Plato. English philosopher John Stuart Mill was a student of Jeremy Bentham.

85. Declarative : Procedural :: Explicit : Implicit

The answer is **c.** In the area of memory, there are two major divisions. Declarative memory is also known as explicit memory and procedural memory is also known as implicit memory.

86. Blue : **Rose** :: Femme aux Bras Croisés : Garçon à la pipe

The answer is **a.** Spanish painter Pablo Picasso painted Femme aux Bras Croisés during a phase of his career known as his "Blue Period." He painted Garçon à la pipe during his "Rose period."

87. Concise : Epigram :: Sweeping : Epic

The answer is **a.** Concise describes an epigram, and sweeping describes an epic.

88. Brew : **Contrive** :: Fret : Worry

The answer is **d.** To brew means to contrive, and to fret means to worry.

89. Bergman : Buñuel :: **Cries and Whispers** : The Discreet Charm of the Bourgeoisie

The answer is **c.** Cries and Whispers is a 1972 film by Swedish filmmaker Ingmar Bergman. The Discreet Charm of the Bourgeoisie is a 1972 film by Mexican filmmaker Luis Buñuel.

90. Bacon : Renaissance :: Locke : Enlightenment

The answer is **d.** Bacon was a philosopher during the Renaissance. Locke was a philosopher during the Enlightenment.

91. 20 : 70 :: **40** : 140

The answer is **a.** The sum of 2 complementary angles is 90 degrees (20 + 70 = 90). The sum of 2 supplementary angles is 180 degrees (40 + 140 = 180).

92. Parrot : Mimic :: Dog : **Hound**

The answer is **d.** To parrot means to mimic, and to dog means to hound.

93. *The Silver Chair* : A Wrinkle in Time :: *Harry Potter and the Goblet of Fire* : The Two Towers

The answer is **d.** *The Silver Chair* is one of seven books in the Chronicles of Narnia series by C. S. Lewis and *Harry Potter and the Goblet of Fire* is one of seven books in the Harry Potter series by J.K. Rowling. *A Wrinkle in Time* is a book in a trilogy by Madeleine L'Engle and *The Two Towers* is a book in the Lord of the Rings trilogy by J.R.R. Tolkien.

94. Vinaya Pitaka : **Buddhism** :: Kalpa Sūtra : Jainsim

The answer is **b.** The Vinaya Pitaka is a holy text used by Buddhists; the Kalpa Sūtra is a holy text used by Jains.

95. Salutation : Mission statement :: Letterhead : Key projections

The answer is **a.** Salutation and letterhead are parts of a business letter. Mission statement and key projections are parts of a business plan.

96. Precambrian : 85 :: Cenozoic : **1**

The answer is **a.** The Precambrian Era accounts for about 85% of geologic time; the Cenozoic Era accounts for about 1% of geologic time.

97. Prime : 11 :: Perfect : **28**

The answer is **d.** 11 is a prime number. The only divisors are 1 and 11. 28 is a perfect number. 28 is the sum of its proper divisors.

98. Triassic : **Quaternary** :: Mesosoic : Cenozoic

The answer is **d.** The Triassic period was part of the Mesozoic Era; the Quarternary period was part of the Cenozoic Era.

99. Barber license : **Broadcast license** :: Accountant license : Drug manufacturing license

The answer is **b.** A barber license and an accountant license are both state licenses. A broadcast license and a drug manufacturing license are both federal licenses.

100. **Stevens** : Ford :: Souter : Bush

The answer is **b.** Justice Stevens was appointed to the U.S. Supreme Court by President Ford. Justice Souter was appointed by President Bush.

101. Adore : Abhor :: Censure : **Extol**

The answer is **c.** to adore is the opposite of abhor, and censure is the opposite of extol.

102. Yeomanly : **Disloyal** :: Perilous : Safe

The answer is **b.** Yeomanly is an antonym for disloyal, and perilous is an antonym for safe.

103. Brooklyn : **Mitte** :: New York City : Berlin

The answer is **b.** Brooklyn is one of the five boroughs of New York. Mitte is one of the 12 boroughs of Berlin.

104. Beaufort : Wind :: Saffir-Simpson : **Hurricanes**

The answer is **c.** The Beaufort scale measures the intensity of wind; the Saffir-Simpson scale measures the intensity of hurricanes.

105. Chayefsky : Emerson :: Scene : **Stanza**

The answer is **b.** Paddy Chayefsky is a screenwriter whose scripts are divided into scenes. Ralph Waldo Emerson is a poet whose poems are divided into stanzas.

106. $\frac{3}{5} : \frac{1}{5} :: \frac{6}{7} : \frac{2}{7}$

The answer is **d.** $\frac{1}{3}$ times $\frac{3}{5}$ equals $\frac{1}{5}$. $\frac{1}{3}$ times $\frac{6}{7}$ equals $\frac{2}{7}$.

107. **Flagon** : Half Gallon :: Peck : $\frac{1}{4}$ Bushel

The answer is **a.** A half gallon is equal to a flagon; a peck is equal to $\frac{1}{4}$ bushel.

108. Honshu : Japan :: Sumatra : **Indonesia**

The answer is **c.** Honshu is one of the main islands of Japan. Sumatra is one of the main islands of Indonesia.

109. Hutton : Geology :: Dalton : **Atomic Theory**

The answer is **a.** James Hutton was the father of modern geology; John Dalton was the father of atomic theory.

110. Folded : Fault-Block :: **Blue** : Red

The answer is **a.** Folded and fault-block both describe types of mountains, with folded being the largest; blue and red both describe types of stars, with blue being the largest.

111. Alabama : **Camelia** :: Illinois : Violet

The answer is **a.** The state flower of Alabama is the camelia. The state flower of Illinois is the violet.

112. Mythologize : Debunk :: Exile : **Welcome**

The answer is **b.** Mythologize is an antonym of debunk, and exile is an antonym of welcome.

113. Abate : Reduce :: Beat : **Surpass**

The answer is **a.** Abate and reduce are synonyms, as are beat and surpass.

114. Bachelor : **Fire hall** :: Studio : Fire House

The answer is **d.** In Canada, a one-room apartment is called a bachelor; in the United States, it is called a studio. In Canada, a fire station is called a fire hall; it is called a fire house in the United States.

115. Corporate : Career :: **International** : Junior

The answer is **c.** Corporate and international are two types of universities. Career and junior are two types of colleges.

116. Moldavia : **Turkey** :: Romania : Bessarabia

The answer is **a.** Moldavia, Turkey, Romania, and Bessarabia are all former names of the country now known as Moldova.

117. Rosh Hashanah : **Purim** :: Yom Kippur : Passover

The answer is **a.** In Judaism, Yom Kippur is the holiday that immediately follows Rosh Hashanah and Passover is the holiday that immediately follows Purim.

118. Spanakopita : Spinach :: Taramosalata : **Caviar**

The answer is **b.** The main ingredient of the Greek dish spanakopita is spinach; the main ingredient of the Greek dish taramosalata is caviar.

119. 4^1 : 4^2 :: 2^1 : **2^3**

The answer is **d.** $4^1 = 4$ and $4^2 = 16$. The ratio of 4 to 16 is 1 to 4. $2^1 = 2$ and $2^3 = 8$. The ratio of 2 to 8 is 1 to 4.

120. Infuse : Permeate :: Kindle : **Light**

The answer is **a.** Infuse means permeate, and kindle means light.

Scoring Your MAT Practice Test

As mentioned in Chapter 1, when you receive your personal score report for the official MAT, you'll be provided with a scaled score and two percentile ranks, all of which are derived from the number of items you answered correctly—known as your raw score.

Because there are different forms and formats of the official MAT, and typically 20 of the 120 questions on the official MAT are experimental and do not count toward your official scaled score and percentile ranks, it is impossible to create an accurate raw score to scaled score or raw score to percentile chart for this and the other practice tests found in this book. In the end, you are striving to correctly answer the highest number of questions as possible and familiarize yourself with the MAT format so you're fully prepared to do your best on test day. For now, what's much more important than your overall score is how you did on each of the content areas tested by the exam. You need to diagnose your strengths and weaknesses so that you can concentrate your efforts as you prepare. The question types are mixed in the practice exam, so in order to tell where your strengths and weaknesses lie, you'll need to compare your answer sheet with the following **MAT Practice Test 3 Review**, which shows which of the content areas each question falls into.

Use your performance here in conjunction with the LearningExpress Test Preparation System in Chapter 2 to help you devise a study plan. You should plan to spend more time studying areas that correspond to the questions you found hardest and less time on the content areas in which you did well. Once you have spent some time reviewing, take the next MAT Practice Test to see if you've improved.

MAT PRACTICE TEST 3 REVIEW	
CONTENT AREA	**QUESTION NUMBERS**
Language and Vocabulary	3, 4, 7, 9, 10, 17, 23, 24, 33, 45, 46, 50, 60, 61, 68, 69, 76, 87, 88, 92, 101, 102, 112, 113, 120
Humanities	1, 2, 5, 8, 11, 15, 40, 42, 44, 47, 48, 54, 63, 81, 82, 84, 86, 89, 93, 94, 105
Social Science	6, 16, 18, 20, 22, 25, 28, 56, 58, 62, 64, 65, 79, 85, 90, 100, 103, 108, 116
Natural Science	12, 14, 26, 27, 29, 30, 38, 49, 51, 52, 59, 67, 70, 71, 73, 83, 96, 98, 104, 107, 109, 110
General	19, 21, 31, 32, 34, 35, 37, 41, 43, 55, 57, 72, 74, 75, 77, 78, 95, 99, 111, 114, 115, 117, 118
Mathematics	13, 36, 39, 53, 66, 80, 91, 97, 106, 119

MAT Practice Test 4

CHAPTER SUMMARY

Here's another sample MAT test for you to practice with.

For this practice test, simulate the actual test-taking experience as closely as you can. Find a quiet place to work where you won't be disturbed. If you own this book, use the answer sheet on the following pages and find some #2 pencils to fill in the circles with. Use a timer or stopwatch to time yourself—you'll have 60 minutes to complete the official MAT. After you take the test, use the detailed answer explanations that follow to review.

MAT Practice Test 4

1.	ⓐ	ⓑ	ⓒ	ⓓ
2.	ⓐ	ⓑ	ⓒ	ⓓ
3.	ⓐ	ⓑ	ⓒ	ⓓ
4.	ⓐ	ⓑ	ⓒ	ⓓ
5.	ⓐ	ⓑ	ⓒ	ⓓ
6.	ⓐ	ⓑ	ⓒ	ⓓ
7.	ⓐ	ⓑ	ⓒ	ⓓ
8.	ⓐ	ⓑ	ⓒ	ⓓ
9.	ⓐ	ⓑ	ⓒ	ⓓ
10.	ⓐ	ⓑ	ⓒ	ⓓ
11.	ⓐ	ⓑ	ⓒ	ⓓ
12.	ⓐ	ⓑ	ⓒ	ⓓ
13.	ⓐ	ⓑ	ⓒ	ⓓ
14.	ⓐ	ⓑ	ⓒ	ⓓ
15.	ⓐ	ⓑ	ⓒ	ⓓ
16.	ⓐ	ⓑ	ⓒ	ⓓ
17.	ⓐ	ⓑ	ⓒ	ⓓ
18.	ⓐ	ⓑ	ⓒ	ⓓ
19.	ⓐ	ⓑ	ⓒ	ⓓ
20.	ⓐ	ⓑ	ⓒ	ⓓ
21.	ⓐ	ⓑ	ⓒ	ⓓ
22.	ⓐ	ⓑ	ⓒ	ⓓ
23.	ⓐ	ⓑ	ⓒ	ⓓ
24.	ⓐ	ⓑ	ⓒ	ⓓ
25.	ⓐ	ⓑ	ⓒ	ⓓ
26.	ⓐ	ⓑ	ⓒ	ⓓ
27.	ⓐ	ⓑ	ⓒ	ⓓ
28.	ⓐ	ⓑ	ⓒ	ⓓ
29.	ⓐ	ⓑ	ⓒ	ⓓ
30.	ⓐ	ⓑ	ⓒ	ⓓ
31.	ⓐ	ⓑ	ⓒ	ⓓ
32.	ⓐ	ⓑ	ⓒ	ⓓ
33.	ⓐ	ⓑ	ⓒ	ⓓ
34.	ⓐ	ⓑ	ⓒ	ⓓ
35.	ⓐ	ⓑ	ⓒ	ⓓ
36.	ⓐ	ⓑ	ⓒ	ⓓ
37.	ⓐ	ⓑ	ⓒ	ⓓ
38.	ⓐ	ⓑ	ⓒ	ⓓ
39.	ⓐ	ⓑ	ⓒ	ⓓ
40.	ⓐ	ⓑ	ⓒ	ⓓ
41.	ⓐ	ⓑ	ⓒ	ⓓ
42.	ⓐ	ⓑ	ⓒ	ⓓ
43.	ⓐ	ⓑ	ⓒ	ⓓ
44.	ⓐ	ⓑ	ⓒ	ⓓ
45.	ⓐ	ⓑ	ⓒ	ⓓ

46.	ⓐ	ⓑ	ⓒ	ⓓ
47.	ⓐ	ⓑ	ⓒ	ⓓ
48.	ⓐ	ⓑ	ⓒ	ⓓ
49.	ⓐ	ⓑ	ⓒ	ⓓ
50.	ⓐ	ⓑ	ⓒ	ⓓ
51.	ⓐ	ⓑ	ⓒ	ⓓ
52.	ⓐ	ⓑ	ⓒ	ⓓ
53.	ⓐ	ⓑ	ⓒ	ⓓ
54.	ⓐ	ⓑ	ⓒ	ⓓ
55.	ⓐ	ⓑ	ⓒ	ⓓ
56.	ⓐ	ⓑ	ⓒ	ⓓ
57.	ⓐ	ⓑ	ⓒ	ⓓ
58.	ⓐ	ⓑ	ⓒ	ⓓ
59.	ⓐ	ⓑ	ⓒ	ⓓ
60.	ⓐ	ⓑ	ⓒ	ⓓ
61.	ⓐ	ⓑ	ⓒ	ⓓ
62.	ⓐ	ⓑ	ⓒ	ⓓ
63.	ⓐ	ⓑ	ⓒ	ⓓ
64.	ⓐ	ⓑ	ⓒ	ⓓ
65.	ⓐ	ⓑ	ⓒ	ⓓ
66.	ⓐ	ⓑ	ⓒ	ⓓ
67.	ⓐ	ⓑ	ⓒ	ⓓ
68.	ⓐ	ⓑ	ⓒ	ⓓ
69.	ⓐ	ⓑ	ⓒ	ⓓ
70.	ⓐ	ⓑ	ⓒ	ⓓ
71.	ⓐ	ⓑ	ⓒ	ⓓ
72.	ⓐ	ⓑ	ⓒ	ⓓ
73.	ⓐ	ⓑ	ⓒ	ⓓ
74.	ⓐ	ⓑ	ⓒ	ⓓ
75.	ⓐ	ⓑ	ⓒ	ⓓ
76.	ⓐ	ⓑ	ⓒ	ⓓ
77.	ⓐ	ⓑ	ⓒ	ⓓ
78.	ⓐ	ⓑ	ⓒ	ⓓ
79.	ⓐ	ⓑ	ⓒ	ⓓ
80.	ⓐ	ⓑ	ⓒ	ⓓ
81.	ⓐ	ⓑ	ⓒ	ⓓ
82.	ⓐ	ⓑ	ⓒ	ⓓ
83.	ⓐ	ⓑ	ⓒ	ⓓ
84.	ⓐ	ⓑ	ⓒ	ⓓ
85.	ⓐ	ⓑ	ⓒ	ⓓ
86.	ⓐ	ⓑ	ⓒ	ⓓ
87.	ⓐ	ⓑ	ⓒ	ⓓ
88.	ⓐ	ⓑ	ⓒ	ⓓ
89.	ⓐ	ⓑ	ⓒ	ⓓ
90.	ⓐ	ⓑ	ⓒ	ⓓ

91.	ⓐ	ⓑ	ⓒ	ⓓ
92.	ⓐ	ⓑ	ⓒ	ⓓ
93.	ⓐ	ⓑ	ⓒ	ⓓ
94.	ⓐ	ⓑ	ⓒ	ⓓ
95.	ⓐ	ⓑ	ⓒ	ⓓ
96.	ⓐ	ⓑ	ⓒ	ⓓ
97.	ⓐ	ⓑ	ⓒ	ⓓ
98.	ⓐ	ⓑ	ⓒ	ⓓ
99.	ⓐ	ⓑ	ⓒ	ⓓ
100.	ⓐ	ⓑ	ⓒ	ⓓ
101.	ⓐ	ⓑ	ⓒ	ⓓ
102.	ⓐ	ⓑ	ⓒ	ⓓ
103.	ⓐ	ⓑ	ⓒ	ⓓ
104.	ⓐ	ⓑ	ⓒ	ⓓ
105.	ⓐ	ⓑ	ⓒ	ⓓ
106.	ⓐ	ⓑ	ⓒ	ⓓ
107.	ⓐ	ⓑ	ⓒ	ⓓ
108.	ⓐ	ⓑ	ⓒ	ⓓ
109.	ⓐ	ⓑ	ⓒ	ⓓ
110.	ⓐ	ⓑ	ⓒ	ⓓ
111.	ⓐ	ⓑ	ⓒ	ⓓ
112.	ⓐ	ⓑ	ⓒ	ⓓ
113.	ⓐ	ⓑ	ⓒ	ⓓ
114.	ⓐ	ⓑ	ⓒ	ⓓ
115.	ⓐ	ⓑ	ⓒ	ⓓ
116.	ⓐ	ⓑ	ⓒ	ⓓ
117.	ⓐ	ⓑ	ⓒ	ⓓ
118.	ⓐ	ⓑ	ⓒ	ⓓ
119.	ⓐ	ⓑ	ⓒ	ⓓ
120.	ⓐ	ⓑ	ⓒ	ⓓ

Directions: For each question, select the answer choice in the parentheses that best completes the analogy.

1. Turncoat : Traitor :: (**a.** Scamp **b.** Pillow **c.** Blush **d.** Tricky) : Rogue

2. (**a.** Clockwork **b.** Anger **c.** Jealousy **d.** Fruit) : Wrath :: Orange : Grape

3. Carpenter : Wrench :: Baker : (**a.** Saw **b.** Spatula **c.** Plate **d.** Chef)

4. Hanker : (**a.** Junk **b.** Fool **c.** Yearn **d.** Bunker) :: Ponder : Think

5. Deplete : Decrease :: (**a.** Danger **b.** Dislike **c.** Miss **d.** Shun) : Avoid

6. Publish : (**a.** Page **b.** Book **c.** Song **d.** Movie) :: Release : Record

7. Carnegie : (**a.** Comedy **b.** Sports **c.** Music **d.** Film) :: Globe : Drama

8. Quotient : Division :: (**a.** Sum **b.** Factor **c.** Product **d.** Remainder) : Multiplication

9. Chatter : Talk :: Flutter : (**a.** Dance **b.** Wobble **c.** Sing **d.** Flap)

10. Triangle : Rectangle :: 180 : (**a.** 90 **b.** 180 **c.** 270 **d.** 360)

11. Nursery : (**a.** Teach **b.** School **c.** Junior **d.** College) :: Kindergarten : Graduate

12. Epithelial : (**a.** Attaching **b.** Beating **c.** Covering **d.** Alerting) :: Cardiac : Pumping

13. Protagonist : (**a.** Evil **b.** Character **c.** Dénouement **d.** Antagonist) :: Hero : Villain

14. Union : Confederacy :: Blue : (**a.** Gray **b.** White **c.** Green **d.** Red)

15. Essay : (**a.** Speech **b.** Song **c.** Villanelle **d.** Lyric) :: Ode : Sestina

16. (**a.** Portuguese **b.** Brazilian **c.** Spanish **d.** French) : Brazil :: English : Australia

17. Bull : (**a.** Hawk **b.** Bear **c.** Cow **d.** Sheep) :: Rising : Falling

18. 98.6 : Fahrenheit :: 37 : (**a.** Kelvin **b.** Celsius **c.** Illness **d.** Health)

19. Carve : Wood :: (**a.** Cut **b.** Bake **c.** Mold **d.** Statue) : Clay

20. Andes : South America :: Alps : (**a.** Switzerland **b.** Central American **c.** Himalayas **d.** Europe)

21. Plead : (**a.** Avoid **b.** Dismiss **c.** Ask **d.** Covet) :: Submerge : Dip

22. Doze : Sleep :: Tiptoe : (**a.** Walk **b.** Flat **c.** Shelf **d.** Swim)

23. Notre Dame : Taj Mahal :: France : (**a.** Indonesia **b.** Taiwan **c.** Iran **d.** India)

24. (**a.** Argentina **b.** Columbia **c.** Brazil **d.** Honduras) : Paraguay :: Central : South

25. Seismology : Earthquakes :: Cosmology : (**a.** Universe **b.** Constellations **c.** Earth **d.** Skin)

26. Strep : Bacteria :: (**a.** Ringworm **b.** Conjunctivitis **c.** Athlete's Foot **d.** Influenza) : Virus

27. Algae : Moneran :: Mammal : (**a.** Protista **b.** Animalia **c.** Plantae **d.** Fungi)

28. Garfield : Carter :: (**a.** Mining **b.** Preaching **c.** Teaching **d.** Editing) : Farming

29. Pachyderm : Insect :: (**a.** Rhinoceros **b.** Moose **c.** Camel **d.** Goat) : Ant

30. Zipper : Cuff :: (**a.** Lapel **b.** Button **c.** Shirt **d.** Vest) : Collar

31. True blue : Hold your horses :: (**a.** Loyal **b.** Evil **c.** Strange **d.** Slow) : Hesitate

32. Exoskeleton : Crab :: Endoskeleton : (**a.** Spider **b.** Bear **c.** Fungus **d.** Insect)

33. Ledger : Accounts :: (**a.** Pundit **b.** Weather **c.** Astrology **d.** Diary) : Observations

34. Grape : Wine :: Potato : (**a.** Gin **b.** Beer **c.** Vodka **d.** Scotch)

35. Perimeter : Area :: (**a.** l + w **b.** 2l + 2w **c.** 4lw **d.** 4l + 4w) : lw

36. Hoe : Farmer :: Calculator : (**a.** Abacus **b.** Tractor **c.** Mathematician **d.** Arithmetic)

37. (**a.** Cash **b.** Wealth **c.** Purse **d.** Inheritance) : Money :: Urn : Ashes

38. Pie : Bee :: Sky : (**a.** Wings **b.** Bonnet **c.** Scary **d.** Small)

39. Folk : (**a.** Sonnet **b.** Cautionary **c.** Naturalism **d.** Prose) :: Epistolary : Picaresque

40. Camus : (**a.** Dostoyevsky **b.** Kafka **c.** Nietzsche **d.** Sartre) :: The Stranger : No Exit

41. Garble : Distort :: Garner : (**a.** Learn **b.** Warble **c.** Earn **d.** Distress)

42. Stradivarius : Rickenbacker :: Violin : (**a.** Trombone **b.** Piano **c.** Guitar **d.** Harp)

43. (**a.** Haig **b.** Baker **c.** Christopher **d.** Rice) : Albright :: Rice : Clinton

44. Black Nativity : Anna Christie :: Hughes : (**a.** O'Neill **b.** Simon **c.** Pinter **d.** Hurston)

45. (**a.** Pirouette **b.** Falsetto **c.** Ballet **d.** Minuet) : Trill :: Jeté : Glissando

46. Heart : Apple :: Stone : (**a.** Eye **b.** Blink **c.** See **d.** Wall)

47. Ontology : Axiology :: (**a.** Existence **b.** Philosophy **c.** Science **d.** Mind) : Value

48. Tundra : Boggy :: Taiga : (**a.** Windy **b.** Dry **c.** Permafrost **d.** Coniferous)

49. Skew : Gloomy :: Slant : (**a.** Glee **b.** Foible **c.** Desperate **d.** Gloaming)

50. Danish : Denmark :: (**a.** Belarusian **b.** French **c.** Bulgarian **d.** Finnish) : Belgium

51. Kepler : Planetary Motion :: Mcclintock : (**a.** Quantum Mechanics **b.** Transposons **c.** Theory of Relativity **d.** Evolution)

52. Fuzzy : Clarity :: (**a.** Flexible **b.** Rigid **c.** Clear **d.** Forthright) : Flexibility

53. Fillmore : Whig :: Wilson : (**a.** Democrat **b.** Republican **c.** Bull moose **d.** Separatist)

54. (**a.** Gardener **b.** Lumberjack **c.** Forest **d.** Log) : Landscaper :: Tree : Grass

55. Defy : Obey :: (**a.** Please **b.** Aggravate **c.** Submit **d.** Change) : Placate

56. Baste : Cooking :: (**a.** Pinch **b.** Mulch **c.** Heat **d.** Paste) : Gardening

57. Thatcher : Major :: Chirac : (**a.** Fillon **b.** Sarkozy **c.** Mitterrand **d.** Pompidou)

58. Lincoln : Kennedy :: Jackson : (**a.** Bush **b.** Reagan **c.** Nixon **d.** Clinton)

59. Persist : (**a.** Habituate **b.** Quit **c.** Torment **d.** Pest) :: Eject : Welcome

60. 1066 : 1812 :: Battle of Hastings : (**a.** Battle of the Bulge **b.** King Phillip's War **c.** Defeat of Napoleon **d.** Bay of Pigs)

61. (**a.** Hirohito **b.** Kyoto **c.** Akihito **d.** Kan) : Mussolini :: Japan : Italy

62. Cent : (**a.** Quarter **b.** Nickel **c.** Dollar **d.** Penny) :: Kilogram : Quintal

63. (**a.** Watt **b.** Ampere **c.** Hertz **d.** Fermi) : Current :: Fahrenheit : Temperature

64. Arbus : Adams :: People : (**a.** Animals **b.** Photography **c.** Landscapes **d.** Architecture)

65. Hydric : Moist :: (**a.** Tonic **b.** Sciatic **c.** Phlegmatic **d.** Pyric) : Burning

66. Eddie Adams : Bob Woodward :: (**a.** Television **b.** Radio **c.** Magazine **d.** Photo) : Newspaper

67. Mesosaurus : Continental Drift :: Lucy : (**a.** Evolution **b.** Meiosis **c.** Australopithecus **d.** Johansen)

68. Tissue : Organ :: (**a.** Order **b.** Domain **c.** Classification **d.** System) : Kingdom

69. Luge : (**a.** Ski **b.** Lane **c.** Lunge **d.** Feet) :: Toe : Tone

70. Cup : (**a.** Pint **b.** Quart **c.** Litre **d.** Gallon) :: Quart : Gallon

71. Volume : (**a.** Voltometer **b.** Thermometer **c.** Graduated Cylinder **d.** Telescope) :: Mass : Balance

72. (**a.** Rabbi **b.** Torah **c.** Yarmulke **d.** Haskalah) : Zucchetto :: Jewish : Catholic

73. Lady Bird : (**a.** Imelda **b.** Evita **c.** Marie **d.** Senorita) :: United States : Argentina

74. First Law : (**a.** Newton **b.** Second Law **c.** Third Law **d.** Gravity) :: Inertia : Acceleration

75. Lions : (**a.** Pistons **b.** Tigers **c.** Orioles **d.** Marlins) :: Football : Baseball

76. Heat : (**a.** Restaurant **b.** Agriculture **c.** Bank **d.** Real estate) :: Electricity : Consulting Firm

77. (**a.** Light **b.** Leaden **c.** Slow **d.** Boss) : Heavy :: Ravenous : Hungry

78. (**a.** Clinging **b.** Electric **c.** Alive **d.** Kinetic) : Static :: Deficient : Complete

79. Black Forest : (**a.** Tiramisu **b.** Florida **c.** Pot **d.** Pasty) :: Key Lime : Shoofly

80. Teaspoon : Tablespoon :: (**a.** Inch **b.** Foot **c.** Centimeter **d.** Meter) : Yard

81. 4 : 8 :: 25 : (**a.** 5 **b.** 10 **c.** 25 **d.** 125)

82. Alfred Hitchcock : Federico Fellini :: Bernard Herrmann : (**a.** Nino Rota **b.** John Williams **c.** Marcello Mastrioanni **d.** Cary Grant)

83. (**a.** Cherry **b.** Buko **c.** Pecan **d.** Quiche) : Homity :: Mince : Custard

84. (**a.** Realism **b.** Period **c.** De Stijl **d.** Arabesque) : Motif :: Futurism : Movement

85. The Homecoming : *Catch-22* :: (**a.** The Canterbury Tales **b.** Leave it to Psmith **c.** Punch **d.** Babbitt) : *A Modest Proposal*

86. Blood : Circulatory :: (**a.** Bones **b.** Liver **c.** Skin **d.** Carpuscles) : Integumentary

87. Elizabeth Bishop : 1949 :: (**a.** Josephine Jacobson **b.** James Dickey **c.** Robert Frost **d.** Allen Tate) : 1959

88. Objectivism : (**a.** *The Fountainhead* **b.** Steppenwolf **c.** Rand **d.** Nausea) :: Buddhism : Siddhartha

89. (**a.** Varna **b.** Hindi **c.** Brahmin **d.** Sankara) : Kshatriya :: Vaishya : Shudra

90. 97 : 3 :: Salt : (**a.** Fresh **b.** Ocean **c.** River **d.** Iodine)

91. Curie : Physics and Chemistry :: (**a.** Pauling **b.** Sanger **c.** Bardeen **d.** Chomsky) : Chemistry and Peace

92. Game : Series :: (**a.** Winner **b.** Sentence **c.** Syllable **d.** Event) : Word

93. West End : London :: (**a.** Lower East Side **b.** Chelsea **c.** Harlem **d.** Broadway) : Manhattan

94. Curling : Shuffleboard :: (**a.** Puck **b.** Hammer **c.** Sweep **d.** Stone) : Biscuit

95. Qattara Depression : Libyan : Badwater Basin : (**a.** Sahara **b.** Sonoran **c.** Patagonian **d.** Mojave)

96. (**a.** Upbraid **b.** Umbrage **c.** Mumble **d.** Broadcast) : Enunciate :: Praise : Insult

97. Lithe : (**a.** Filth **b.** Asleep **c.** Giant **d.** Dancer) :: Slovenly : Slob

98. Kigali : Rwanda :: Kinshasa : (**a.** Malaysia **b.** Democratic Republic of Congo **c.** Zambia **d.** Sri Lanka)

99. Teide : (**a.** Italy **b.** Alaska **c.** Spain **d.** Russia) :: Rinjani : Indonesia

100. Leaves of Grass : (**a.** Paradise Lost **b.** Romeo and Juliet **c.** Sonnet **d.** Trees) :: Little Father : The Princess

101. King Harald V : Queen Beatrix :: Norway : (**a.** Sweden **b.** Finland **c.** Netherlands **d.** Denmark)

102. X-Axis : Female :: Y-Axis : (**a.** Punnett **b.** Male **c.** Chromosone **d.** Gene)

103. Sagacious : Undiscerning :: Amusing : (**a.** Clever **b.** Droll **c.** Humorless **d.** Confusing)

104. Newton : Coulomb :: Force : (**a.** Charge **b.** Negative **c.** Positive **d.** Watt)

105. Rocinante : Cervantes :: (**a.** Aragon **b.** Gamgee **c.** Quixote **d.** Hasufel) : Tolkein

106. Thymine : DNA :: (**a.** Adenine **b.** Cytosine **c.** Guanine **d.** Uracil) : mRNA

107. Potassium : (**a.** Nervous **b.** Circulatory **c.** Respiratory **d.** Skeletal) :: Zinc : Immune

108. Milliner : (**a.** Lens **b.** Hats **c.** Ties **d.** Gloves) :: Optician : Eyeglasses

109. $12 : 2 \times 2 \times 3 :: 40 :$ (**a.** $2 \times 2 \times 10$ **b.** $2 \times 4 \times 5$ **c.** $2 \times 2 \times 2 \times 5$ **d.** $2 \times 2 \times 3 \times 5$)

110. Overlock : Blind :: (**a.** Chain **b.** Herringbone **c.** Yarn **d.** Stitch) : Slip

111. New Mexico : Virginia :: (**a.** Bluebird **b.** Pope **c.** Roadrunner **d.** Yucca) : Cardinal

112. 540 Million : (**a.** Proerozoic **b.** Phanerozoic **c.** Cambrian **d.** Precambrian) :: 3.9 Billion : Archeozoic

113. (**a.** Scalene **b.** Right **c.** Isosceles **d.** Obtuse) : Equilateral :: Unequal : Equal

114. Adivasi : Mbuti :: (**a.** Australia **b.** India **c.** Egypt **d.** Africa) : The Democratic Republic of the Congo

115. Machiavellian : (**a.** Unscrupulous **b.** Disconsolate **c.** Sincere **d.** Penurious) :: Orwellian : Intrusive

116. Izba : (**a.** Russia **b.** Japan **c.** Pakistan **d.** Brazil) :: Konak : Turkish

117. $9\frac{1}{2} : 16\frac{1}{2} ::$ (**a.** $16\frac{1}{2}$ **b.** $25\frac{1}{2}$ **c.** $36\frac{1}{2}$ **d.** $49\frac{1}{2}$) : $64\frac{1}{2}$

118. $25{,}000 : 2.5 \times 10^4 ::$ (**a.** 2.5 **b.** .25 **c.** .025 **d.** .0025) : 2.5×10^{-3}

119. Prosaic : (**a.** Ordinary **b.** Tropical **c.** Abundant **d.** Sparse) :: Profuse : Lush

120. (**a.** Goat **b.** Zephyr **c.** Cipher **d.** Champion) : Zero :: Ampersand : And

Answers

1. Turncoat : Traitor :: **Scamp** : Rogue

The answer is **a.** Turncoat is another word for traitor and scamp is another word for rogue.

2. **Clockwork** : Wrath :: Orange : Grape

The answer is **a.** *A Clockwork Orange* is a 1962 novel by Anthony Burgess and *The Grapes of Wrath* is a 1939 novel by John Steinbeck.

3. Carpenter : Wrench :: Baker : **Spatula**

The answer is **b.** A wrench is a tool used by a carpenter. A spatula is a tool used by a baker.

4. Hanker : **Yearn** :: Ponder : Think

The answer is **c.** Hanker is another word for yearn and ponder is another word for think.

5. Deplete : Decrease :: **Shun** : Avoid

The answer is **d.** To deplete is to decrease completely, and to shun is to avoid completely.

6. Publish : **Book** :: Release : Record

The answer is **b.** To make a book available to the public is to publish it. To make a record available to the public is to release it.

7. Carnegie : **Music** :: Globe : Drama

The answer is **c.** Carnegie Hall in Manhattan is a famous venue for music performances. The Globe Theater in London is a famous playhouse.

8. Quotient : Division :: **Product** : Multiplication

The answer is **c.** A quotient is the result of division. A product is the result of multiplication.

9. Chatter : Talk :: Flutter : **Flap**

The answer is **d.** To chatter is to talk rapidly, and to flutter is to flap rapidly.

10. Triangle : Rectangle :: 180 : **360**

The answer is **d.** There are 180 degrees in a triangle and 360 degrees in a rectangle.

11. Nursery : **College** :: Kindergarten : Graduate

The answer is **d.** Nursery school and kindergarten are both parts of preschool education. College and graduate school are both parts of higher education.

12. Epithelial : **Covering** :: Cardiac : Pumping

The answer is **c.** Epithelial tissue covers the body; cardiac tissue pumps blood.

13. Protagonist : **Antagonist** :: Hero : Villain

The answer is **d.** Protagonist is a literary term for hero. Antagonist is a literary term for villain.

14. Union : Confederacy :: Blue : **Gray**

The answer is **a.** Union soldiers wore blue uniforms during the Civil War and Confederate soldiers wore gray.

15. Essay : **Speech** :: Ode : Sestina

The answer is **a.** An essay and a speech are two forms of prose writing. An ode and a sestina are two forms of poetry.

16. Portuguese : Brazil :: English : Australia

The answer is **a.** Portuguese is the most widely spoken language in Brazil and English is the most widely spoken language in Australia.

17. Bull : **Bear** :: Rising : Falling

The answer is **b.** A rising market is called a bull market and a falling market is called a bear market.

18. 98.6 : Fahrenheit :: 37 : **Celsius**

The answer is **b.** 98.6 degrees Fahrenheit is equivalent to 37 degrees Celsius.

19. Carve : Wood :: **Mold** : Clay

The answer is **c.** A sculptor shapes wood by carving it and shapes clay by molding it.

20. Andes : South America :: Alps : **Europe**

The answer is **d.** The Andes mountain range is in South America and the Alps range is in Europe.

21. Plead : **Ask** :: Submerge : Dip

The answer is **c.** To plead is to ask urgently, and to submerge is to dip completely.

22. Doze : Sleep :: Tiptoe : **Walk**

The answer is **a.** To doze is to sleep lightly, and to tiptoe is to walk lightly.

23. Notre Dame : Taj Mahal :: France : **India**

The answer is **d.** Notre Dame is located in France. The Taj Mahal is located in India.

24. Honduras : Paraguay :: Central : South

The answer is **d.** Paraguay is a country in South America. Honduras is a country in Central America.

25. Seismology : Earthquakes :: Cosmology : **Universe**

The answer is **a.** Seismology is the study of earthquakes; cosmology is the study of the universe.

26. Strep : Bacteria :: **Influenza** : Virus

The answer is **d.** Strep is caused by a bacteria; influenza is caused by a virus.

27. Algae : Moneran :: Mammal : **Animalia**

The answer is **b.** Algae belong to the Moneran Kingdom; mammals belong to the Animalia Kingdom.

28. Garfield : Carter :: **Preaching** : Farming

The answer is **b.** Garfield was a preacher before he became president. Carter was a farmer before he became president.

29. Pachyderm : Insect :: **Rhinoceros** : Ant

The answer is **a.** A rhinoceros is a pachyderm; an ant is an insect.

30. Zipper : Cuff :: **Button** : Collar

The answer is **b.** Zippers and buttons are both used to fasten clothing. Cuffs and collars are both edges on clothing.

31. True blue : Hold your horses :: **Loyal** : Hesitate

The answer is **a.** True blue is an expression meaning loyal. Hold your horses is an expression meaning hesitate.

32. Exoskeleton : Crab :: Endoskeleton : **Bear**

The answer is **b.** A crab has an exoskeleton; a bear has an endoskeleton.

33. Ledger : Accounts :: **Diary** : Observations

The answer is **d.** A ledger is a book that contains accounts, and a diary is a book that contains observations.

34. Grape : Wine :: Potato : **Vodka**

The answer is **c.** Grapes are used to make wine and potatoes are used to make vodka.

35. Perimeter: Area :: **2l + 2w** : lw

The answer is **b.** lw is the formula for the area of a rectangle. 2l + 2w is the formula for the perimeter of a rectangle.

36. Hoe : Farmer :: Calculator : **Mathematician**

The answer is **c.** A hoe is a tool used by a farmer. A calculator is a tool used by a mathematician.

37. **Purse** : Money :: Urn : Ashes

The answer is **c.** A purse is used to hold money, and an urn is used to hold ashes.

38. Pie : Bee :: Sky : **Bonnet**

The answer is **b.** The common expression "pie in the sky" refers to something unrealistic. The expression "bee in the bonnet" means angry.

39. Folk : **Cautionary** :: Epistolary : Picaresque

The answer is **b.** Two kinds of tales are folk tales and cautionary tales. Two kinds of novels are epistolary novels and picaresque novels.

40. Camus : **Sartre** :: The Stranger : No Exit

The answer is **d.** *The Stranger* is a 1942 novel by Albert Camus. No Exit is a 1944 play by Jean-Paul Sartre.

41. Garble : Distort :: Garner : **Earn**

The answer is **c.** Garble means distort, and garner means earn.

42. Stradivarius : Rickenbacker :: Violin : **Guitar**

The answer is **c.** Stradivarius is a famous brand of high-quality violins. Rickenbacker is a famous brand of high-quality guitars.

43. Christopher : Albright :: Rice : Clinton

The answer is **c.** Hillary Rodham Clinton became Secretary of State after Condoleeza Rice; Madeleine Albright became Secretary of State after Warren Christopher.

44. Black Nativity : Anna Christie :: Hughes : **O'Neill**

The answer is **a.** Black Nativity is a play by Langston Hughes. Anna Christie is a play by Eugene O'Neill.

45. Pirouette : Trill :: Jeté : Glissando

The answer is **a.** Pirouette and Jeté are both dance maneuvers. Falsetto and glissando are musical gestures.

46. Heart : Apple :: Stone : **Eye**

The answer is **a.** The metaphor "heart of stone" refers to an unfeeling person; the metaphor "apple of my eye" refers to a beloved person.

47. Ontology : Axiology :: **Existence** : Value

The answer is **a.** Ontology is the philosophical study of existence. Axiology is the philosophical study of value.

48. Tundra : Boggy :: Taiga : **Coniferous**

The answer is **d.** Tundra is generally boggy; taiga is known for its coniferous forests.

49. Skew : Gloomy :: Slant : **Desperate**

The answer is **c.** To skew is a synonym of to slant, and to be gloomy is a synonym for desperate.

50. Danish : Denmark :: **French** : Belgium

The answer is **b.** Danish is the official language of Denmark. French is the official language of Belgium.

51. Kepler : Planetary Motion :: Mcclintock : **Transposons**

The answer is **b.** Johannes Kepler developed the laws of planetary motion; Barbara McClintock discovered transposons.

52. Fuzzy : Clarity :: **Rigid** : Flexibility

The answer is **b.** Fuzzy means lacking in clarity, and rigid means lacking flexibility.

53. Fillmore : Whig :: Wilson : **Democrat**

The answer is **a.** Wilson was a member of the Democratic Party and Fillmore was a member of the Whig Party.

54. Lumberjack : Landscaper :: Tree : Grass

The answer is **b.** A lumberjack cuts trees. A landscaper cuts grass.

55. Defy : Obey :: **Aggravate** : Placate

The answer is **b.** To defy is the opposite of to obey, and to aggravate is the opposite of to placate.

56. Baste : Cooking :: **Mulch** : Gardening

The answer is **b.** Baste is a cooking term, and mulch is a gardening term.

57. Thatcher : Major :: Chirac : **Sarkozy**

The answer is **b.** In England, Margaret Thatcher preceded John Major as Prime Minister. In France, Jacques Chirac preceded Nicolas Sarkozy as President.

58. Lincoln : Kennedy :: Jackson : **Reagan**

The answer is **b.** Both Presidents Lincoln and Kennedy were assassinated. There was an assassination attempt on both President Jackson and President Reagan.

59. Persist : **Quit** :: Eject : Welcome

The answer is **b.** To persist is the opposite of to quit, and to eject is the opposite of to welcome.

60. 1066 : 1812 :: Battle of Hastings : **Defeat of Napoleon**

The answer is **c.** The Battle of Hastings took place in 1066. Napoleon was defeated in Russia in 1812.

61. **Hirohito** : Mussolini :: Japan : Italy

The answer is **a.** Hirohito was the leader of Japan during World War II. Mussolini was the leader of Italy.

62. Cent : **Dollar** :: Kilogram : Quintal

The answer is **c.** A dollar is 100 cents; a quintal is 100 kilograms.

63. **Ampere** : Current :: Fahrenheit : Temperature

The answer is **b.** Andre-Marie Ampere is the French physicist whose name was given to a unit of electrical current; Daniel Gabriel Fahrenheit was a German physicist whose name was given to a measure of temperature.

64. Arbus : Adams :: People : **Landscapes**

The answer is **c.** Diane Arbus is famous for photographing people. Ansel Adams is famous for photographing landscapes.

65. Hydric : Moist :: **Pyric** : Burning

The answer is **d.** Hydric is associated with something moist, and pyric is associated with something burning.

66. Eddie Adams : Bob Woodward :: **Photo** : Newspaper

The answer is **d.** Eddie Adams was a famous photojournalist. Bob Woodward was a famous newspaper journalist.

67. Mesosaurus : Continental Drift :: Lucy : **Evolution**

The answer is **a.** The mesosaurus provides evidence for continental drift; Lucy provides evidence for evolution.

68. Tissue : Organ :: **Order** : Kingdom

The answer is **a.** Organs are made up of tissues; kingdoms are made up of orders.

69. Luge : **Lunge** :: Toe : Tone

The answer is **c.** Luge with an added "n" is lunge, and toe with an added "n" is tone.

70. Cup : **Quart** :: Quart : Gallon

The answer is **b.** There are 4 quarts in one gallon. There are 4 cups in one quart.

71. Volume : **Graduated Cylinder** :: Mass : Balance

The answer is **c.** A balance is used to measure mass; a graduated cylinder is used to measure volume.

72. **Yarmulke** : Zucchetto :: Jewish : Catholic

The answer is **c.** A yarmulke is a skullcap worn by clerics in the Jewish religion. A zucchetto is a skullcap worn by clerics in the Catholic religion.

73. Lady Bird : **Evita** :: United States : Argentina

The answer is **b.** Both Claudia Taylor Johnson, who was a first lady of the United States, and Maria Eva Peron, who was a first lady of Argentina, were known by their nicknames, Lady Bird and Evita.

74. First Law : **Second Law** :: Inertia : Acceleration

The answer is **b.** Newton's First Law describes inertia; Newton's Second Law describes acceleration.

75. Lions : **Tigers** :: Football : Baseball

The answer is **b.** Detroit's Football team is called the Lions and its baseball team is called the Tigers.

76. Heat : **Restaurant** :: Electricity : Consulting firm

The answer is **a.** Heat and electricity are both utilities. A restaurant and a consulting firm are both service businesses.

77. **Leaden** : Heavy :: Ravenous : Hungry

The answer is **b.** To be leaden is to be oppressively heavy, and to be ravenous is to be excessively hungry.

78. **Kinetic** : Static :: Deficient : Complete

The answer is **d.** Kinetic means to be in motion and static means to be at rest, and deficient means lacking and complete means to be whole.

79. Black Forest : **Tiramisu** :: Key lime : Shoofly

The answer is **a.** Black Forest and tiramisu are both types of cakes. Key lime and shoofly are types of pies.

80. Teaspoon : Tablespoon :: **Foot** : Yard

The answer is **b.** There are three teaspoons in one tablespoon. There are three feet in one yard.

81. 4 : 8 :: 25 : **125**

The answer is **d.** 2^2 equals 4 and 2^3 equals 8. 5^2 equals 25 and 5^3 equals 125.

82. Alfred Hitchcock : Federico Fellini :: Bernard Herrmann : **Nino Rota**

The answer is **a.** English filmmaker Alfred Hitchcock often used Bernard Herrmann to compose the soundtracks to his films. Italian filmmaker Federico Fellini often worked with composer Nino Rota.

83. **Quiche** : Homity :: Mince : Custard

The answer is **d.** Quiche and homity are both savory pies. Mince and custard are both sweet pies.

84. **Arabesque** : Motif :: Futurism : Movement

The answer is **d.** An arabesque is an artistic motif. Futurism was an artistic movement.

85. *The Homecoming* : *Catch-22* :: **Leave it to Psmith** : *A Modest Proposal*

The answer is **b.** Harold Pinter's play The Homecoming and P.G. Wodehouse's novel *Leave It to Psmith* are both comedies of manners. Joseph Heller's novel *Catch-22* and Jonathan Swift's essay *A Modest Proposal* are satires.

86. Blood : Circulatory :: **Skin** : Integumentary

The answer is **c.** The circulatory system is mostly comprised of blood; the integumentary system is mostly comprised of skin.

87. Elizabeth Bishop : 1949 :: **Robert Frost** : 1959

The answer is **c.** Elizabeth Bishop was appointed Poet Laureate of the United States in 1949. Robert Frost was appointed Poet Laureate of the United States in 1959.

88. Objectivism : **The Fountainhead** :: Buddhism : Siddhartha

The answer is **a.** Ayn Rand's wrote her 1943 novel *The Fountainhead* in accordance with her belief in a philosophy she called objectivism. Herman Hesse wrote his 1922 novel *Siddhartha* in accordance with Buddhist philosophy.

89. **Brahmin** : Kshatriya :: Vaishya : Shudra

The answer is **c.** Brahmin, Kshatriya, Vaishya and Shudra are the four varnas, castes in Hinduism.

90. 97 : 3 :: Salt : **Fresh**

The answer is **a.** Earth's water is approximately 97 percent salt and 3 percent fresh.

91. Curie : Physics and Chemistry :: **Pauling** : Chemistry and Peace

The answer is **a.** Curie won two Nobel Prizes: one for physics and one for chemistry. Pauling also won two: one for chemistry and one for peace.

92. Game : Series :: **Syllable** : Word

The answer is **c.** A game is part of a series, and a syllable is part of a word.

93. West End : London :: **Broadway** : Manhattan

The answer is **d.** The West End is the most famous theater district in London, England; Broadway is the most famous theater district in Manhattan.

94. Curling : Shuffleboard :: **Stone** : Biscuit

The answer is **d.** The disc used in the sport of curling is called a stone. The disc used in the game of shuffleboard is called a biscuit.

95. Qattara Depression : Libyan : Badwater Basin : **Mojave**

The answer is **d.** The Qattara Depression is the lowest point in the Libyan Desert. Badwater Basin is the lowest point in the Mojave Desert.

96. **Mumble** : Enunciate :: Praise : Insult

The answer is **c.** To mumble is the opposite of to enunciate, and to praise is the opposite of to insult.

97. Lithe : **Dancer** :: Slovenly : Slob

The answer is **d.** Lithe can describe a dancer, and slovenly can describe a slob.

98. Kigali : Rwanda :: Kinshasa : **Democratic Republic of Congo**

The answer is **b.** Kigali is the capital of Rwanda and Kinshasa is the capital of the Democratic Republic of Congo.

99. Teide : **Spain** :: Rinjani : Indonesia

The answer is **c.** Mount Teide is a volcano in Spain. Mount Rinjani is a volcano in Indonesia.

100. Leaves of Grass : **Paradise Lost** :: Little Father : The Princess

The answer is **a.** Walt Whitman's "Leaves of Grass" and Li-Young Lee's "Little Father" were both composed in free verse. John Milton's "Paradise Lost" and Alfred Tennyson's "The Princess" are written in blank verse.

101. King Harald V : Queen Beatrix :: Norway : **Netherlands**

The answer is **c.** King Harald V is the reigning monarch of Norway and Queen Beatrix is the reigning monarch of the Netherlands.

102. X-Axis : Female :: Y-Axis : **Male**

The answer is **b.** In a Punnett square, the x-axis lists the female genes and the y-axis lists the male genes.

103. Sagacious : Undiscerning :: Amusing : **Humorless**

The answer is **c.** To be sagacious is to be the opposite of undiscerning and to be amusing is to be the opposite of humorless.

104. Newton : Coulomb :: Force : **Positive**

The answer is **c.** A newton is a measure of force; a coulomb is a measure of charge.

105. Rocinante : Cervantes :: **Hasufel** : Tolkein

The answer is **d.** Rocinante is the name of a horse in Miguel de Cervantes's novel *Don Quixote*. Hasufel is the name of a horse in J.R.R. Tolkein's novel *The Two Towers*.

106. Thymine : DNA :: **Uracil** : mRNA

The answer is **d.** Thymine is found in DNA just as Uracil is found in mRNA.

107. Potassium : **Nervous** :: Zinc : Immune

The answer is **a.** Potassium builds the nervous system; zinc improves immunity.

108. Milliner : **Hats** :: Optician : Eyeglasses

The answer is **b.** A person who sells hats is called a milliner. A person who sells eyeglasses is called an optician.

109. 12 : 2 × 2 × 3 :: 40 : **2 × 2 × 2 × 5**

The answer is **c.** 2 × 2 × 3 is the prime factorization of 12. 2 × 2 × 2 × 5 is the prime factorization of 40.

110. Overlock : Blind :: **Chain** : Slip

The answer is **a.** Overlock and blind are two types of sewing stitches. Chain and slip are two types of crochet stitches.

111. New Mexico : Virginia :: **Roadrunner** : Cardinal

The answer is **c.** The state bird of New Mexico is the roadrunner. The state bird of Virginia is the cardinal.

112. 540 Million : **Phanerozoic** :: 3.9 Billion : Archeozoic

The answer is **b.** Archeozoic and Phanerozoic are both eons. The Archeozoic eon was approxi-

mately 3.9 billion years ago; the Phanerozoic eon was approximately 540 million years ago.

113. **Scalene :** Equilateral :: Unequal : Equal

The answer is **a.** In an equilateral triangle all of the sides are equal. In a scalene triangle, all of the sides are unequal.

114. Adivasi : Mbuti :: **India** : The Democratic Republic of the Congo

The answer is **b.** The Adivasi are a nomadic tribe from India. The Mbuti are a nomadic tribe from the Democratic Republic of the Congo.

115. Machiavellian : **Unscrupulous** :: Orwellian : Intrusive

The answer is **a.** Something Machiavellian is considered unscrupulous, and Orwellian describes something as intrusive.

116. Izba : **Russia** :: Konak : Turkey

The answer is **a.** An izba is a type of house in Russia. A konak is a type of house in Turkey.

117. $9^{\frac{1}{2}}$: $16^{\frac{1}{2}}$ :: $36^{\frac{1}{2}}$: $64^{\frac{1}{2}}$

The answer is **c.** $9^{\frac{1}{2}} = 3$, the square root of 9, and $16^{\frac{1}{2}} = 4$, the square root of 16 (ratio is 3 to 4); $36^{\frac{1}{2}} = 6$, the square root of 36, and $64^{\frac{1}{2}} = 8$, the square root of 64 (ratio is 3 to 4).

118. 25,000 : 2.5 × 104 :: **.0025** : 2.5 × 10-3

The answer is **d.** 25,000 in scientific notation is written as 2.5 × 104. In scientific notation .0025 is written as 2.5 × 10-3.

119. Prosaic : **Ordinary** :: Profuse : Lush

The answer is **a.** Prosaic means ordinary, and profuse means lush.

120. Cipher : Zero :: Ampersand : And

The answer is **c.** A cipher is a symbol for a zero, and an ampersand is a symbol for *and*.

Scoring Your MAT Practice Test

As mentioned in Chapter 1, when you receive your personal score report for the official MAT, you'll be provided with a scaled score and two percentile ranks, all of which are derived from the number of items you answered correctly—known as your raw score.

Because there are different forms and formats of the official MAT, and typically 20 of the 120 questions on the official MAT are experimental and do not count toward your official scaled score and percentile ranks, it is impossible to create an accurate raw score to scaled score or raw score to percentile chart, for this and the other practice tests found in this book. In the end, you are striving to correctly answer the highest number of questions as possible and familiarize yourself with the MAT format—so you're fully prepared to do your best on test day. For now, what's much more important than your overall score is how you did on each of the content areas tested on the exam. You need to diagnose your strengths and weaknesses so that you can concentrate your efforts as you prepare. The question types are mixed in the practice exam, so in order to tell where your strengths and weaknesses lie, you'll need to compare your answer sheet with the following **MAT Practice Test 4 Review**, which shows which of the content areas each question falls into.

Use your performance here in conjunction with the LearningExpress Test Preparation System in Chapter 2 to help you devise a study plan. You should plan to spend more time studying areas that correspond to the questions you found hardest and less time on the content areas in which you did well. Once you have spent some time reviewing, take the next MAT Practice Test to see if you've improved.

MAT PRACTICE TEST 4 REVIEW	
CONTENT AREA	**QUESTION NUMBERS**
Language and Vocabulary	1, 4, 5, 9, 21, 22, 33, 37, 41, 49, 52, 55, 56, 59, 65, 69, 77, 78, 92, 96, 97, 103, 115, 119, 120
Humanities	2, 6, 7, 13, 15, 19, 39, 40, 42, 44, 45, 47, 64, 82, 84, 85, 87, 88, 93, 100, 105
Social Science	14, 16, 17, 20, 23, 24, 28, 43, 53, 57, 58, 60, 61, 73, 89, 91, 95, 98, 99, 101
Natural Science	12, 18, 25, 26, 27, 29, 32, 48, 51, 62, 63, 67, 68, 71, 74, 86, 90, 102, 104, 106, 107, 112
General	3, 11, 30, 31, 34, 36, 38, 46, 50, 54, 66, 72, 75, 76, 79, 83, 94, 108, 110, 111, 114, 116
Mathematics	8, 10, 35, 70, 80, 81, 109, 113, 117, 118

CHAPTER

MAT Practice Test 5

CHAPTER SUMMARY

Here's another sample MAT test for you to practice with.

For this practice test, simulate the actual test-taking experience as closely as you can. Find a quiet place to work where you won't be disturbed. If you own this book, use the answer sheet on the following pages and find some #2 pencils to fill in the circles with. Use a timer or stopwatch to time yourself— you'll have 60 minutes to complete the official MAT. After you take the test, use the detailed answer explanations that follow to review.

MAT Practice Test 5

1.	ⓐ	ⓑ	ⓒ	ⓓ
2.	ⓐ	ⓑ	ⓒ	ⓓ
3.	ⓐ	ⓑ	ⓒ	ⓓ
4.	ⓐ	ⓑ	ⓒ	ⓓ
5.	ⓐ	ⓑ	ⓒ	ⓓ
6.	ⓐ	ⓑ	ⓒ	ⓓ
7.	ⓐ	ⓑ	ⓒ	ⓓ
8.	ⓐ	ⓑ	ⓒ	ⓓ
9.	ⓐ	ⓑ	ⓒ	ⓓ
10.	ⓐ	ⓑ	ⓒ	ⓓ
11.	ⓐ	ⓑ	ⓒ	ⓓ
12.	ⓐ	ⓑ	ⓒ	ⓓ
13.	ⓐ	ⓑ	ⓒ	ⓓ
14.	ⓐ	ⓑ	ⓒ	ⓓ
15.	ⓐ	ⓑ	ⓒ	ⓓ
16.	ⓐ	ⓑ	ⓒ	ⓓ
17.	ⓐ	ⓑ	ⓒ	ⓓ
18.	ⓐ	ⓑ	ⓒ	ⓓ
19.	ⓐ	ⓑ	ⓒ	ⓓ
20.	ⓐ	ⓑ	ⓒ	ⓓ
21.	ⓐ	ⓑ	ⓒ	ⓓ
22.	ⓐ	ⓑ	ⓒ	ⓓ
23.	ⓐ	ⓑ	ⓒ	ⓓ
24.	ⓐ	ⓑ	ⓒ	ⓓ
25.	ⓐ	ⓑ	ⓒ	ⓓ
26.	ⓐ	ⓑ	ⓒ	ⓓ
27.	ⓐ	ⓑ	ⓒ	ⓓ
28.	ⓐ	ⓑ	ⓒ	ⓓ
29.	ⓐ	ⓑ	ⓒ	ⓓ
30.	ⓐ	ⓑ	ⓒ	ⓓ
31.	ⓐ	ⓑ	ⓒ	ⓓ
32.	ⓐ	ⓑ	ⓒ	ⓓ
33.	ⓐ	ⓑ	ⓒ	ⓓ
34.	ⓐ	ⓑ	ⓒ	ⓓ
35.	ⓐ	ⓑ	ⓒ	ⓓ
36.	ⓐ	ⓑ	ⓒ	ⓓ
37.	ⓐ	ⓑ	ⓒ	ⓓ
38.	ⓐ	ⓑ	ⓒ	ⓓ
39.	ⓐ	ⓑ	ⓒ	ⓓ
40.	ⓐ	ⓑ	ⓒ	ⓓ
41.	ⓐ	ⓑ	ⓒ	ⓓ
42.	ⓐ	ⓑ	ⓒ	ⓓ
43.	ⓐ	ⓑ	ⓒ	ⓓ
44.	ⓐ	ⓑ	ⓒ	ⓓ
45.	ⓐ	ⓑ	ⓒ	ⓓ

46.	ⓐ	ⓑ	ⓒ	ⓓ
47.	ⓐ	ⓑ	ⓒ	ⓓ
48.	ⓐ	ⓑ	ⓒ	ⓓ
49.	ⓐ	ⓑ	ⓒ	ⓓ
50.	ⓐ	ⓑ	ⓒ	ⓓ
51.	ⓐ	ⓑ	ⓒ	ⓓ
52.	ⓐ	ⓑ	ⓒ	ⓓ
53.	ⓐ	ⓑ	ⓒ	ⓓ
54.	ⓐ	ⓑ	ⓒ	ⓓ
55.	ⓐ	ⓑ	ⓒ	ⓓ
56.	ⓐ	ⓑ	ⓒ	ⓓ
57.	ⓐ	ⓑ	ⓒ	ⓓ
58.	ⓐ	ⓑ	ⓒ	ⓓ
59.	ⓐ	ⓑ	ⓒ	ⓓ
60.	ⓐ	ⓑ	ⓒ	ⓓ
61.	ⓐ	ⓑ	ⓒ	ⓓ
62.	ⓐ	ⓑ	ⓒ	ⓓ
63.	ⓐ	ⓑ	ⓒ	ⓓ
64.	ⓐ	ⓑ	ⓒ	ⓓ
65.	ⓐ	ⓑ	ⓒ	ⓓ
66.	ⓐ	ⓑ	ⓒ	ⓓ
67.	ⓐ	ⓑ	ⓒ	ⓓ
68.	ⓐ	ⓑ	ⓒ	ⓓ
69.	ⓐ	ⓑ	ⓒ	ⓓ
70.	ⓐ	ⓑ	ⓒ	ⓓ
71.	ⓐ	ⓑ	ⓒ	ⓓ
72.	ⓐ	ⓑ	ⓒ	ⓓ
73.	ⓐ	ⓑ	ⓒ	ⓓ
74.	ⓐ	ⓑ	ⓒ	ⓓ
75.	ⓐ	ⓑ	ⓒ	ⓓ
76.	ⓐ	ⓑ	ⓒ	ⓓ
77.	ⓐ	ⓑ	ⓒ	ⓓ
78.	ⓐ	ⓑ	ⓒ	ⓓ
79.	ⓐ	ⓑ	ⓒ	ⓓ
80.	ⓐ	ⓑ	ⓒ	ⓓ
81.	ⓐ	ⓑ	ⓒ	ⓓ
82.	ⓐ	ⓑ	ⓒ	ⓓ
83.	ⓐ	ⓑ	ⓒ	ⓓ
84.	ⓐ	ⓑ	ⓒ	ⓓ
85.	ⓐ	ⓑ	ⓒ	ⓓ
86.	ⓐ	ⓑ	ⓒ	ⓓ
87.	ⓐ	ⓑ	ⓒ	ⓓ
88.	ⓐ	ⓑ	ⓒ	ⓓ
89.	ⓐ	ⓑ	ⓒ	ⓓ
90.	ⓐ	ⓑ	ⓒ	ⓓ

91.	ⓐ	ⓑ	ⓒ	ⓓ
92.	ⓐ	ⓑ	ⓒ	ⓓ
93.	ⓐ	ⓑ	ⓒ	ⓓ
94.	ⓐ	ⓑ	ⓒ	ⓓ
95.	ⓐ	ⓑ	ⓒ	ⓓ
96.	ⓐ	ⓑ	ⓒ	ⓓ
97.	ⓐ	ⓑ	ⓒ	ⓓ
98.	ⓐ	ⓑ	ⓒ	ⓓ
99.	ⓐ	ⓑ	ⓒ	ⓓ
100.	ⓐ	ⓑ	ⓒ	ⓓ
101.	ⓐ	ⓑ	ⓒ	ⓓ
102.	ⓐ	ⓑ	ⓒ	ⓓ
103.	ⓐ	ⓑ	ⓒ	ⓓ
104.	ⓐ	ⓑ	ⓒ	ⓓ
105.	ⓐ	ⓑ	ⓒ	ⓓ
106.	ⓐ	ⓑ	ⓒ	ⓓ
107.	ⓐ	ⓑ	ⓒ	ⓓ
108.	ⓐ	ⓑ	ⓒ	ⓓ
109.	ⓐ	ⓑ	ⓒ	ⓓ
110.	ⓐ	ⓑ	ⓒ	ⓓ
111.	ⓐ	ⓑ	ⓒ	ⓓ
112.	ⓐ	ⓑ	ⓒ	ⓓ
113.	ⓐ	ⓑ	ⓒ	ⓓ
114.	ⓐ	ⓑ	ⓒ	ⓓ
115.	ⓐ	ⓑ	ⓒ	ⓓ
116.	ⓐ	ⓑ	ⓒ	ⓓ
117.	ⓐ	ⓑ	ⓒ	ⓓ
118.	ⓐ	ⓑ	ⓒ	ⓓ
119.	ⓐ	ⓑ	ⓒ	ⓓ
120.	ⓐ	ⓑ	ⓒ	ⓓ

Directions: For each question, select the best answer in the parentheses that best completes the analogy.

1. Lancelot : Robin Hood :: (**a.** Guinevere **b.** Arthur **c.** Little John **d.** Legend) : Marian

2. Perimeter : Polygon :: (**a.** Circumference **b.** Radius **c.** Diameter **d.** Chord) : Circle

3. Approach : (**a.** Pounce **b.** Arrive **c.** Demand **d.** Airport) :: Leave : Bolt

4. Lawless : Order :: Captive : (**a.** Trouble **b.** Punishment **c.** Jail **d.** Freedom)

5. Chord : Note :: (**a.** Clef **b.** Music **c.** Key **d.** Staff) : Line

6. (**a.** Halloween **b.** Thanksgiving **c.** Holiday **d.** Christmas Eve) : Christmas :: 31 : 25

7. Madison : (**a.** G. H. Bush **b.** Reagan **c.** G. W. Bush **d.** Quayle) :: War of 1812 : Gulf War

8. Crop : Photograph :: (**a.** Shoot **b.** Process **c.** Display **d.** Edit) : Film

9. (**a.** Michelangelo **b.** Da Vinci **c.** Wright **d.** Frost) : Architect :: Rodin : Sculptor

10. Gold : Silver :: Au : (**a.** Ag **b.** Fe **c.** Ge **d.** Hg)

11. (**a.** Duet **b.** Singer **c.** Trio **d.** Violin) : 2 :: Quartet : 4

12. Jesus : Vishnu :: Christianity : (**a.** Hinduism **b.** Judaism **c.** God **d.** Religion)

13. Oswald : Kennedy :: Ruby : (**a.** Oswald **b.** Nixon **c.** Hinckley **d.** Booth)

14. Monotheism : (**a.** Atheism **b.** Polytheism **c.** Deism **d.** Theism) :: One : Many

15. Donkey : (**a.** Elephant **b.** Horse **c.** Eagle **d.** Cat) :: Democrat : Republican

16. France : Franc :: Netherlands : (**a.** Mark **b.** Guilder **c.** Pound **d.** Lira)

17. Speed : Distance :: (**a.** Decibel **b.** Coulomb **c.** Knot **d.** Stone) : League

18. (**a.** Argentina **b.** Nicaragua **c.** New Mexico **d.** Paraguay) : Central :: Uruguay : South

19. Siam : (**a.** Laos **b.** Vietnam **c.** Macau **d.** Thailand) :: Khmer Republic : Cambodia

20. Search : (**a.** Peer **b.** Ransack **c.** Destroy **d.** Find) :: Defeat : Vanquish

21. Hint : (**a.** Demand **b.** Point **c.** Surprise **d.** Secret) :: Whisper : Shout

22. Sphygmomanometer : Blood :: Chronometer : (**a.** Heat **b.** Time **c.** Distance **d.** Pressure)

23. Seine : Thames :: (**a.** Scotland **b.** Switzerland **c.** France **d.** Italy) : England

24. Moss : Cow :: (**a.** Monera **b.** Protista **c.** Fungi **d.** Plantae) : Animalia

25. Frog : Emu :: (**a.** Amphibian **b.** Mammalian **c.** Insectival **d.** Reptilian) : Avian

26. (**a.** Office **b.** School **c.** Executive **d.** Campus) : Assistant :: Administrator : Teacher

27. Sloth : Action :: (**a.** Unscrupulousness **b.** Teachers **c.** Hero **d.** Conscientious) : Principles

28. (**a.** Hindenburg **b.** Spirit of St. Louis **c.** Orient Express **d.** Mayflower) : Airplane :: Titanic : Steamship

29. MFA : Artist :: MBA : (**a.** Basketball **b.** Doctor **c.** Executive **d.** Sculptor)

30. Calculus : (**a.** Social Studies **b.** Science **c.** Math **d.** Arithmetic) :: Grammar : English

31. Grove : Forest :: (**a.** Pond **b.** Ocean **c.** Tree **d.** Boat) : Lake

32. Shower : Deluge :: (**a.** Wet **b.** Window **c.** Ignore **d.** Glance) : Stare

33. Idaho : (**a.** Crop **b.** State **c.** Illinois **d.** Iowa) :: Potato : Corn

34. Milk : Lactose :: Fruit : (**a.** Glucose **b.** Sucrose **c.** Fructose **d.** Ribose)

35. November 1 : Scorpio :: March 1 : (**a.** Capricorn **b.** Taurus **c.** Cancer **d.** Pisces)

36. .5 : .25 :: .02 : (**a.** .00004 **b.** .0004 **c.** .04 **d.** .4)

37. Circumference : Diameter :: 3.14 : (**a.** 1 **b.** 2 **c.** 4 **d.** 5)

38. Quadrilateral : 4 :: Hexagon : (**a.** 5 **b.** 6 **c.** 7 **d.** 8)

39. Gregor : (**a.** Franz **b.** Grete **c.** Karl **d.** Josef) :: Metamorphosis : Trial

40. Clavinet : (**a.** Accordion **b.** Zither **c.** Clavichord **d.** Spinet) :: Hurdy gurdy : Sitar

41. (**a.** Earth **b.** Fly **c.** Mud **d.** Acre) : Land :: Slice : Cake

42. Pool : Loop :: Lap : (**a.** Lifeguard **b.** Track **c.** Heat **d.** Pal)

43. Plath : (**a.** Ariel **b.** The Colossus **c.** The Bell Jar **d.** Mademoiselle) :: Lowry : Under the Volcano

44. (**a.** A cappella **b.** Obbligato **c.** Tutti **d.** Chamber) : Unaccompanied :: Concerto : Accompanied

45. Trypsin : Proteins :: Lipase : (**a.** Amalase **b.** Sugars **c.** Carbohydrates **d.** Fats)

46. Spike : (**a.** Bronx **b.** Brooklyn **c.** Staten Island **d.** Queens) :: Woody : Manhattan

47. (**a.** Maslow **b.** Jung **c.** Freud **d.** Skinner) : Lewin :: Analytic Theory : Field Theory

48. The Birth of a Nation : A Trip to the Moon :: Sunset Boulevard : (**a.** Intolerance **b.** Black and white **c.** The African Queen **d.** Steamboat Bill Jr.)

49. Polyphony : Melodic :: Cacophony : (**a.** Beatific **b.** Neutral **c.** Complex **d.** Inharmonious)

50. Purr : (**a.** Cat **b.** Whiff **c.** Contentment **d.** Anger) :: Huff : Indignation

51. Lap : Pool :: (**a.** Pass **b.** Gene **c.** Light year **d.** Slide) : Space

52. Pelosi : House of Representatives :: (**a.** Albright **b.** Woodhull **c.** Ginsburg **d.** O'Connor) : Supreme Court

53. Adenine : Thymine :: (**a.** Guanine **b.** DNA **c.** RNA **d.** Uracil) : Cytosine

54. (**a.** Barter **b.** Market **c.** Driven **d.** Welfare): Capitalism :: Planned : Socialism

55. Jefferson : Monticello :: Jackson : (**a.** Hermitage **b.** Springfield **c.** Tennessee **d.** Springwood)

56. Matzo : Jewish :: (**a.** Curry **b.** Kheeri **c.** Rice **d.** Roti) : Indian

57. St. Louis : Gateway City :: Kansas City : (**a.** Monument City **b.** City of Fountains **c.** Music City **d.** Garden City)

58. Earthquake : (**a.** Tectonic **b.** Tsunami **c.** Richter Scale **d.** Tornado) :: Greenhouse Gases : Global Warming

59. Tinker : Kettle :: Cobbler : (**a.** Pan **b.** Shoe **c.** Pot **d.** Clock)

60. Eraser : Pencil :: (**a.** Write **b.** Delete **c.** Nib **d.** Calligraphy) : Pen

61. (**a.** Horse **b.** Divine **c.** Mask **d.** Shield) : Armor :: Equipment : Gear

62. Patrol : (**a.** Subway **b.** Response **c.** Car **d.** Taxi) :: Bus : Train

63. Smith : Marx :: (**a.** Capitalism **b.** Feudalism **c.** Socialism **d.** Behaviorism) : Communism

64. (**a.** Rugby **b.** Hockey **c.** Baseball **d.** Grasshopper) : The United States :: Cricket : Bermuda

65. Oxygen : (**a.** Hydrogen **b.** Helium **c.** Carbon Dioxide **d.** Heart) :: Arteries : Veins

66. Turban : (**a.** Robe **b.** Toga **c.** Headdress **d.** Nomad) :: Turbine : Engine

67. Slither : Snake :: Rotate : (**a.** Rock **b.** Support **c.** Fan **d.** Turn)

68. White Blood Cells : Protection :: Platelets : (**a.** Clotting **b.** Bleeding **c.** Immunity **d.** Red Blood Cells)

69. $\frac{2}{5} : \frac{6}{15} :: \frac{3}{7} :$ (**a.** $\frac{3}{21}$ **b.** $\frac{6}{14}$ **c.** $\frac{9}{14}$ **d.** $\frac{9}{21}$)

70. $\frac{1}{2} : \frac{1}{6} ::$ (**a.** $\frac{1}{2}$ **b.** 2 **c.** 3 **d.** $\frac{2}{3}$) : 1

71. Calcium : Iron :: Bones : (**a.** White Blood Cells **b.** Muscles **c.** Red Blood Cells **d.** Digestion)

72. B1 : Thiamin :: (**a.** C **b.** B2 **c.** D **d.** E) : Riboflavin

73. (**a.** Princeton **b.** Hofstra **c.** Dartmouth **d.** Rice) : College :: Harvard : University

74. Neurosurgeon : Cobbler :: Operation : (**a.** Apple **b.** Shoe **c.** Repair **d.** Instruct)

75. Indonesia : (**a.** Island **b.** Peninsula **c.** Archipelago **d.** Volcanic) :: Malawi : landlocked

76. Lungs : Heart :: (**a.** Digestive **b.** Respiratory **c.** Nervous **d.** Muscular) : Circulatory

77. Ralph : Ricky :: (**a.** Alice **b.** Wilma **c.** Ethel **d.** Trixie) : Lucy

78. Supermarket : (**a.** Financial **b.** Information **c.** Retail **d.** Industry) :: Limousine service : Transportation

79. (**a.** Snip **b.** Bouquet **c.** Teeth **d.** Excise) : Cut :: Flowers : Bloom

80. Circumference : (**a.** Diameter **b.** Radius **c.** Area **d.** Diagonal) :: 2pr : r2

81. A Tale of Two Cities : The Red Badge of Courage :: The Scarlet Pimpernel : (**a.** The Good Shepherd **b.** Shiloh **c.** Slaughterhouse Five **d.** A Farewell to Arms)

82. (**a.** Sukiyaki **b.** Chowder **c.** Carpaccio **d.** Bistek) : Goulash :: Steak tartare : Flaki

83. Arrastre : Drag :: Barrida : (**a.** Hop **b.** Pull **c.** Sweep **d.** Fall)

84. Potato : Kiwi :: (**a.** Lemon balm **b.** Ferula **c.** Eggplant **d.** Feijoa) : Persimmon

85. Tabula Rasa : (**a.** Ad finem **b.** Existentialism **c.** Vice versa **d.** Nihilism) :: Locke : Turgenev

86. Development : Sprawl :: Famine : (**a.** Malnutrition **b.** Crawl **c.** Urban **d.** Obesity)

87. Also Sprach Zarathustra : (**a.** The Elephant Man **b.** Raging Bull **c.** 2001: A Space Odyssey **d.** Barry Lyndon) :: Pachelbel's Canon : Ordinary People

88. Teeth & Bones : (**a.** Iron **b.** Phosphorus **c.** Magnesium **d.** Zinc) :: DNA : Folic Acid

89. Muscle Tissue : (**a.** Nervous Tissue **b.** Connective Tissue **c.** Organ Tissue **d.** Epithelial Tissue) :: Contraction : Coverage

90. Union : Towns :: Confederacy : (**a.** Cities **b.** Streams **c.** Mountains **d.** States)

91. (**a.** Chekhov **b.** Baryshnikov **c.** Glinka **d.** Brunov) : Russian :: Bruhn : Danish

92. (**a.** Uganda **b.** Ghana **c.** Chad **d.** South Africa) : New Zealand :: Zululand : Maori

93. Cheap : Peach :: (**a.** King **b.** Regal **c.** Orange **d.** Majestic) : Large

94. Carthage : (**a.** Milan **b.** Rome **c.** Troy **d.** Greece) :: Athens : Sparta

95. 4! : 24 :: 5! : (**a.** 40 **b.** 60 **c.** 80 **d.** 120)

96. (**a.** Carbon Layer **b.** Ultraviolet Light **c.** Ozone Layer **d.** Troposphere) : Stratosphere :: Mesosphere : Ionosphere

97. Lorenz : Geese :: Goodall : (**a.** Chimps **b.** Antelopes **c.** Peacocks **d.** Meerkats)

98. Sachs : *The End of Poverty* :: Smith : (**a.** *The Wealth of Nations* **b.** *The Protestant Ethics and the Spirit of Capitalism* **c.** *Patterns of Culture* **d.** *The Apocalypse*)

99. Manacle : Hands :: (**a.** Shin **b.** Fetter **c.** Stock **d.** Fodder) : Feet

100. Flip : Impertinent :: Dice : (**a.** Cut **b.** Cards **c.** Bounce **d.** Gamble)

101. (**a.** Bolshevik **b.** Rasputin **c.** Marx **d.** Trotsky) : Lenin :: Kerensky : Plekhanov

102. Cyrillic : (**a.** Ancient Egyptian **b.** Germanic **c.** Slavic **d.** Ancient Greek) :: Devanagari : Indian

103. Vitamin E : Antioxidant :: Folic Acid : (**a.** Red Blood Cell Producer **b.** Vision Enhancer **c.** Immunity Booster **d.** Bone Strengthener)

104. Synodic : Sidereal :: Lunation : (**a.** Moon **b.** Phase **c.** Orbital **d.** Period)

105. Pitepalt : (**a.** Peanut **b.** Pork **c.** Pickle **d.** Pasta) :: Pierogi : Potato

106. (**a.** Linger **b.** Arrive **c.** Announce **d.** Depart) : Leave :: Vacillate : Decide

107. Wasabi : Mustard :: (**a.** Horseradish **b.** Cabbage **c.** Blueberry **d.** Plum) : Cherry

108. Cumbia : Bourrée :: Colombia : (**a.** Bolgaria **b.** France **c.** Bolivia **d.** Austria)

109. Gregg Toland :: Jack Warner : Cinematographer : (**a.** Producer **b.** Editor **c.** Assistant director **d.** Cameraman)

110. (**a.** Sudden **b.** Gloomy **c.** Overt **d.** Off) : Hidden :: Ebullient : Glum

111. Gloaming : (**a.** Gloom **b.** Beaming **c.** Morning **d.** Dusk) :: Bearing : Manner

112. President : Operations Director :: Banker : (**a.** CEO **b.** Board of Director **c.** Managing Director **d.** Executive Assistant)

113. 11 : 1-1 :: 12 : (**a.** 20 **b.** 21 **c.** 21 **d.** 22)

114. (**a.** Dean **b.** Janitor **c.** Groundskeeper **d.** Porter) : College :: Concierge : Hotel

115. Archeozoic : Proterozoic :: Bacteria : (**a.** Dinosaurs **b.** Sponges **c.** Birds **d.** Mammals)

116. Gateleg : (**a.** Tuffet **b.** Fauteuil **c.** Headboard **d.** Armoire) :: Refectory : Credenza

117. Log 10 : Log 100 :: (**a.** Log 1 **b.** Log 10 **c.** Log 100 **d.** Log 1000) : Log 10000

118. Irreverent : Respect :: Slipshod : (**a.** Messy **b.** Slippery **c.** Care **d.** Wit)

119. $\sqrt{18}$: $\sqrt{50}$ :: 3 : (**a.** 1 **b.** 2 **c.** 4 **d.** 5)

120. The Snake Charmer: (**a.** Clément **b.** Delaunay **c.** Rousseau **d.** Terk) :: The Fiddler : Chagall

Answers

1. Lancelot : Robin Hood :: **Guinevere** : Marian

The answer is **a.** In Arthurian legend, Sir Lancelot and Lady Guinevere were lovers. Legendary English outlaw Robin Hood and Lady Marian of Leaford were also lovers.

2. Perimeter : Polygon :: **Circumference** : Circle

The answer is **a.** The perimeter of a polygon is the sum of the lengths of its sides. The circumference is the length around the outside of a circle.

3. Approach : **Pounce** :: Leave : Bolt

The answer is **a.** To pounce is to approach suddenly, and to bolt is to leave suddenly.

4. Lawless : Order :: Captive : **Freedom**

The answer is **d.** To be lawless is to lack order, and to be captive is to lack freedom.

5. Chord : Note :: **Staff** : Line

The answer is **d.** In music, a chord is made up of notes and a staff is made up of lines.

6. **Halloween** : Christmas :: 31 : 25

The answer is **a.** Halloween is celebrated on October 31. Christmas is celebrated on December 25.

7. Madison : **G. H. Bush** :: War of 1812 : Gulf War

The answer is **a.** Madison was the president during the War of 1812. G. H. Bush was the president during the Gulf War.

8. Crop : Photograph :: **Edit** : Film

The answer is **d.** To trim a photograph is to crop it. To trim film is to edit it.

9. **Wright** : Architect :: Rodin : Sculptor

The answer is **c.** Frank Lloyd Wright is a famous architect; Auguste Rodin is a famous sculptor.

10. Gold : Silver :: Au : **Ag**

The answer is **a.** The symbol for gold is Au; the symbol for silver is Ag.

11. **Duet** : 2 :: Quartet : 4

The answer is **a.** A duet is an ensemble of two musicians or singers. A quartet is an ensemble of four singers or musicians.

12. Jesus : Vishnu :: Christianity : **Hinduism**

The answer is **a.** In Christianity, Jesus Christ is regarded as an incarnation of God on Earth. In Hinduism, Vishnu is regarded as an incarnation of God on Earth.

13. Oswald : Kennedy :: Ruby : **Oswald**

The answer is **a.** Lee Harvey Oswald assassinated President Kennedy. Later, Jack Ruby assassinated Lee Harvey Oswald.

14. Monotheism : **Polytheism** :: One : Many

The answer is **b.** Monotheism is the belief in a single god. Polytheism is the belief in many gods.

15. Donkey : **Elephant** :: Democrat : Republican

The answer is **a.** A donkey is the symbol of the Democratic Party and an elephant is the symbol of the Republican Party.

16. France : Franc :: Netherlands : **Guilder**

The answer is **b.** Prior to adopting the euro, the franc was the unit of currency in France and the guilder was the currency of the Netherlands.

17. Speed : Distance :: **Knot** : League

The answer is **c.** A knot is a measure of speed at sea; a league is a measure of distance at sea.

18. **Nicaragua** : Central :: Uruguay : South

The answer is **b.** Nicaragua is in Central America and Uruguay is in South America.

19. Siam : **Thailand** :: Khmer Republic : Cambodia

The answer is **d.** Siam is the former name of Thailand. Khmer Republic is the former name of Cambodia.

20. Search : **Ransack** :: Defeat : Vanquish

The answer is **b.** To ransack is to search thoroughly, and to vanquish is defeat thoroughly.

21. Hint : **Demand** :: Whisper : Shout

The answer is **a.** To hint is to ask subtly and to demand is to ask insistently; to whisper is to talk quietly and to shout is to talk loudly.

22. Sphygmomanometer : Blood :: Chronometer : **Time**

The answer is **b.** A sphygmomanometer measures blood; a chronometer measures time.

23. Seine : Thames :: **France** : England

The answer is **c.** The Seine River is in France and the Thames River is in England.

24. Moss : Cow :: **Plantae** : Animalia

The answer is **d.** Mosses belong to the kingdom Plantae; cows belong to the kingdom Animalia.

25. Frog : Emu :: **Amphibian** : Avian

The answer is **a.** A frog is amphibian; an emu is avian.

26. **Executive** : Assistant :: Administrator : Teacher

The answer is **c.** An executive manages an assistant, and an administrator manages a teacher.

27. Sloth : Action :: **Unscrupulousness** : Principles

The answer is **a.** Sloth is a lack of action, and unscrupulousness is a lack of principles.

28. **Spirit of St. Louis** : Airplane :: Titanic : Steamship

The answer is **b.** The Spirit of St. Louis is a famous airplane; the Titanic was a famous steamship.

29. MFA : Artist :: MBA : **Executive**

The answer is **c.** An MFA , or Master of Fine Arts, is a degree for artists. An MBA, or Master of Business Administration, is a degree for business executives.

30. Calculus : **Math** :: Grammar : English

The answer is **c.** Calculus is a subject one studies in math class. Grammar is a subject one studies in English class.

31. Grove : Forest :: **Pond** : Lake

The answer is **a.** A grove is a smaller version of a forest, and a pond is a smaller version of a lake.

32. Shower : Deluge :: **Glance** : Stare

The answer is **d.** A shower is a less intense version of a deluge, and a glance is a less intense version of a stare.

33. Idaho : **Iowa** :: Potato : Corn

The answer is **d.** One of the main crops of Idaho is the potato. One of the main crops of Iowa is corn.

34. Milk : Lactose :: Fruit : **Fructose**

The answer is **c.** Lactose is the sugar in milk; fructose is the sugar in fruit.

35. November 1 : Scorpio :: March 1: **Pisces**

The answer is **d.** According to astrology, someone who is born on November 1 is born under the Scorpio star sign; someone who is born on March 1 is born under the Pisces star sign.

36. .5 : .25 :: .02 : **.0004**

The answer is **b.** .5 squared equals .25 and .02 squared equals .0004.

37. Circumference : Diameter :: 3.14 : **1**

The answer is **a.** The circumference of a circle is 3.14 times the diameter.

38. Quadrilateral : 4 :: Hexagon : **6**

The answer is **b.** A quadrilateral is a polygon that has 4 sides and a hexagon is a polygon that has 6 sides.

39. Gregor : **Josef** :: Metamorphosis : Trial

The answer is **d.** Gregor Samsa is the protagonist in Franz Kafka's 1915 *novella The Metamorphosis*. Josef K. is the protagonist in Kafka's 1925 novel *The Trial*.

40. Clavinet : **Zither** :: Hurdy gurdy : Sitar

The answer is **b.** The clavinet and the hurdy gurdy are both keyboard instruments. The zither and the sitar are both string instruments.

41. **Acre** : Land :: Slice : Cake

The answer is **d.** An acre is a piece of land, and a slice is a piece of cake.

42. Pool : Loop :: Lap: **Pal**

The answer is **d.** Pool is loop spelled backward, and lap is pal spelled backward.

43. Plath : **The Bell Jar** :: Lowry : Under the Volcano

The answer is **c.** *The Bell Jar* is a semi-auto-biographical novel by Sylvia Plath. *Under the Volcano* is a semi-autobiographical novel by Malcolm Lowry.

44. **A cappella** : Unaccompanied :: Concerto : Accompanied

The answer is **a.** An a cappella musical composition is written for an unaccompanied solo voice. A concerto is a musical composition written for a solo instrument, accompanied by an orchestra.

45. Trypsin : Proteins :: Lipase : **Fats**

The answer is **d.** Trypsin is a pancreatic enzyme that digests protein; lipase is a pancreatic enzyme that digests fats.

46. Spike : **Brooklyn** :: Woody : Manhattan

The answer is **b.** Spike Lee is a filmmaker known for his movies set in the Brooklyn borough of New York City. Woody Allen is a filmmaker known for setting movies in the Manhattan borough of New York City.

47. **Jung** : Lewin :: Analytic Theory : Field Theory

The answer is **b.** Both Jung and Lewin developed theories of personality. Jung's is called analytic theory and Lewin's is called field theory.

48. The Birth of a Nation : A Trip to the Moon :: Sunset Boulevard : **The African Queen**

The answer is **c.** The Birth of a Nation and A Trip to the Moon are both silent films. Sunset Boulevard and The African Queen are both sound films.

49. Polyphony : Melodic :: Cacophony : **Inharmonious**

The answer is **d.** Polyphony is the use of two or more instruments to create a melodic sound. Cacophony is the use of two or more instruments to create a harsh, inharmonious sound.

50. Purr : **Contentment** :: Huff : Indignation

The answer is **c.** To purr is a sign of contentment, and to huff is a sign of indignation.

51. Lap : Pool :: **Light year** : Space

The answer is **c.** Lap is a distance covered in a pool, and light year is a distance covered in space.

52. Pelosi : House of Representatives :: **O'Connor** : Supreme Court

The answer is **d.** Nancy Pelosi was the first female Speaker of the House of Representatives. Sandra Day O'Connor was the first female justice of the Supreme Court.

53. Adenine : Thymine :: **Guanine** : Cytosine

The answer is **a.** In DNA molecules, adenine always bonds with thymine, and guanine always bonds with cytosine.

54. **Market** : Capitalism :: Planned : Socialism

The answer is **b.** Capitalism is a market economy. Socialism is a planned economy.

55. Jefferson : Monticello :: Jackson : **Hermitage**

The answer is **a.** Jefferson's estate was known as Monticello and Jackson's estate was known as Hermitage.

56. Matzo : Jewish :: **Roti** : Indian

The answer is **d.** Matzo is a type of Jewish bread. Roti is a type of Indian bread.

57. St. Louis : Gateway City :: Kansas City : **City of Fountains**

The answer is **b.** Kansas City is known as the City of Fountains and St. Louis is known as the Gateway City.

58. Earthquake : **Tsunami** :: Greenhouse Gases : Global Warming

The answer is **b.** Earthquakes are one of the causes of tsunamis, and greenhouse gases are one of the causes of global warming.

59. Tinker : Kettle :: Cobbler : **Shoe**

The answer is **b.** A tinker is a person who mends kettles. A cobbler is a person who mends shoes.

60. Eraser : Pencil :: **Nib** : Pen

The answer is **c.** The eraser is part of a pencil, and the nib is part of a pen.

61. Shield : Armor :: Equipment : Gear

The answer is **d.** A shield is a synonym of armor, and equipment is a synonym of gear.

62. Patrol : **Response** :: Bus : Train

The answer is **b.** A patrol car and a response car are two types of police cars. A bus and a train are two types of public transportation vehicles.

63. Smith : Marx :: **Capitalism** : Communism

The answer is **a.** Smith was a noted writer on capitalism and Marx is a noted writer on communism.

64. Baseball : The United States :: Cricket : Bermuda

The answer is **c.** Baseball is the de facto national sport of the United States. Cricket is the de facto national sport of Bermuda.

65. Oxygen : **Carbon Dioxide** :: Arteries : Veins

The answer is **c.** Oxygen is abundant in the arteries, while carbon dioxide is abundant in the veins.

66. Turban : **Headdress** :: Turbine : Engine

The answer is **c.** A turban is a type of headdress, and a turbine is a type of engine.

67. Slither : Snake :: Rotate : **Fan**

The answer is **c.** Slither describes the movement of a snake, and rotate describes the movement of a fan.

68. White Blood Cells : Protection :: Platelets : **Clotting**

The answer is **a.** White blood cells provide protection; platelets provide clotting.

69. $\frac{2}{5} : \frac{6}{15} :: \frac{3}{7} : \frac{9}{21}$

The answer is **d.** $\frac{2}{5} \times \frac{3}{3} = \frac{6}{15}$. $\frac{3}{7} \times \frac{3}{3} = \frac{9}{21}$.

70. $\frac{1}{2} : \frac{1}{6} :: \mathbf{3} : \mathbf{1}$

The answer is **c.** The fraction $\frac{1}{2}$ is 3 times as large as the fraction $\frac{1}{6}$, which is equal to the ratio 3 : 1.

71. Calcium : Iron :: Bones : **Red Blood Cells**

The answer is **c.** Calcium strengthens bones; iron strengthens red blood cells.

72. B1 : Thiamin :: **B2** : Riboflavin

The answer is **b.** Thiamin is another name for vitamin B1; Riboflavin is another name for vitamin B2.

73. Dartmouth : College :: Harvard : University

The answer is **c.** The respective schools are referred to as Dartmouth College and Harvard University.

74. Neurosurgeon : Cobbler :: Operation : **Repair**

The answer is **c.** A neurosurgeon performs operations. A cobbler performs repairs.

75. Indonesia : **Archipelago** :: Malawi : Landlocked

The answer is **c.** Indonesia is an archipelago, a cluster of islands. Malawi is a landlocked African country.

76. Lungs : Heart :: **Respiratory** : Circulatory

The answer is **b.** The lungs are the central organ in the respiratory system, and the heart is the central organ in the circulatory system.

77. Ralph : Ricky :: **Alice** : Lucy

The answer is **a.** Ralph and Alice Kramden were married characters on the classic television comedy "The Honeymooners." Ricky and Lucy Ricardo were married characters (and actors) on the classic television comedy "I Love Lucy."

78. Supermarket : **Retailer** :: Limousine service : Transportation

The answer is **c.** A supermarket is a kind of retail business. A limousine service is a kind of transportation business.

79. Teeth : Cut :: Flowers : Bloom

The answer is **c.** Teeth cut and flowers bloom.

80. Circumference : **Area** :: 2p*r* : p*r*2

The answer is **c.** 2p*r* is the formula for the circumference of a circle. p*r*2 is the formula for the area of a circle.

81. *A Tale of Two Cities* : *The Red Badge of Courage* :: *The Scarlet Pimpernel* : Shiloh

The answer is **b.** Charles Dickens' novel *A Tale of Two Cities* and Baroness Emmuska Orczy's novel *The Scarlet Pimpernel* are set during the French Revolution. Stephen Crane's novel *The Red Badge of Courage* and Shelby Foote's novel *Shiloh* are both set during the American Civil War.

82. **Carpaccio** : Goulash :: Steak tartare : Flaki

The answer is **c.** Carpaccio and steak tartare are both dishes made with raw beef. Goulash and flaki are dishes made with cooked beef.

83. Arrastre : Drag :: Barrida : **Sweep**

The answer is **c.** In dance, an arrastre is a drag and a barrida is a sweep.

84. Potato : Kiwi :: **Eggplant** : Persimmon

The answer is **c.** The potato and the eggplant are both perennial vegetables. The kiwi and the persimmon are perennial fruits.

85. Tabula Rasa : **Nihilism** :: Locke : Turgenev

The answer is **d.** The philosophical term tabula rasa, a Latin phrase meaning blank slate, was coined by John Locke. The philosophical term nihilism, which means a belief in nothing, was coined by Russian writer Ivan Turgenev.

86. Development : Sprawl :: Famine : **Malnutrition**

The answer is **a.** Development is a cause of sprawl, and famine is a cause of malnutrition.

87. Also Sprach Zarathustra : ***2001: A Space Odyssey*** :: Pachelbel's Canon : *Ordinary People*

The answer is **c.** Richard Strauss's composition "Also Sprach Zarathustra" is famous for being used in the 1968 film *2001: A Space Odyssey*. "Pachelbel's Canon" by composer Johann Pachelbel is famous for its use in the 1980 film *Ordinary People*.

88. Teeth & Bones : **Phosphorus** :: DNA : Folic Acid

The answer is **b.** Phosphorus aids in the formation of teeth and bones; folic acid aids in the formation of DNA.

89. Muscle Tissue : **Epithelial Tissue** :: Contraction : Coverage

The answer is **d.** Muscle tissue provides contraction; epithelial tissue provides coverage.

90. Union : Towns :: Confederacy : **Streams**

The answer is **b.** In the American Civil War, the Union named battles after towns and the Confederates named battles after streams.

91. **Baryshnikov** : Russian :: Bruhn : Danish

The answer is **b.** Mikhail Baryshnikov is a Russian ballet dancer and Erik Bruhn is a Danish ballet dancer.

92. **South Africa** : New Zealand :: Zululand : Maori

The answer is **d.** Zululand is a sub-national monarchy in South Africa. Maori is a sub-national monarchy in New Zealand.

93. Cheap : Peach :: **Regal** : Large

The answer is **b.** Cheap is an anagram for peach, and regal is an anagram for large.

94. Carthage : **Rome** :: Athens : Sparta

The answer is **b.** In the Punic Wars, Carthage and Rome were opposing sides. In the Peloponnesian Wars, Athens and Sparta were opposing sides.

95. 4! : 24 :: 5! : **120**

The answer is **d.** 4! Means $4 \times 3 \times 2 \times 1$ which equals 24, and 5! means $5 \times 4 \times 3 \times 2 \times 1$ which equals 120.

96. **Ozone Layer** : Stratosphere :: Mesoshpere : Ionosphere

The answer is **c.** The stratosphere contains the ozone layer; the ionosphere contains the mesosphere.

97. Lorenz : Geese :: Goodall : **Chimps**

The answer is **a.** Konrad Lorenz studied geese; Jane Goodall studied chimps.

98. Sachs : *The End of Poverty* :: Smith : *The Wealth of Nations*

The answer is **a.** Both economists, Sachs wrote *The End of Poverty* and Smith wrote *The Wealth of Nations*.

99. Manacle : Hands :: **Fetter** : Feet

The answer is **b.** A manacle is a shackle for the hands, and a fetter is a shackle for the feet.

100. Flip : Impertinent :: Dice : **Cut**

The answer is **a.** Flip is a synonym for impertinent, and dice is a synonym of cut.

101. **Trotsky** : Lenin :: Kerensky : Plekhanov

The answer is **d.** Trotsky and Lenin were the leaders of the Reds in the Russian Civil War and Kerensky and Plekhanov were the leaders of the Whites.

102. Cyrillic : **Slavic** :: Devanagari : Indian

The answer is **c.** The Cyrillic alphabet is used in Slavic languages and the devanagari alphabet is used in Indian writing with syllabic features.

103. Vitamin E : Antioxidant :: Folic Acid : **Red Blood Cell Producer**

The answer is **a.** Vitamin E works as an antioxidant; folic acid works as a red blood cell producer.

104. Synodic : Sidereal :: Lunation : **Phase**

The answer is **b.** When talking about the moon's cycle, synodic is another name for lunation; sidereal is another name for phase.

105. Pitepalt : **Pork** :: Pierogi : Potato

The answer is **b.** A pitepalt is a Swedish dumpling filled with pork. A pierogi is a Polish dumpling filled with potato.

106. **Linger** : Leave :: Vacillate : Decide

The answer is **a.** To linger means to be slow to leave, and to vacillate is to be slow to decide.

107. Wasabi : Mustard :: **Plum** : Cherry

The answer is **d.** Wasabi and mustard both belong to a family of flowering plants called brassicaceae. The plum and the cherry belong to the drupe fruit family.

108. Cumbia : Bourrée :: Colombia : **France**

The answer is **b.** Cumbia is a folk dance from Colombia. Bourrée is a dance that originated in France.

109. Gregg Toland : Jack Warner :: Cinematographer : **Producer**

The answer is **a.** Gregg Toland was a famous cinematographer. Jack Warner was a famous movie producer.

110. **Overt** : Hidden :: Ebullient : Glum

The answer is **c.** Overt is an antonym of hidden, and ebullient is an antonym of glum.

111. Gloaming : **Dusk** :: Bearing : Manner

The answer is **d.** Gloaming is another word for dusk, and bearing is another word for manner.

112. President : Operations director :: Banker : **Executive Assistant**

The answer is **d.** In business, president and operations director are both executive titles. Banker and Executive Assistant are non-executive titles.

113. $11 : 1^{-1} :: 12 : 2^0$

The answer is **a.** 1 raised to any power equals 1. Any number raised to the 0 power equals 1.

114. **Porter** : College :: Concierge : Hotel

The answer is **d.** The caretaker of a college is called a porter. The caretaker of a hotel is called a concierge.

115. Archeozoic : Proterozoic :: Bacteria : **Sponges**

The answer is **b.** Bacteria developed in the Archeozoic Eon (3.9 to 2.5 billion years ago); multi-cellular organisms, such as sponges, evolved during the Proterozoic Eon.

116. Gateleg : **Armoire** :: Refectory : Credenza

The answer is **d.** A gateleg and a refectory are two types of tables. An armoire and a credenza are two types of cabinets.

117. Log 10 : Log 100 :: **Log 100** : Log 10000

The answer is **c.** Log 10 = 1 and log 100 = 2; the ratio is 1 to 2. log 100 = 2 and log 10000 = 4; the ratio is 1 to 2.

118. Irreverent : Respect :: Slipshod : **Care**

The answer is **c.** Irreverent means lacking in respect, and slipshod means lacking in care.

119. $\sqrt{18} : \sqrt{50} :: 3 : 5$

The answer is **d.** $\sqrt{18}$ simplified is equal to $3\sqrt{2}$. $\sqrt{50}$ simplified is equal to $5\sqrt{2}$; the ratio is 3 to 5.

120. The Snake Charmer : **Rousseau** :: The Fiddler : Chagall

The answer is **c.** The Snake Charmer is a 1907 painting by Henri Rousseau. The Fiddler is a 1912 painting by Marc Chagall.

Scoring Your MAT Practice Test

As mentioned in Chapter 1, when you receive your personal score report for the official MAT, you'll be provided with a scaled score and two percentile ranks, all of which are derived from the number of items you answered correctly—known as your raw score.

Because there are different forms and formats of the official MAT, and typically 20 of the 120 questions on the official MAT are experimental and do not count toward your official scaled score and percentile ranks, it is impossible to create an accurate raw score to scaled score or raw score to percentile chart for this and the other practice tests found in this book. In the end, you are striving to correctly answer the highest number of questions as possible and familiarize yourself with the MAT format so you're fully prepared to do your best on test day. For now, what's much more important than your overall score is how you did on each of the content areas tested by the exam. You need to diagnose your strengths and weaknesses so that you can concentrate your efforts as you prepare. The question types are mixed in the practice exam, so in order to tell where your strengths and weaknesses lie, you'll need to compare your answer sheet with the **MAT Practice Test 5 Review** below, which shows which of the content areas each question falls into.

Use your performance here in conjunction with the LearningExpress Test Preparation System in Chapter 2 to help you devise a study plan. You should plan to spend more time studying areas that correspond to the questions you found hardest and less time on the content areas in which you did well. Once you have spent some time reviewing, take the next MAT Practice Test to see if you've improved.

MAT PRACTICE TEST 5 REVIEW	
CONTENT AREA	**QUESTION NUMBERS**
Language and Vocabulary	3, 4, 20, 21, 26, 27, 31, 32, 41, 42, 50, 51, 60, 61, 66, 67, 79, 86, 93, 99, 100, 106, 110, 111, 118
Humanities	1, 5, 8, 9, 11, 14, 39, 40, 43, 44, 46, 48, 49, 81, 83, 85, 87, 91, 108, 109, 120
Social Science	7, 13, 15, 16, 18, 19, 23, 47, 52, 54, 55, 57, 63, 75, 90, 92, 94, 98, 101, 102
Natural Science	10, 17, 22, 24, 25, 34, 37, 45, 53, 58, 65, 68, 71, 72, 76, 88, 89, 96, 97, 103, 104, 115
General	6, 12, 28, 29, 30, 33, 35, 56, 59, 62, 64, 73, 74, 77, 78, 82, 84, 105, 107, 112, 114, 116
Mathematics	2, 36, 38, 69, 70, 80, 95, 113, 117, 119

CHAPTER

▶ MAT Practice Test 6

CHAPTER SUMMARY

Here's another sample MAT test for you to practice with.

For this practice test, simulate the actual test-taking experience as closely as you can. Find a quiet place to work where you won't be disturbed. If you own this book, use the answer sheet on the following pages and find some #2 pencils to fill in the circles. Use a timer or stopwatch to time yourself— you'll have 60 minutes to complete the official MAT. After you take the test, use the detailed answer explanations that follow to review any questions you missed.

MAT Practice Test 6

1.	ⓐ	ⓑ	ⓒ	ⓓ
2.	ⓐ	ⓑ	ⓒ	ⓓ
3.	ⓐ	ⓑ	ⓒ	ⓓ
4.	ⓐ	ⓑ	ⓒ	ⓓ
5.	ⓐ	ⓑ	ⓒ	ⓓ
6.	ⓐ	ⓑ	ⓒ	ⓓ
7.	ⓐ	ⓑ	ⓒ	ⓓ
8.	ⓐ	ⓑ	ⓒ	ⓓ
9.	ⓐ	ⓑ	ⓒ	ⓓ
10.	ⓐ	ⓑ	ⓒ	ⓓ
11.	ⓐ	ⓑ	ⓒ	ⓓ
12.	ⓐ	ⓑ	ⓒ	ⓓ
13.	ⓐ	ⓑ	ⓒ	ⓓ
14.	ⓐ	ⓑ	ⓒ	ⓓ
15.	ⓐ	ⓑ	ⓒ	ⓓ
16.	ⓐ	ⓑ	ⓒ	ⓓ
17.	ⓐ	ⓑ	ⓒ	ⓓ
18.	ⓐ	ⓑ	ⓒ	ⓓ
19.	ⓐ	ⓑ	ⓒ	ⓓ
20.	ⓐ	ⓑ	ⓒ	ⓓ
21.	ⓐ	ⓑ	ⓒ	ⓓ
22.	ⓐ	ⓑ	ⓒ	ⓓ
23.	ⓐ	ⓑ	ⓒ	ⓓ
24.	ⓐ	ⓑ	ⓒ	ⓓ
25.	ⓐ	ⓑ	ⓒ	ⓓ
26.	ⓐ	ⓑ	ⓒ	ⓓ
27.	ⓐ	ⓑ	ⓒ	ⓓ
28.	ⓐ	ⓑ	ⓒ	ⓓ
29.	ⓐ	ⓑ	ⓒ	ⓓ
30.	ⓐ	ⓑ	ⓒ	ⓓ
31.	ⓐ	ⓑ	ⓒ	ⓓ
32.	ⓐ	ⓑ	ⓒ	ⓓ
33.	ⓐ	ⓑ	ⓒ	ⓓ
34.	ⓐ	ⓑ	ⓒ	ⓓ
35.	ⓐ	ⓑ	ⓒ	ⓓ
36.	ⓐ	ⓑ	ⓒ	ⓓ
37.	ⓐ	ⓑ	ⓒ	ⓓ
38.	ⓐ	ⓑ	ⓒ	ⓓ
39.	ⓐ	ⓑ	ⓒ	ⓓ
40.	ⓐ	ⓑ	ⓒ	ⓓ
41.	ⓐ	ⓑ	ⓒ	ⓓ
42.	ⓐ	ⓑ	ⓒ	ⓓ
43.	ⓐ	ⓑ	ⓒ	ⓓ
44.	ⓐ	ⓑ	ⓒ	ⓓ
45.	ⓐ	ⓑ	ⓒ	ⓓ

46.	ⓐ	ⓑ	ⓒ	ⓓ
47.	ⓐ	ⓑ	ⓒ	ⓓ
48.	ⓐ	ⓑ	ⓒ	ⓓ
49.	ⓐ	ⓑ	ⓒ	ⓓ
50.	ⓐ	ⓑ	ⓒ	ⓓ
51.	ⓐ	ⓑ	ⓒ	ⓓ
52.	ⓐ	ⓑ	ⓒ	ⓓ
53.	ⓐ	ⓑ	ⓒ	ⓓ
54.	ⓐ	ⓑ	ⓒ	ⓓ
55.	ⓐ	ⓑ	ⓒ	ⓓ
56.	ⓐ	ⓑ	ⓒ	ⓓ
57.	ⓐ	ⓑ	ⓒ	ⓓ
58.	ⓐ	ⓑ	ⓒ	ⓓ
59.	ⓐ	ⓑ	ⓒ	ⓓ
60.	ⓐ	ⓑ	ⓒ	ⓓ
61.	ⓐ	ⓑ	ⓒ	ⓓ
62.	ⓐ	ⓑ	ⓒ	ⓓ
63.	ⓐ	ⓑ	ⓒ	ⓓ
64.	ⓐ	ⓑ	ⓒ	ⓓ
65.	ⓐ	ⓑ	ⓒ	ⓓ
66.	ⓐ	ⓑ	ⓒ	ⓓ
67.	ⓐ	ⓑ	ⓒ	ⓓ
68.	ⓐ	ⓑ	ⓒ	ⓓ
69.	ⓐ	ⓑ	ⓒ	ⓓ
70.	ⓐ	ⓑ	ⓒ	ⓓ
71.	ⓐ	ⓑ	ⓒ	ⓓ
72.	ⓐ	ⓑ	ⓒ	ⓓ
73.	ⓐ	ⓑ	ⓒ	ⓓ
74.	ⓐ	ⓑ	ⓒ	ⓓ
75.	ⓐ	ⓑ	ⓒ	ⓓ
76.	ⓐ	ⓑ	ⓒ	ⓓ
77.	ⓐ	ⓑ	ⓒ	ⓓ
78.	ⓐ	ⓑ	ⓒ	ⓓ
79.	ⓐ	ⓑ	ⓒ	ⓓ
80.	ⓐ	ⓑ	ⓒ	ⓓ
81.	ⓐ	ⓑ	ⓒ	ⓓ
82.	ⓐ	ⓑ	ⓒ	ⓓ
83.	ⓐ	ⓑ	ⓒ	ⓓ
84.	ⓐ	ⓑ	ⓒ	ⓓ
85.	ⓐ	ⓑ	ⓒ	ⓓ
86.	ⓐ	ⓑ	ⓒ	ⓓ
87.	ⓐ	ⓑ	ⓒ	ⓓ
88.	ⓐ	ⓑ	ⓒ	ⓓ
89.	ⓐ	ⓑ	ⓒ	ⓓ
90.	ⓐ	ⓑ	ⓒ	ⓓ

91.	ⓐ	ⓑ	ⓒ	ⓓ
92.	ⓐ	ⓑ	ⓒ	ⓓ
93.	ⓐ	ⓑ	ⓒ	ⓓ
94.	ⓐ	ⓑ	ⓒ	ⓓ
95.	ⓐ	ⓑ	ⓒ	ⓓ
96.	ⓐ	ⓑ	ⓒ	ⓓ
97.	ⓐ	ⓑ	ⓒ	ⓓ
98.	ⓐ	ⓑ	ⓒ	ⓓ
99.	ⓐ	ⓑ	ⓒ	ⓓ
100.	ⓐ	ⓑ	ⓒ	ⓓ
101.	ⓐ	ⓑ	ⓒ	ⓓ
102.	ⓐ	ⓑ	ⓒ	ⓓ
103.	ⓐ	ⓑ	ⓒ	ⓓ
104.	ⓐ	ⓑ	ⓒ	ⓓ
105.	ⓐ	ⓑ	ⓒ	ⓓ
106.	ⓐ	ⓑ	ⓒ	ⓓ
107.	ⓐ	ⓑ	ⓒ	ⓓ
108.	ⓐ	ⓑ	ⓒ	ⓓ
109.	ⓐ	ⓑ	ⓒ	ⓓ
110.	ⓐ	ⓑ	ⓒ	ⓓ
111.	ⓐ	ⓑ	ⓒ	ⓓ
112.	ⓐ	ⓑ	ⓒ	ⓓ
113.	ⓐ	ⓑ	ⓒ	ⓓ
114.	ⓐ	ⓑ	ⓒ	ⓓ
115.	ⓐ	ⓑ	ⓒ	ⓓ
116.	ⓐ	ⓑ	ⓒ	ⓓ
117.	ⓐ	ⓑ	ⓒ	ⓓ
118.	ⓐ	ⓑ	ⓒ	ⓓ
119.	ⓐ	ⓑ	ⓒ	ⓓ
120.	ⓐ	ⓑ	ⓒ	ⓓ

Directions: For each question, select the answer choice in the parentheses that best completes the analogy.

1. (**a.** Episode **b.** Chapter **c.** Prequel **d.** Part) : Sequel :: Before : After

2. Brig : Military :: (**a.** Ship **b.** Jail **c.** Cage **d.** Bar) : Civilian

3. Gobble : Eat :: (**a.** Deny **b.** Embrace **c.** Acquiesce **d.** Infer) : Accept

4. Stoker : Shelley :: (**a.** Hyde **b.** Van Helsing **c.** Hook **d.** Lugosi) : Frankenstein

5. $\frac{2}{3} : \frac{3}{2} :: \frac{4}{5} :$ (**a.** $\frac{1}{2}$ **b.** $\frac{5}{2}$ **c.** $\frac{1}{4}$ **d.** $\frac{5}{4}$)

6. (**a.** Jay Gatsby **b.** Nostromo **c.** Goodman Brown **d.** Henry Chinaski) : Hawthorne :: Billy Budd : Melville

7. Beantown : Windy City :: (**a.** New York City **b.** Boston **c.** Baltimore **d.** San Francisco) : Chicago

8. Mineral : Specific :: Rock : (**a.** Mixture **b.** Gem **c.** Chemical **d.** Hard)

9. Ethnocracy : Plutocracy :: Ethnic Group : (**a.** Many **b.** People **c.** Wealthy **d.** Majority)

10. Belfast : Northern Ireland :: (**a.** Barcelona **b.** Seville **c.** Gibraltar **d.** Madrid) : Spain

11. (**a.** Bike **b.** Ice **c.** Wheel **d.** Roadway) : Skid :: Obstacle : Swerve

12. Iceland : Italy :: Ísland : (**a.** Europe **b.** Italia **c.** Roma **d.** Italian)

13. Luther : Lutheranism :: (**a.** Calvin **b.** Wesley **c.** Henry VIII **d.** Queen Elizabeth) : Anglicanism

14. Invertebrates : Paleozoic :: (**a.** Reptiles **b.** Amphibians **c.** Mammals **d.** Fishes) : Cenozoic

15. (**a.** Tree **b.** Coffee **c.** Pestle **d.** Saw) : Grind :: Ax : Chop

16. Continents : Pangaea :: Elements : (**a.** Ion **b.** Compound **c.** Nucleus **d.** Geography)

17. Rabbi : Pastor :: (**a.** Ordain **b.** Preside **c.** Judaism **d.** Lutheran) : Christianity

18. Short-Term : Carbohydrates :: Long-Term : (**a.** Protein **b.** Amino Acids **c.** Sugars **d.** Lipids)

19. Jellyfish : Whale :: Invertebrate : (**a.** Mollusk **b.** Vertebrate **c.** Shark **d.** Mammal)

20. Ham : Bacon :: (**a.** Pork **b.** Meat **c.** Veal **d.** Cutlet) : Beef

21. (**a.** Refrigerator **b.** Stove **c.** Ice **d.** Defrost) : Cool :: Oven : Cook

22. (**a.** Diamond **b.** Club **c.** Sand **d.** Hole) : Baseball :: Gridiron : Football

23. The Last Supper : Jesus Christ :: (**a.** Saint George and the Dragon **b.** Pietà **c.** Canvas **d.** The Creation of Adam) : God

24. The Raven : (**a.** A Red, Red Rose **b.** Seeker of Truth **c.** Stanza **d.** Seagull) :: Poe : Burns

25. Left Wing : (**a.** Center field **b.** 10 Yard Line **c.** Home base **d.** Center court) :: Face-off Spot : End Zone

26. Jann Wenner : Hunter S. Thompson :: (**a.** Manager **b.** Boss **c.** Author **d.** Editor) : Writer

27. $\frac{1}{2}$: .5 :: (**a.** $\frac{1}{3}$ **b.** $\frac{1}{4}$ **c.** $\frac{1}{5}$ **d.** $\frac{1}{6}$) : .25

28. Virginia : Georgia :: Maryland : (**a.** New Hampshire **b.** Vermont **c.** Maine **d.** Tennessee)

29. 45 : (**a.** 40 **b.** 37 **c.** 35 **d.** 34) :: 22 : 14

30. Paleontology : (**a.** Geology **b.** Astronomy **c.** Microscopy **d.** Archeology) :: Anatomy : Biology

31. Nixon : (**a.** Goldwater **b.** Agnew **c.** Rockefeller **d.** Reagan) :: Kennedy : Johnson

32. (**a.** Coffee **b.** Dig **c.** Tumbler **d.** Tavern) : Mug :: Trowel : Spade

33. Carousel : Luggage :: Escalator : (**a.** Raise **b.** Elevator **c.** People **d.** Building)

34. Mercury : Jupiter :: (**a.** Hydrogen **b.** Boron **c.** Magnesium **d.** Potassium) : Ununoctium

35. Irrelevant : Significance :: Relaxed : (**a.** Care **b.** Calm **c.** Thoughtful **d.** Asleep)

36. Follow : Chase :: Nudge : (**a.** Thrust **b.** Pursue **c.** Catch **d.** Precede)

37. Metropolis : Future :: (**a.** Blade Runner **b.** Bonnie and Clyde **c.** Comedy **d.** City) : Past

38. Cancel : Delay :: Surrender : (**a.** Anticipate **b.** Yield **c.** Fire **d.** Army)

39. (**a.** Humanism **b.** Analytical **c.** Gestalt **d.** Existentialism) : Jung :: Behaviorism : Watson

40. (**a.** Gluten **b.** Sodium **c.** Glucose **d.** Lactose) : Soy :: Seitan : Tofu

41. Cotton : (**a.** Silk **b.** Nylon **c.** Rattan **d.** Flax) :: Hemp : Fiberglass

42. Romeo : Juliet :: Poison : (**a.** Tragedy **b.** Gun **c.** Dagger **d.** Drown)

43. (**a.** Pacifism **b.** Marx **c.** Heidegger **d.** Hayek) : Existentialism :: Stirner : Egoism

44. Trench : (**a.** Retraction **b.** Subduction **c.** Tectonic **d.** Geographic) :: Mountain : Collision

45. Banjo : Five :: Violin : (**a.** Two **b.** Three **c.** Four **d.** Six)

46. Suriname : Brazil :: (**a.** Dutch **b.** English **c.** French **d.** Spanish) : Portuguese

47. Hawaii : (**a.** New Zealand **b.** Sydney **c.** Tasmania **d.** Auckland) :: United States : Australia

48. Global Warming : Flooding :: Low Pressure Systems : (**a.** Clear Skies **b.** Calm **c.** Cyclones **d.** Earthquakes)

49. (**a.** North Korea **b.** China **c.** Vietnam **d.** Japan) : Cambodia :: Chile : Argentina

50. Receipt : (**a.** Money **b.** Store **c.** Purchase **d.** Husband) :: License : Marriage

51. Thousand Lakes : (a. Minneapolis b. Finland c. Netherlands d. Venice) :: Midnight Sun : Norway

52. Finesse : Cunning :: (a. Agility b. Vision c. Purpose d. Jealousy) : Resentment

53. Everest : Blanc :: Himalayas : (a. Rockies b. Apennines c. Black d. Alps)

54. Washington : Jefferson :: (a. Roosevelt b. Madison c. Jackson d. Kennedy) : Lincoln

55. Atmosphere : (a. Pressure b. Stratosphere c. Amp d. Measure) :: Degree : Temperature

56. Citrus : Nuts :: C : (a. A b. B c. D d. E)

57. 125 : 25 :: 27 : (a. 3 b. 9 c. 15 d. 81)

58. Brig : (a. Limerick b. Crate c. Prison d. Trickery) :: Sham : Hoax

59. Igneous : Sedimentary :: (a. Magma b. Metamorphic c. Surface d. Pressure) : Sediment

60. Barometer : Atmospheric Pressure :: (a. Hydrometer b. Precipitation c. Rain Gauge d. Thermometer) : Intensity of Rain

61. Tokyo : Japan :: (a. San Jose b. San Juan c. Puerto Limon d. Cartago) : Costa Rica

62. Arctic : Borealis :: Antarctic : (a. Lights b. Australis c. Aurora d. Ionosphere)

63. Earthquakes : (a. Rocky Mountain West b. Ring of Fire c. Mid-Atlantic Region d. Eastern Europe) :: Tornadoes : Southern United States

64. Bold : Brass :: (a. Merry b. Fresh c. Neat d. Modest) : Maiden

65. Romulus : (a. Cane b. Adam c. Qabil d. Eve) :: Remus : Abel

66. Justice : (a. License b. Second c. Rope d. Tie) :: Nature : String

67. Honda : Aston Martin :: Mitsubishi : (a. Vauxhall b. Ales c. Hope d. Isuzu)

68. Battalion : (a. Army b. Troop c. Rifles d. Battle) :: Dollar : Cent

69. Cineast : Film :: Gastronome : (a. Gnomes b. Files c. Food d. Stars)

70. (a. O'Keefe b. Monet c. Renoir d. Bazille) : van Gogh :: Water Lilies : Sunflowers

71. (a. Head I b. New Atlantis c. Triptych d. Existentialist) : The Scream :: Bacon : Munch

72. Haute Couture : (a. Outerwear b. Accessory c. Ready-to-Wear d. Fashion) :: Kids Wear : Knitwear

73. Librarian : Bookkeeper :: Organize : (a. Store b. Balance c. Office d. Direct)

74. Log 10 : Log 100 :: 1 : (a. 2 b. 4 c. 10 d. 20)

75. Bolt : Steel :: (a. Needle b. Cloth c. Pin d. Thread) : Fabric

76. mm : (a. cm b. dm c. m d. hm) :: m : km

77. Dolly : (a. Ticket b. Ship c. Camera d. Ocean) :: Ferry : Passenger

78. Efficient : Wasteful :: (**a.** Sly **b.** Detective **c.** Honest **d.** Cautious) : Deceptive

79. (**a.** Hike **b.** Grass **c.** Mold **d.** Trail) : Spoil :: Walk : Path

80. M : Breathless :: German Expressionism : (**a.** French New Wave **b.** Feminism **c.** Parody **d.** Surrealism)

81. Shakespeare : (**a.** 15 **b.** 16 **c.** 17 **d.** 18) :: Shaw : 20

82. Andretti : Car :: (**a.** DeLonge **b.** Rogers **c.** Shoemaker **d.** Wayne) : Horse

83. New York City : (**a.** Taco **b.** Hamburger **c.** Pizza **d.** Cake) :: Philadelphia : Cheesesteak

84. *Remembrance of Things Past* : *Up From Slavery* :: (**a.** *A Farewell to Arms* **b.** *The Diary of Anne Frank* **c.** *The Autobiography of Mark Twain* **d.** *Moll Flanders*) : *Confessions*

85. (**a.** Circumference **b.** Automation **c.** Sextant **d.** Hydration) : Navigation :: Abacus : Calculation

86. Dither : Settle :: Display : (**a.** Corrupt **b.** Bother **c.** Hide **d.** Count)

87. Rob Roy : Scott :: Eugénie Grandet : (**a.** Hugo **b.** Gogol **c.** Balzac **d.** Stendhal)

88. Koffka : Kohler :: Perls : (**a.** Wertheimer **b.** Freud **c.** Durkheim **d.** Pavlov)

89. Cleaver : Tenderizer :: Snake : (**a.** Slicer **b.** Palette **c.** Roller **d.** Auger)

90. Epigram : Elegy :: (**a.** Lengthy **b.** Sorrowful **c.** Angry **d.** Witty) : Mournful

91. Art Deco : 20 :: (**a.** Fauvisim **b.** Cubism **c.** Art Brut **d.** Impressionism) : 19

92. Cambrian : Paleozoic :: Triassic : (**a.** Mesozoic **b.** Cenozoic **c.** Azoic **d.** Archeozoic)

93. 30 : 150 :: (**a.** 100 **b.** 70 **c.** 140 **d.** 150) : 110

94. (**a.** Nobel **b.** Lakoff **c.** Braille **d.** Chomsky) : Langacker :: Generative Grammar : Cognitive Linguistics

95. Clumsy : Dexterity :: (**a.** Passive **b.** Oaf **c.** Submit **d.** Wish) : Will

96. Gavrilo Princip : John Wilkes Booth :: (**a.** President Kennedy **b.** Pope John Paul II **c.** Archduke Ferdinand **d.** Benito Mussolini) : President Lincoln

97. Maasai : (**a.** New Zealand **b.** Mexico **c.** Africa **d.** Iceland) :: Palawah : Australia

98. Prokaryote : Eukaryote :: (**a.** White Blood Cell **b.** Neuron **c.** Organelle **d.** Bacteria) : Skin Cell

99. Mnemonics : (**a.** Memory **b.** Future **c.** Hieroglyphics **d.** Movement) :: Phonetics : Language

100. ATP : Protein :: (**a.** Mitochondria **b.** Nucleolus **c.** Lysosomes **d.** Chemical) : Ribosomes

101. Lipase : (**a.** Trypsin **b.** Sucrose **c.** Amylase **d.** Enzyme) :: Fats : Carbohydrates

102. Hamstring : (**a.** Ride **b.** Cripple **c.** Scratch **d.** Wager) :: Stake : Bet

103. *Double Indemnity* : (**a.** *White Heat* **b.** *The 400 Blows* **c.** *Open City* **d.** *Suspiria*) :: Film noir : Italian neorealism

104. Horseshoe Crab : Scorpion :: (**a.** Malpighian **b.** Crustacean **c.** Chelicerate **d.** Pedipalp) : Arachnid

105. Helium : Noble :: Flourine : (**a.** Inert **b.** Alkali **c.** Halogen **d.** Transition)

106. Yard : Meter :: (**a.** Inch **b.** Foot **c.** Centimeter **d.** Mile) : Kilometer

107. Analogous : Wings :: (**a.** Vestigial **b.** Homologous **c.** Reptiles **d.** Vertebrates) : Tarsals

108. Alizarin : Crimson :: (**a.** Camel **b.** Ao **c.** Sienna **d.** Slate) : Capri

109. (**a.** Dermatologist **b.** Apprentice **c.** Professor **d.** Docent) : Patient :: Pedagogue : Pupil

110. Exasperate : Irk :: (**a.** Prevent **b.** Leather **c.** Argue **d.** Dismiss) : Dissuade

111. Cask : Sack :: Thin : (**a.** Fire **b.** Satchel **c.** Rope **d.** Hint)

112. (**a.** Carlyle **b.** Hume **c.** Bentham **d.** Place) : A Treatise of Human Nature :: Mill : On Liberty

113. Jean-Paul Sartre : Literature :: Le Duc Tho : (**a.** Chemistry **b.** Peace **c.** Economics **d.** Literature)

114. Pogo : Doonesbury :: (**a.** Davis **b.** Breathed **c.** Wilson **d.** Kelly) : Trudeau

115. Windmill : Rudder :: (**a.** Electronic **b.** Turbine **c.** Engine **d.** Compressor) : Airfoil

116. $18 : 80 :: 41 :$ (**a.** 40 **b.** $4\text{-}1$ **c.** $(\frac{1}{4})\text{-}1$ **d.** $(\frac{1}{4})1$)

117. Real : Imaginary :: $\sqrt{5}$: (**a.** $\sqrt{0}$ **b.** $\sqrt{1}$ **c.** $\sqrt{-1}$ **d.** $\sqrt{4}$)

118. (**a.** Tiding **b.** Mystery **c.** Patio **d.** Jargon) : Patois :: Plot : Design

119. (**a.** Miser **b.** Raconteur **c.** Harmonious **d.** Felon) : Entertain :: Bully : Browbeat

120. Nonvascular : Vascular :: (**a.** Mosses **b.** Tomatoes **c.** Corn **d.** Beets) : Beans

Answers

1. Prequel : Sequel :: Before : After

The answer is **c**. A prequel is a work that comes before another work to which it is related. A sequel is a work that comes after a work to which it is related.

2. Brig : Military :: **Jail** : Civilian

The answer is **b**. A brig is a military place of detention. A jail is a civilian place of detention.

3. Gobble : Eat :: **Embrace** : Accept

The answer is **b**. To gobble is to eat to eagerly, and to embrace is to accept readily.

4. Stoker : Shelley :: **Van Helsing** : Frankenstein

The answer is **b**. Abraham Van Helsing is a character in the horror novel *Dracula* by Bram Stoker. Victor Frankenstein is a character in Mary Wollstonecraft Shelley's horror novel *Frankenstein*.

5. $\frac{2}{3} : \frac{3}{2} :: \frac{4}{5} : \frac{5}{4}$

The answer is **d**. $\frac{3}{2}$ is the reciprocal of $\frac{2}{3}$ and $\frac{5}{4}$ is the reciprocal of $\frac{4}{5}$.

6. Goodman Brown : Hawthorne :: Billy Budd : Melville

The answer is **c**. Goodman Brown is a literary character created by Nathaniel Hawthorne. Billy Budd is a literary character created by Herman Melville.

7. Beantown : Windy City :: **Boston** : Chicago

The answer is **b**. Beantown is a nickname for Boston; Windy City is a nickname for Chicago.

8. Mineral : Specific :: Rock : **Mixture**

The answer is **a**. A mineral is made up of a specific element; a rock is a mixture of minerals.

9. Ethnocracy : Plutocracy :: Ethnic Group : **Wealthy**

The answer is **c**. In an ethnocracy, a particular ethnic group rules the government. In a plutocracy, the government is ruled by the wealthy.

10. Belfast : Northern Ireland :: **Madrid** : Spain

The answer is **d**. Belfast is the capital of Northern Ireland and Madrid is the capital of Spain.

11. Ice : Skid :: Obstacle : Swerve

The answer is **b**. Ice can cause something to skid, and an obstacle can cause something to swerve.

12. Iceland : Italy :: Ísland : **Italia**

The answer is **b**. The domestic name of Iceland is Ísland. The domestic name of Italy is Italia.

13. Luther : Lutheranism :: **Henry VIII** : Anglicanism

The answer is **c**. Martin Luther founded Lutheranism. King Henry VIII of England founded Anglicanism.

14. Invertebrates : Paleozoic :: **Mammals** : Cenozoic

The answer is **c.** Invertebrates made their appearance on earth during the Paleozoic Era; mammals made their appearance during the Cenozoic Era.

15. Pestle : Grind :: Ax : Chop

The answer is **c.** A pestle is a tool for grinding, and an ax is a tool for chopping.

16. Continents : Pangaea :: Elements : **Compound**

The answer is **b.** Pangaea was formed by continents bonded together; compounds are formed by elements bonded together.

17. Rabbi : Pastor :: **Judaism** : Christianity

The answer is **c.** An ordained person in Judaism is called a rabbi. An ordained person in Christianity is called a pastor.

18. Short-Term : Carbohydrates :: Long-Term : **Lipids**

The answer is **d.** Carbohydrates provide short-term energy; lipids store energy for long-term needs.

19. Jellyfish : Whale :: Invertebrate : **Vertebrate**

The answer is **b.** A jellyfish is an invertebrate; a whale is a vertebrate.

20. Ham : Bacon :: **Veal** : Beef

The answer is **c.** Ham and bacon are both meats taken from pigs. Veal and beef are both meats taken from cows.

21. Refrigerator : Cool :: Oven : Cook

The answer is **a.** A refrigerator is an appliance that cools food. An oven is an appliance that cooks food.

22. Diamond : Baseball :: Gridiron : Football

The answer is **a.** The area on which baseball is played is referred to as the diamond. The area on which football is played is referred to as the gridiron.

23. The Last Supper : Jesus Christ :: **The Creation of Adam** : God

The answer is **d.** Jesus Christ is depicted in Leonardo da Vinci's painting The Last Supper. The Christian God is portrayed in The Creation of Adam, a section of Michelangelo's fresco on the ceiling of the Sistine Chapel.

24. The Raven : **A Red, Red Rose** :: Poe : Burns

The answer is **a.** "The Raven" is a poem by Edgar Allan Poe. "A Red, Red Rose" is a poem by Robert Burns.

25. Left Wing : **10 Yard Line** :: Face-off Spot : End Zone

The answer is **b.** The left wing and face-off spot are parts of a hockey rink. The 10 yard line and end zone are parts of a football field.

26. Jann Wenner : Hunter S. Thompson :: **Editor** : Writer

The answer is **d.** Jann Wenner is the editor of the magazine *Rolling Stone*. Hunter S. Thompson wrote articles for the magazine.

27. $\frac{1}{2}$: .5 :: $\frac{1}{4}$: .25

The answer is **b.** .5 is the decimal equivalent of $\frac{1}{2}$ and .25 is the decimal equivalent of $\frac{1}{4}$.

28. Virginia : Georgia :: Maryland : **New Hampshire**

The answer is **a.** All four states are related because they were each one of the original 13 colonies.

29. 45 : **37** :: 22 : 14

The answer is **b.** 8 subtracted from 22 is 14 and 8 subtracted from 45 is 37.

30. Paleontology : **Geology** :: Anatomy : Biology

The answer is **a.** Paleontology is a branch of geology; anatomy is a branch of biology.

31. Nixon : **Goldwater** :: Kennedy : Johnson

The answer is **a.** Nixon lost the 1960 presidential election to Kennedy. Goldwater lost the 1964 election to Johnson.

32. **Tumbler** : Mug :: Trowel : Spade

The answer is **c.** Both a tumbler and a mug are used as drinking vessels, and a trowel and a spade are used as garden tools.

33. Carousel : Luggage :: Escalator : **People**

The answer is **c.** A carousel is used to move luggage, and an escalator is used to move people.

34. Mercury : Jupiter :: **Hydrogen** : Ununoctium

The answer is **a.** Mercury is the smallest planet; Jupiter is the largest. Hydrogen has the smallest atomic number; Ununoctium has the largest.

35. Irrelevant : Significance :: Relaxed : **Care**

The answer is **a.** To be irrelevant is to lack significance, and to be relaxed is to be free of care.

36. Follow : Chase :: Nudge : **Thrust**

The answer is **a.** To follow is less intense than to chase, and to nudge is less intense than to thrust.

37. *Metropolis* : Future :: ***Bonnie and Clyde*** : Past

The answer is **b.** Fritz Lang's 1927 film *Metropolis* is set in the future. Arthur Penn's 1967 film *Bonnie and Clyde* is set in the past.

38. Cancel : Delay :: Surrender : **Yield**

The answer is **b.** To cancel is more intense than to delay, and to surrender is more intense than to yield.

39. **Analytical** : Jung :: Behaviorism : Watson

The answer is **b.** The analytical school of psychology was founded by Carl Jung. The psychological philosophy of Behaviorism was founded by John B. Watson.

40. **Gluten** : Soy :: Seitan : Tofu

The answer is **a.** The basis of the food seitan is wheat gluten; the basis of the food tofu is soy beans.

41. Cotton : **Nylon** :: Hemp : Fiberglass

The answer is **b.** Cotton and hemp are both natural fibers. Nylon and fiberglass are man-made fibers.

42. Romeo : Juliet :: Poison : **Dagger**

The answer is **c.** In William Shakespeare's play Romeo and Juliet, Romeo takes his own life with poison and Juliet takes her own life with a dagger.

43. **Heidegger** : Existentialism :: Stirner : Egoism

The answer is **c.** Philosopher Martin Heidegger believed in existentialism. Philosopher Max Stirner believed in egoism.

44. Trench : **Subduction** :: Mountain : Collision

The answer is **b.** Mountains are formed through the collision of tectonic plates; trenches are formed through the subduction of tectonic plates.

45. Banjo : Five :: Violin : **Four**

The answer is **c.** A banjo has five strings and a violin has four strings.

46. Suriname : Brazil :: **Dutch** : Portuguese

The answer is **a.** The major language in Brazil is Portuguese. In Suriname, it is Dutch.

47. Hawaii : **Tasmania** :: United States : Australia

The answer is **c.** Hawaii is an island state of the United States. An island state of Australia is Tasmania.

48. Global warming : Flooding :: Low pressure systems : **Clear skies**

The answer is **a.** Global warming can cause coastal flooding; low pressure systems can cause cyclones.

49. **Vietnam** : Cambodia :: Chile : Argentina

The answer is **c.** Vietnam borders Cambodia; Chile borders Argentina.

50. Receipt : **Purchase** :: License : Marriage

The answer is **c.** A receipt is an acknowledgement or document of a purchase, and a license is a document acknowledging a marriage.

51. Thousand lakes : **Finland** :: Midnight sun : Norway

The answer is **b.** Finland is known as the Land of a Thousand Lakes. Norway is known as the Land of the Midnight Sun.

52. Finesse : Cunning :: **Jealousy** : Resentment

The answer is **d.** Finesse is a synonym for cunning, and jealousy is a synonym for resentment.

53. Everest : Blanc :: Himalayas : **Alps**

The answer is **d.** Mount Everest is the highest peak in the Himalayas and Mount Blanc is the highest peak in the Alps.

54. Washington : Jefferson :: **Roosevelt** : Lincoln

The answer is **a.** Washington, Jefferson, Roosevelt, and Lincoln are the four U.S. presidents whose likenesses are carved into Mount Rushmore.

55. Atmosphere : **Pressure** :: Degree : Temperature

The answer is **a.** Pressure is measured in atmospheres; temperature is measured in degrees.

56. Citrus : Nuts :: C : **E**

The answer is **d.** Vitamin C is found in citrus; Vitamin E is found in nuts.

57. 125 : 25 :: 27 : **9**

The answer is **b.** 5^3 equals 125 and 5^2 equals 25. 3^3 equals 27 and 3^2 equals 9.

58. Brig : **Prison** :: Sham : Hoax

The answer is **c.** A brig is another word for a prison, and a sham is another word for a hoax.

59. Igneous : Sedimentary :: **Magma** : Sediment

The answer is **a.** Igneous rock is composed of magma; sedimentary rock is composed of sediment.

60. Barometer : Atmospheric Pressure :: **Rain Gauge** : Intensity of Rain

The answer is **c.** A barometer measures atmospheric pressure; a rain guage measures the intensity of rain.

61. Tokyo : Japan :: **San Jose** : Costa Rica

The answer is **a.** Tokyo is the capital of Japan; San Jose is the capital of Costa Rica.

62. Arctic : Borealis :: Antarctic : **Australis**

The answer is **b.** The northern lights—aurora borealis—are visible within the Arctic circle. The southern lights—aurora australis—are visible within the Antarctic circle.

63. Earthquakes : **Ring of Fire** :: Tornadoes : Southern United States

The answer is **b.** The Ring of Fire in the Pacific Ocean is home to much of the world's seismic activity.

64. Bold : Brass :: **Modest** : Maiden

The answer is **d.** The common similes "bold as brass" and "modest as a maid" can both be used to describe people.

65. Romulus : Cane :: Remus : **Abel**

The answer is **a.** In Roman mythology, Romulus and Remus are brothers. In the Bible, Cain and Abel are brothers.

66. Justice : **License** :: Nature : String

The answer is **a.** Justice and license are both words that complete common expressions beginning with the word "poetic": poetic justice is a rightful outcome and poetic license is harmless dishonesty. Nature and string are both words that complete common expressions beginning with the word "second": second nature refers to a habit so regular it seems natural, and second string is a backup resource.

67. Honda : Aston Martin :: Mitsubishi : **Vauxhall**

The answer is **a.** Honda and Mitsubishi are both Japanese car manufacturers. Aston Martin and Vauxhall are British car manufacturers.

68. Battalion : **Troop** :: Dollar : Cent

The answer is **b.** A troop is a unit of a battalion, and a cent is a unit of a dollar.

69. Cineast : Film :: Gastronome : **Food**

The answer is **c.** A cineast loves film, and a gastronome loves food.

70. **Monet** : van Gogh :: Water Lilies : Sunflowers

The answer is **b.** "Water Lilies" is a series of paintings by Claude Monet. "Sunflowers" is a series of paintings by Vincent van Gogh.

71. **Head I** : The Scream :: Bacon : Munch

The answer is **a.** Head I is a painting by Francis Bacon. The Scream is a painting by Edvard Munch.

72. Haute Couture : **Ready-to-Wear** :: Kids Wear : Knitwear

The answer is **c.** Haute couture and ready-to-wear are two markets of fashion. Kids wear and knitwear are two types of fashion design.

73. Librarian : Bookkeeper :: Organize : **Balance**

The answer is **b.** A librarian's job is to organize books; a bookkeeper's job is to balance them.

74. Log 10 : Log 100 :: 1 : 2

The answer is **a.** The log of 10 is 1 and the log of 100 is 2.

75. Bolt : Steel :: **Thread** : Fabric

The answer is **d.** Bolts are used to fasten steel together permanently. Thread is used to fasten fabric together permanently.

76. mm : **m** :: m : km

The answer is **c.** There are 1000 millimeters (mm) in one meter (m). There are 1000 meters (m) in one kilometer (km).

77. Dolly : **Camera** :: Ferry : Passenger

The answer is **c.** A dolly moves a television or motion picture camera, and a ferry moves passengers.

78. Efficient : Wasteful :: **Honest** : Deceptive

The answer is **c.** To be efficient is the opposite of to be wasteful, and to be honest is the opposite of to be deceptive.

79. Mold : Spoil :: Walk : Path

The answer is **c.** Mold is a synonym for spoil, and walk is a synonym for path.

80. M : Breathless :: German Expressionism : **French New Wave**

The answer is **a.** Fritz Lang's 1931 film M is an example of a cinematic movement called German Expressionism. Jean Luc Godard's 1960 film Breathless is an example of a cinematic movement called the French New Wave.

81. Shakespeare : **17** :: Shaw : 20

The answer is **c.** Playwright William Shakespeare died in the 17th century. Playwright George Bernard Shaw died in the 20th century.

82. Andretti : Car :: **Shoemaker** : Horse

The answer is **c.** Mario Andretti is famous for racing cars. Willie Shoemaker was a famous jockey who raced horses.

83. New York City : **Pizza** :: Philadelphia : Cheesesteak

The answer is **c.** New York City is renowned for its pizza, while Philadelphia is renowned for its cheesesteaks.

84. *Remembrance of Things Past* : *Up From Slavery* :: *A Farewell to Arms* : *Confessions*

The answer is **a.** Marcel Proust's *Remembrance of Things Past* and Ernest Hemingway's *A Farewell to Arms* are both semi-autobiographical

novels. Booker T. Washington's *Up from Slavery* and Jean-Jacques Rousseau's *Confessions* are autobiographies.

85. Sextant : Navigation :: Abacus : Calculation

The answer is **c.** A sextant is a tool used in navigation, and an abacus is a tool used in calculation.

86. Dither : Settle :: Display : **Hide**

The answer is **c.** Dither is an antonym for settle, and display is an antonym for hide.

87. *Rob Roy* : Scott :: *Eugénie Grandet* : **Balzac**

The answer is **c.** *Rob Roy* is an 1817 novel by Walter Scott. *Eugénie Grandet* is an 1833 novel by Honoré de Balzac.

88. Koffka : Kohler :: Perls : **Wertheimer**

The answer is **a.** Kurt Koffka, Wolfgang Kohler, Fritz Perls, and Max Wertheimer were all Gestalt psychologists.

89. Cleaver : Tenderizer :: Snake : **Auger**

The answer is **d.** A cleaver and a tenderizer are both tools used by a butcher. A snake and an auger are both tools used by a plumber.

90. Epigram : Elegy :: **Witty** : Mournful

The answer is **d.** An epigram is a witty poetic statement. An elegy is a mournful poetic statement made to remember the dead.

91. Art Deco : 20 :: **Impressionism** : 19

The answer is **d.** Art Deco was an art movement of the 20th Century. Impressionism was an art movement of the 19th Century.

92. Cambrian : Paleozoic :: Triassic : **Mesozoic**

The answer is **a.** The Cambrian period occurred during the Paleozoic era and the Triassic period occurred during the Mesozoic era.

93. 30 : 150 :: **70** : 110

The answer is **b.** Two supplementary angles equal 180 degrees. 30 plus 150 equals 180. 70 plus 110 equals 180.

94. **Chomsky** : Langacker :: Generative grammar : Cognitive linguistics

The answer is **d.** Linguist Noam Chomsky is known for his work in the area of generative grammar and Ronald Langacker is known for his work in cognitive linguistics.

95. Clumsy : Dexterity :: **Passive** : Will

The answer is **a.** Clumsy means lacking in dexterity, and passive means lacking in will.

96. Gavrilo Princip : John Wilkes Booth :: **Archduke Ferdinand** : President Lincoln

The answer is **c.** Princip assassinated Archduke Ferdinand and Booth assassinated President Lincoln.

97. Maasai : **Africa** :: Palawah : Australia

The answer is **c.** The Maasai are native to Africa. The Palawah are native to Australia.

98. Prokaryote : Eukaryote :: **Bacteria** : Skin Cell

The answer is **d.** Bacteria are prokaryotic cells; skin cells are eukaryotic cells.

99. Mnemonics : **Memory** :: Phonetics : Language

The answer is **a.** Mnemonics deals with memory, and phonetics deals with language.

100. ATP : Protein :: **Mitochondria** : Ribosomes

The answer is **a.** ATP is produced by mitochondria; protein is produced by ribosomes.

101. Lipase : **Amylase** :: Fats : Carbohydrates

The answer is **c.** Lipase digests fats; amylase digests carbohydrates.

102. Hamstring : **Cripple** :: Stake : Bet

The answer is **b.** To hamstring means to cripple, and to stake means to bet.

103. *Double Indemnity* : *Open City* :: *Film Noir* : *Italian Neorealism*

The answer is **c.** Billy Wilder's 1944 film *Double Indemnity* is an example of the cinematic style called film noir. Roberto Rossellini's 1945 film *Open City* is an example of the cinematic style called Italian neorealism.

104. Horseshoe crab : Scorpion :: **Chelicerate** : Arachnid

The answer is **c.** Scorpions are arachnids; horseshoe crabs are chelicerates.

105. Helium : Noble :: Flourine : **Halogen**

The answer is **c.** Helium is a noble gas; fluorine is a halogen.

106. Yard : Meter :: **Mile** : Kilometer

The answer is **d.** In the metric system, 1 yard equals .9144 meters. One mile equals 1.6093 kilometers.

107. Analogous : Wings :: **Homologous** : Tarsals

The answer is **b.** Wings from insects and birds are analogous—similar in purpose, but not adapted from the same ancestor. Tarsals in birds, humans, and whales are homologous structures, meaning that they were inherited from a common ancestor.

108. Alizarin : Crimson :: **Ao** : Capri

The answer is **b.** Alizarin and crimson are two shades of red. Ao and capri are two shades of blue.

109. **Dermatologist** : Patient :: Pedagogue : Pupil

The answer is **a.** A dermatologist, a skin doctor, helps a patient. A pedagogue, a teacher, helps a pupil learn.

110. Exasperate : Irk :: **Prevent** : Dissuade

The answer is **a.** To exasperate is to irk entirely, and to prevent is to dissuade entirely.

111. Cask : Sack :: Thin : **Hint**

The answer is **d.** Cask is an anagram for sack, and thin is an anagram for hint.

112. **Hume** : *A Treatise of Human Nature* :: Mill : *On Liberty*

The answer is **b.** Philosopher David Hume wrote *A Treatise of Human Nature.* Philosopher John Stuart Mill wrote *On Liberty.*

113. Jean-Paul Sartre : Literature :: Le Duc Tho : **Peace**

The answer is **b.** Sartre was awarded the Nobel Prize in literature but declined. Tho declined the Nobel Peace Prize.

114. Pogo : Doonesbury :: **Kelly** : Trudeau

The answer is **d.** Pogo is a comic strip created by Walt Kelly. Doonesbury is a comic strip created by Gary Trudeau.

115. Windmill : Rudder :: **Turbine** : Airfoil

The answer is **b.** A windmill is a machine classified as a turbine. A rudder is a device classified as an airfoil.

116. $18 : 81 :: 41 : (\frac{1}{4})^{-1}$

The answer is **c.** 1^8 equals 1 and 8^0 equals 1. 4^1 equals 4 and $(\frac{1}{4})^{-1}$ equals 4.

117. Real : Imaginary :: $\sqrt{5}$: $\sqrt{-1}$

The answer is **c.** The $\sqrt{5}$ is a real number. The $\sqrt{-1}$ is an imaginary number.

118. Jargon : Patois :: Plot : Design

The answer is **d.** Jargon is a synonym for patois, and plot is a synonym for design.

119. Raconteur : Entertain :: Bully : Browbeat

The answer is **b.** A raconteur is someone who entertains, and a bully is someone who browbeats.

120. Nonvascular : Vascular :: **Mosses** : Beans

The answer is **a.** Beans are vascular plants; mosses are nonvascular plants.

Scoring Your MAT Practice Test

As mentioned in Chapter 1, when you receive your personal score report for the official MAT, you'll be provided with a scaled score and two percentile ranks, all of which are derived from the number of items you answered correctly—known as your raw score.

Because there are different forms and formats of the official MAT, and typically 20 of the 120 questions on the official MAT are experimental and do not count toward your official scaled score and percentile ranks, it is impossible to create an accurate raw score to scaled score or raw score to percentile chart for this and the other practice tests found in this book. In the end, you are striving to correctly answer the highest number of questions as possible and familiarize yourself with the MAT format so you're fully prepared to do your best on test day. For now, what's much more important than your overall score is how you did on each of the content areas tested by the exam. You need to diagnose your strengths and weaknesses so that you can concentrate your efforts as you prepare. The question types are mixed in the practice exam, so in order to tell where your strengths and weaknesses lie, you'll need to compare your answer sheet with the following **MAT Practice Test 6 Review**, which shows which of the content areas each question falls into.

Use your performance here in conjunction with the LearningExpress Test Preparation System in Chapter 2 to help you devise a study plan. You should plan to spend more time studying areas that correspond to the questions you found hardest and less time on the content areas in which you did well. Once you have spent some time reviewing, take the next MAT Practice Test to see if you've improved.

CONTENT AREA	QUESTION NUMBERS
Language and Vocabulary	3, 4, 20, 21, 26, 27, 31, 32, 41, 42, 50, 51, 60, 61, 66, 67, 79, 86, 93, 99, 100, 106, 110, 111, 118
Humanities	1, 5, 8, 9, 11, 14, 39, 40, 43, 44, 46, 48, 49, 81, 83, 85, 87, 91, 108, 109, 120
Social Science	7, 13, 15, 16, 18, 19, 23, 47, 52, 54, 55, 57, 63, 75, 90, 92, 94, 98, 101, 102
Natural Science	10, 17, 22, 24, 25, 34, 37, 45, 53, 58, 65, 68, 71, 72, 76, 88, 89, 96, 97, 103, 104, 115
General	6, 12, 28, 29, 30, 33, 35, 56, 59, 62, 64, 73, 74, 77, 78, 82, 84, 105, 107, 112, 114, 116
Mathematics	2, 36, 38, 69, 70, 80, 95, 113, 117, 119

9 ▶ MAT Practice Test 7

CHAPTER SUMMARY

Here's another sample MAT test for you to practice with.

For this practice test, simulate the actual test-taking experience as closely as you can. Find a quiet place to work where you won't be disturbed. If you own this book, use the answer sheet on the following pages and find some #2 pencils to fill in the circles with. Use a timer or stopwatch to time yourself— you'll have 60 minutes to complete the official MAT. After you take the test, use the detailed answer explanations that follow to review any questions you missed.

MAT Practice Test 7

1.	ⓐ	ⓑ	ⓒ	ⓓ	46.	ⓐ	ⓑ	ⓒ	ⓓ	91.	ⓐ	ⓑ	ⓒ	ⓓ
2.	ⓐ	ⓑ	ⓒ	ⓓ	47.	ⓐ	ⓑ	ⓒ	ⓓ	92.	ⓐ	ⓑ	ⓒ	ⓓ
3.	ⓐ	ⓑ	ⓒ	ⓓ	48.	ⓐ	ⓑ	ⓒ	ⓓ	93.	ⓐ	ⓑ	ⓒ	ⓓ
4.	ⓐ	ⓑ	ⓒ	ⓓ	49.	ⓐ	ⓑ	ⓒ	ⓓ	94.	ⓐ	ⓑ	ⓒ	ⓓ
5.	ⓐ	ⓑ	ⓒ	ⓓ	50.	ⓐ	ⓑ	ⓒ	ⓓ	95.	ⓐ	ⓑ	ⓒ	ⓓ
6.	ⓐ	ⓑ	ⓒ	ⓓ	51.	ⓐ	ⓑ	ⓒ	ⓓ	96.	ⓐ	ⓑ	ⓒ	ⓓ
7.	ⓐ	ⓑ	ⓒ	ⓓ	52.	ⓐ	ⓑ	ⓒ	ⓓ	97.	ⓐ	ⓑ	ⓒ	ⓓ
8.	ⓐ	ⓑ	ⓒ	ⓓ	53.	ⓐ	ⓑ	ⓒ	ⓓ	98.	ⓐ	ⓑ	ⓒ	ⓓ
9.	ⓐ	ⓑ	ⓒ	ⓓ	54.	ⓐ	ⓑ	ⓒ	ⓓ	99.	ⓐ	ⓑ	ⓒ	ⓓ
10.	ⓐ	ⓑ	ⓒ	ⓓ	55.	ⓐ	ⓑ	ⓒ	ⓓ	100.	ⓐ	ⓑ	ⓒ	ⓓ
11.	ⓐ	ⓑ	ⓒ	ⓓ	56.	ⓐ	ⓑ	ⓒ	ⓓ	101.	ⓐ	ⓑ	ⓒ	ⓓ
12.	ⓐ	ⓑ	ⓒ	ⓓ	57.	ⓐ	ⓑ	ⓒ	ⓓ	102.	ⓐ	ⓑ	ⓒ	ⓓ
13.	ⓐ	ⓑ	ⓒ	ⓓ	58.	ⓐ	ⓑ	ⓒ	ⓓ	103.	ⓐ	ⓑ	ⓒ	ⓓ
14.	ⓐ	ⓑ	ⓒ	ⓓ	59.	ⓐ	ⓑ	ⓒ	ⓓ	104.	ⓐ	ⓑ	ⓒ	ⓓ
15.	ⓐ	ⓑ	ⓒ	ⓓ	60.	ⓐ	ⓑ	ⓒ	ⓓ	105.	ⓐ	ⓑ	ⓒ	ⓓ
16.	ⓐ	ⓑ	ⓒ	ⓓ	61.	ⓐ	ⓑ	ⓒ	ⓓ	106.	ⓐ	ⓑ	ⓒ	ⓓ
17.	ⓐ	ⓑ	ⓒ	ⓓ	62.	ⓐ	ⓑ	ⓒ	ⓓ	107.	ⓐ	ⓑ	ⓒ	ⓓ
18.	ⓐ	ⓑ	ⓒ	ⓓ	63.	ⓐ	ⓑ	ⓒ	ⓓ	108.	ⓐ	ⓑ	ⓒ	ⓓ
19.	ⓐ	ⓑ	ⓒ	ⓓ	64.	ⓐ	ⓑ	ⓒ	ⓓ	109.	ⓐ	ⓑ	ⓒ	ⓓ
20.	ⓐ	ⓑ	ⓒ	ⓓ	65.	ⓐ	ⓑ	ⓒ	ⓓ	110.	ⓐ	ⓑ	ⓒ	ⓓ
21.	ⓐ	ⓑ	ⓒ	ⓓ	66.	ⓐ	ⓑ	ⓒ	ⓓ	111.	ⓐ	ⓑ	ⓒ	ⓓ
22.	ⓐ	ⓑ	ⓒ	ⓓ	67.	ⓐ	ⓑ	ⓒ	ⓓ	112.	ⓐ	ⓑ	ⓒ	ⓓ
23.	ⓐ	ⓑ	ⓒ	ⓓ	68.	ⓐ	ⓑ	ⓒ	ⓓ	113.	ⓐ	ⓑ	ⓒ	ⓓ
24.	ⓐ	ⓑ	ⓒ	ⓓ	69.	ⓐ	ⓑ	ⓒ	ⓓ	114.	ⓐ	ⓑ	ⓒ	ⓓ
25.	ⓐ	ⓑ	ⓒ	ⓓ	70.	ⓐ	ⓑ	ⓒ	ⓓ	115.	ⓐ	ⓑ	ⓒ	ⓓ
26.	ⓐ	ⓑ	ⓒ	ⓓ	71.	ⓐ	ⓑ	ⓒ	ⓓ	116.	ⓐ	ⓑ	ⓒ	ⓓ
27.	ⓐ	ⓑ	ⓒ	ⓓ	72.	ⓐ	ⓑ	ⓒ	ⓓ	117.	ⓐ	ⓑ	ⓒ	ⓓ
28.	ⓐ	ⓑ	ⓒ	ⓓ	73.	ⓐ	ⓑ	ⓒ	ⓓ	118.	ⓐ	ⓑ	ⓒ	ⓓ
29.	ⓐ	ⓑ	ⓒ	ⓓ	74.	ⓐ	ⓑ	ⓒ	ⓓ	119.	ⓐ	ⓑ	ⓒ	ⓓ
30.	ⓐ	ⓑ	ⓒ	ⓓ	75.	ⓐ	ⓑ	ⓒ	ⓓ	120.	ⓐ	ⓑ	ⓒ	ⓓ
31.	ⓐ	ⓑ	ⓒ	ⓓ	76.	ⓐ	ⓑ	ⓒ	ⓓ					
32.	ⓐ	ⓑ	ⓒ	ⓓ	77.	ⓐ	ⓑ	ⓒ	ⓓ					
33.	ⓐ	ⓑ	ⓒ	ⓓ	78.	ⓐ	ⓑ	ⓒ	ⓓ					
34.	ⓐ	ⓑ	ⓒ	ⓓ	79.	ⓐ	ⓑ	ⓒ	ⓓ					
35.	ⓐ	ⓑ	ⓒ	ⓓ	80.	ⓐ	ⓑ	ⓒ	ⓓ					
36.	ⓐ	ⓑ	ⓒ	ⓓ	81.	ⓐ	ⓑ	ⓒ	ⓓ					
37.	ⓐ	ⓑ	ⓒ	ⓓ	82.	ⓐ	ⓑ	ⓒ	ⓓ					
38.	ⓐ	ⓑ	ⓒ	ⓓ	83.	ⓐ	ⓑ	ⓒ	ⓓ					
39.	ⓐ	ⓑ	ⓒ	ⓓ	84.	ⓐ	ⓑ	ⓒ	ⓓ					
40.	ⓐ	ⓑ	ⓒ	ⓓ	85.	ⓐ	ⓑ	ⓒ	ⓓ					
41.	ⓐ	ⓑ	ⓒ	ⓓ	86.	ⓐ	ⓑ	ⓒ	ⓓ					
42.	ⓐ	ⓑ	ⓒ	ⓓ	87.	ⓐ	ⓑ	ⓒ	ⓓ					
43.	ⓐ	ⓑ	ⓒ	ⓓ	88.	ⓐ	ⓑ	ⓒ	ⓓ					
44.	ⓐ	ⓑ	ⓒ	ⓓ	89.	ⓐ	ⓑ	ⓒ	ⓓ					
45.	ⓐ	ⓑ	ⓒ	ⓓ	90.	ⓐ	ⓑ	ⓒ	ⓓ					

Directions: For each question, select the answer choice in the parentheses that best completes the analogy.

1. Cello : String quartet :: (**a.** Tuba **b.** Violin **c.** Xylophone **d.** Woodwind) : Brass band

2. Rake : Leaves :: (**a.** Homeowner **b.** Profile **c.** Census **d.** Lawn) : Information

3. Crust : Core :: (**a.** Mitochondria **b.** Golgi Apparatus **c.** Membrane **d.** Ribosome) : Nucleus

4. Pinocchio : Fantasia :: (**a.** Julie Andrews **b.** The Wizard of Oz **c.** Disney **d.** Musical) : Mary Poppins

5. Drink : Food :: (**a.** Bite **b.** Grub **c.** Beverage **d.** Glass) : Fare

6. Hansel : (**a.** Apollo **b.** Cinderella **c.** Pluto **d.** Olympus) :: Gretel : Artemis

7. Postmortem : (**a.** Address **b.** Forecast **c.** Morning **d.** Death) :: Rainbow : Downpour

8. (**a.** Spain **b.** Berkeley **c.** Descartes **d.** Cartesian) : France :: Hobbes : England

9. Yale : Harvard :: New Haven : (**a.** Boston **b.** Massachusetts **c.** Cambridge **d.** New York)

10. (**a.** Nut **b.** Swan **c.** Wolf **d.** Beast) : Sleeping :: Lake : Beauty

11. Oral : (**a.** Dependent **b.** Lazy **c.** Verbose **d.** Wan) :: Anal : Stingy

12. Wings : Boat :: (**a.** Sail **b.** Wheel **c.** Tire **d.** Windshield) : Car

13. Knave : (**a.** Retreat **b.** Beauty **c.** Truth **d.** Stoicism) :: Coward : Bravery

14. (**a.** Deck **b.** Water **c.** Periscope **d.** Astronomy) : Ship :: Telescope : Star

15. Rasp : Straw :: Elder : (**a.** Yellow **b.** Cohosh **c.** Glass **d.** Boysen)

16. Venus : (**a.** Neptune **b.** Pluto **c.** Earth **d.** Mars) :: Inner : Outer

17. Vitamin A : Vision :: (**a.** Vitamin D **b.** Vitamin C **c.** Vitamin E **d.** Vitamin G) : Bones

18. U.S. Senate : (**a.** 50 **b.** 100 **c.** 200 **d.** 122) :: House of Representatives : 435

19. Elizabeth Cady Stanton : Susan B. Anthony :: Lucy Stone : (**a.** Julia Ward Howe **b.** Martha Washington **c.** Harriet Tubman **c.** Lydia Becker **d.** Betsy Ross)

20. Quart : Quarter :: (**a.** Cup **b.** Pint **c.** Quart **d.** Gallon) : Dollar

21. Austria : (**a.** Austrian **b.** French **c.** German **d.** Swedish) :: Cambodia : Khmer

22. Weather : Short-Term :: Climate : (**a.** Daily **b.** Brief **c.** Trends **d.** Cold)

23. High Pressure : Calm :: Low Pressure : (**a.** Sunny **b.** Pleasant **c.** Stormy **d.** Weather)

24. Strong : Stubborn :: Ox : (**a.** Horse **b.** Cow **c.** Zebra **d.** Mule)

25. Penguin : Book Publisher :: (**a.** Editorial **b.** Universal **c.** Printer **d.** McGraw-Hill) : Film Production Company

26. Zinc : (**a.** Bones **b.** Immunity **c.** DNA **d.** Skin) :: Iron : Oxygen

27. Privy : Secret :: Sympathetic : (**a.** Spy **b.** Grief **c.** Clandestine **d.** Joy)

28. Minotaur : Perseus :: (**a.** Monstrous **b.** Ethereal **c.** Dainty **d.** Bull) : Heroic

29. 3 : (**a.** 2 **b.** 4 **c.** 5 **d.** 6) :: Earth : Mars

30. Neck : (**a.** Torso **b.** Foot **c.** Waist **d.** Head) :: Shirt : Pants

31. Light : Windy :: (**a.** Paris **b.** London **c.** Rome **d.** San Francisco) : Chicago

32. Mulholland : (**a.** Michigan **b.** Rodeo **c.** Bourbon **d.** Houston) :: California : Louisiana

33. Holster : Pistol :: (**a.** Weapon **b.** Rifle **c.** Sheath **d.** Club) : Knife

34. Red : Black :: Herring : (**a.** Green **b.** Dog **c.** Fish **d.** Sheep)

35. Quart : Gallon :: 1 : (**a.** 4 **b.** 8 **c.** 12 **d.** 16)

36. Diagonal : Rectangle :: (**a.** Radius **b.** Diameter **c.** Chord **d.** Circumference) : Circle

37. Cellar : House :: (**a.** Land **b.** Hold **c.** Ocean **d.** Wave) : Ship

38. Annex : (**a.** Shelf **b.** Building **c.** Page **d.** Wing) :: Insert : Book

39. Charlotte : Emily :: (**a.** Anne **b.** Branwell **c.** Jane **d.** George) : Ira

40. Night and Day : (**a.** Stardust **b.** Too Darn Hot **c.** Silk Stockings **d.** Ella Fitzgerald) :: I Got You Under My Skin : Heart and Soul

41. Haste : Waste :: (**a.** Fast **b.** Three **c.** Group **d.** Makes) : Crowd

42. Purse : Super :: Plea : (**a.** Avoid **b.** Charity **c.** Help **d.** Leap)

43. The Call of the Wild : Yukon :: The Long Winter : (**a.** Midwest **b.** East Coast **c.** America **d.** Prairie)

44. In limbo : Forgotten :: In the doghouse : (**a.** Lost **b.** Isolated **c.** Favor **d.** Trouble)

45. Lesotho : (**a.** South Africa **b.** Kenya **c.** Chad **d.** Uganda) :: San Marino : Italy

46. Nietzsche : (**a.** Absurdism **b.** Nihilism **c.** Empiricism **d.** Absolutism) :: Petrarch : Humanism

47. To : Too :: Loot : (**a.** Two **b.** Steal **c.** Toot **d.** Lute)

48. G : Treble :: (**a.** B **b.** D **c.** E **d.** F) : Bass

49. Stem : Heartbeat :: Cerebrum : (**a.** Breathing **b.** Swimming **c.** Swallowing **d.** Memory)

50. A Raisin in the Sun : (**a.** Chicago **b.** Illinois **c.** Hansberry **d.** Kansas City) :: Bus Stop : Kansas

51. Saudi Arabia : (**a.** Medina **b.** Mecca **c.** Riyadh **d.** Tabuk) :: Egypt : Cairo

52. Sheep : Ruminant :: Pluto : (**a.** Planet **b.** Neptune **c.** Dwarf Planet **d.** Sun)

53. Cerebrum : Cerebellum :: Learning : (**a.** Balance **b.** Respiration **c.** Language **d.** Stem)

54. Congress : Parliament :: Senate : (**a.** Judiciary **b.** Lords **c.** Representatives **d.** Court)

55. (**a.** Erosion **b.** Cloud **c.** Ground **d.** Forecast) : Rainfall :: Condensation : Humidity

56. Democracy : Ochlocracy :: People : (**a.** Elite **b.** Eight **c.** Mob **d.** Dictator)

57. Moot : Kangaroo :: Hypothetical : (**a.** Irregular Procedures **b.** Animation **c.** Australian **d.** Cases of damage)

58. Data Entry : Excavation :: (**a.** Technician **b.** Computer **c.** Program **d.** Spreadsheet) : Backhoe

59. Christianity : (**a.** Islam **b.** Judaism **c.** Paganism **d.** Hinduism) :: Crucifix : Pentacle

60. Rodents : Mammals :: Red Giants : (**a.** Supernovas **b.** Yellow Giants **c.** Stars **d.** Black Holes)

61. Durkheim : *Suicide* :: McLuhan : (**a.** *Understanding Media* **b.** *Homicide* **c.** *A Study of History* **d.** *Outsiders*)

62. Talons : (**a.** Osprey **b.** Sparrow **c.** Hummingbird **d.** Woodpecker) :: Pouch : Pelican

63. Ginsburg : (**a.** Souter **b.** Rehnquist **c.** Breyer **d.** O'Connor) :: Sotomayor : Kagan

64. Echidna : Monotreme :: Koala : (**a.** Rodent **b.** Marsupial **c.** Pouch **d.** Mammal)

65. Hood Ornament : Car :: (**a.** Bow **b.** Stem **c.** Foremast **d.** Figurehead) : Ship

66. Seamstress : Stylist :: Sew : (**a.** Sell **b.** Design **c.** Coordinate **d.** Illustrate)

67. Binge : Begin :: Tea : (**a.** Supper **b.** Coffee **c.** Eat **d.** Water)

68. Scent : Echolocation :: Dog : (**a.** Cat **b.** Hearing **c.** Bat **d.** Hunting)

69. Kidneys : Regulating Water Balance :: (**a.** Pancreas **b.** Duodenum **c.** Liver **d.** Brain) : Secreting Hormones

70. No : Know :: Steal : (**a.** Rob **b.** Negative **c.** Steel **d.** Don't)

71. Napa : (**a.** Milwaukee **b.** Oakland **c.** Austin **d.** Madison) :: Wine : Beer

72. Urologist : Bladder :: Oncologist : (**a.** Cancer **b.** Heart **c.** Diabetes **d.** Liver)

73. Cruiseliner : Passengers :: (**a.** Agent **b.** Author **c.** Volume **d.** Library) : Books

74. (**a.** Sun Tzu **b.** Ryōkan **c.** Napoleon **d.** Shanghai) : Niccolò Machiavelli :: China : Italy

75. x-axis : y-axis :: $(x, 0)$: (**a.** $(0, x)$ **b.** $(y, 0)$ **c.** $(0, y)$ **d.** $(0, 0)$)

76. Compass : Circle :: (**a.** Ruler **b.** Calculator **c.** Protractor **d.** Abacus) : Angle

77. Schopenhauer : Bizet :: (**a.** Wagner **b.** Godard **c.** Nietzsche **d.** Brahms) : Debussy

78. $\frac{3}{4}$: .75 :: $\frac{1}{8}$: (**a.** .125 **b.** 1.25 **c.** 2.15 **d.** 2.25)

79. Son : Sun :: (**a.** So **b.** Sob **c.** Needle **d.** Daughter) : Sew

80. (**a.** Godunov **b.** Bolshoi **c.** Burlaka **d.** Mussorsky) : Moscow :: Joffrey : Chicago

81. *The Divine Comedy* : (**a.** *Pilgrim's Progress* **b.** *Ulysses* **c.** *Their Eyes Were Watching God* **d.** *This Side of Paradise*) :: *An American Tragedy* : *Thérèse*

82. January 3 : (**a.** February 2 **b.** June 3 **c.** July 4 **d.** October 5) :: Perihelion : Aphelion

83. Plato : Nomanalism :: (**a.** Socrates **b.** Bodin **c.** Locke **d.** Hobbes) : Empiricism

84. (**a.** Jack Cole **b.** Jerome Robbins **c.** Loie Fuller **d.** Gwen Verdon) : Katherine Dunham :: Isadora Duncan : Gus Giordano

85. Odin : Frigga :: Zeus : (**a.** Hera **b.** Freyja **c.** Jupiter **d.** Venus)

86. Butterfly : Utility :: (**a.** Gavel **b.** Machete **c.** Hatchet **d.** Bayonet) : Splitting maul

87. (**a.** Tull **b.** Edison **c.** Carver **d.** Eastman) : Seed drill :: Dewar : Thermos

88. Clastres : Paraguay :: (**a.** Levi-Strauss **b.** Goodall **c.** Mead **d.** Durkheim) : Brazil

89. (**a.** Metaphysics **b.** Epistemology **c.** Aesthetics **d.** Ontology) : Nature of Knowledge :: Logic : Arguments

90. Mollusk : Arthropod :: (**a.** Clam **b.** Lobster **c.** Cray Fish **d.** Annelid): House Fly

91. 78 : 21 :: Nitrogen : (**a.** Oxygen **b.** Argon **c.** Carbon Dioxide **d.** Helium)

92. Degas : (**a.** Zerbe **b.** Cassatt **c.** Bloom **d.** Embry) :: de Kooning : Beauchamp

93. Maodun : China :: Bagutta : (**a.** Italy **b.** Germany **c.** France **d.** Spain)

94. (**a.** Nimbostratus **b.** Stratocumulus **c.** Altostratus **d.** Cirrus) : 20,000 Feet :: Stratus : 6,000 Feet

95. Nictitate : (**a.** Wink **b.** Stomp **c.** Quit **d.** Smoke) :: Expectorate : Spit

96. Paramecium : Moss :: (**a.** Monera **b.** Protista **c.** Fungi **d.** Animalia) : Plantae

97. 21 : Down Syndrome :: 15 : (**a.** Sickle Cell Anemia **b.** Braxton Hicks **c.** Tay-Sachs **d.** Hereditary)

98. 30 : 150 :: (**a.** 100 **b.** 70 **c.** 140 **d.** 150) : 110

99. Fecund : Infertile :: (**a.** Rapid **b.** Slow **c.** Fertilizer **d.** Damp) : Fleet

100. First : Third :: Autotrophs : (**a.** Plants **b.** Herbivores **c.** Bacteria **d.** Carnivores)

101. (**a.** Buba **b.** Yoruba **c.** Batik **d.** Dashiki) : Men :: Kaftan : Women

102. Egregious : Bad :: (**a.** Minuscule **b.** Tall **c.** Wicked **d.** Cheap) : Small

103. Crosshatching : Repoussé :: (**a.** Sculpting **b.** Whittling **c.** Illustration **d.** Collage) : Metalworking

104. Twilight Zone : (**a.** I Love Lucy **b.** Alfred Hitchcock Presents **c.** The Outer Limits **d.** Night Gallery) :: Eye of the Beholder : Lamb to the Slaughter

105. Ouzo : Mediterranean :: (**a.** Schnapps **b.** Jenever **c.** Aquavit **d.** Rakia) : Scandinavia

106. Screw : Lever :: Spring : (**a.** Incline plane **b.** Clock **c.** Axle **d.** Wedge)

107. Trot : (**a.** Drive **b.** Canter **c.** Horse **d.** Speed) :: Jog : Sprint

108. Caliper : (**a.** Odometer **b.** Planimeter **c.** Millimeter **d.** Centimeter) :: Length : Area

109. 18 : 80 :: 41 : (**a.** 40 **b.** 4-1 **c.** $(\frac{1}{4})$-1 **d.** $(\frac{1}{4})$1)

110. Gambol : (**a.** Skip **b.** Win **c.** Bat **d.** Worship) :: Gamble : Bet

111. Yard : Meter :: (**a.** Inch **b.** Foot **c.** Centimeter **d.** Mile) : Kilometer

112. Dolorous : (**a.** Woozy **b.** Weepy **c.** Dull **d.** Sleepy) :: Sonorous : Loud

113. Penurious : (**a.** Generous **b.** Stingy **c.** Decrepit **d.** Cavernous) :: Deep : Significant

114. Kohler : Chimps :: Thorndike : (**a.** Dogs **b.** Mice **c.** Cats **d.** Gorillas)

115. Friedman : Keynes :: Keynes : (**a.** Krugman **b.** Vickery **c.** Marx **d.** Smith)

116. Somnolent : Nap :: Truculent : (**a.** Sleepwalker **b.** Journey **c.** War **d.** Mood)

117. (**a.** Pungent **b.** Quiet **c.** Noisy **d.** Combustible) : Plangent :: Contemptible : Estimable

118. (**a.** Smooth Strokes **b.** Backlighting **c.** Filbert **d.** Round) : Scumbling :: Chiaroscuro : Glazing

119. Real : Imaginary :: $\sqrt{5}$: (**a.** $\sqrt{0}$ **b.** $\sqrt{1}$ **c.** $\sqrt{-1}$ **d.** $\sqrt{4}$)

120. Amiens : (**a.** World War II **b.** War of 1812 **c.** Spanish American War **d.** French Revolution) :: Versailles : World War I

Answers

1. Cello : String quartet :: **Tuba** : Brass band

   The answer is **a.** The cello is a common instrument in a string quartet. A tuba is a common instrument in a brass band.

2. Rake : Leaves :: **Census** : Information

   The answer is **c.** A rake is used to gather grass, and a census is used to gather information.

3. Crust : Core :: **Membrane** : Nucleus

   The answer is **c.** The crust is the earth's outermost layer, and the core is at its center; a cell's membrane is its outermost layer, and its nucleus is at its center.

4. Pinocchio : Fantasia :: **The Wizard of Oz** : Mary Poppins

   The answer is **b.** Pinocchio and Fantasia are both animated films. The Wizard of Oz and Mary Poppins are live-action films.

5. Drink : Food :: **Beverage** : Fare

   The answer is **c.** Drink is another word for beverage. Food is another word for fare.

6. Hansel : **Apollo** :: Gretel : Artemis

   The answer is **a.** According to the fairy tale, Hansel and Gretel were brother and sister. According to Greek mythology, Apollo and Artemis were brother and sister.

7. Postmortem : **Death** :: Rainbow : Downpour

   The answer is **d.** A postmortem follows a death, and a rainbow occurs after a downpour.

8. **Descartes** : France :: Hobbes : England

   The answer is **c.** René Descartes was a philosopher from France. Thomas Hobbes was a philosopher from England.

9. Yale : Harvard :: New Haven : **Cambridge**

   The answer is **c.** Yale University is located in New Haven, CT and Harvard University is located in Cambridge, MA.

10. **Swan** : Sleeping :: Lake : Beauty

    The answer is **b.** Swan Lake and Sleeping Beauty are both ballets by Pyotr Tchaikovsky.

11. Oral : **Dependent** :: Anal : Stingy

    The answer is **a.** In psychodynamic theory a dependent person displays an oral trait and a stingy person displays an anal trait.

12. Wings : Boat :: **Sail** : Car

    The answer is **a.** A boat lacks wings and a car lacks a sail.

13. Knave : **Truth** :: Coward : Bravery

    The answer is **c.** A knave is one who does not exhibit the truth, and a coward does not exhibit bravery.

14. Periscope : Ship :: Telescope : Star

The answer is **c.** A periscope is used to look for ships, and a telescope is used to look for stars.

15. Rasp : Straw :: Elder : **Boysen**

The answer is **d.** Raspberry, strawberry, elderberry and boysenberry are all types of berries.

16. Venus : **Neptune** :: Inner : Outer

The answer is **a.** Venus is considered an inner planet; Neptune is considered an outer planet. Pluto is no longer classified as a planet.

17. Vitamin A : Vision :: **Vitamin D** : Bones

The answer is **a.** Vitamin A strengthens vision; Vitamin D strengthens bones.

18. U.S. Senate : **100** :: House of Representatives : 435

The answer is **b.** The United States Senate has 100 voting members and the House of Representatives has 435 voting members.

19. Elizabeth Cady Stanton : Susan B. Anthony :: Lucy Stone : **Julia Ward Howe**

The answer is **a.** Elizabeth Cady Stanton, Susan B. Anthony, Lucy Stone, and Julia Ward Howe were all leaders in the women's suffrage movement in the United States.

20. Quart : Quarter :: **Gallon** : Dollar

The answer is **d.** There are four quarters in one dollar. There are four quarts in one gallon.

21. Austria : **German** :: Cambodia : Khmer

The answer is **c.** The official language of Austria is German. The official language of Cambodia is Khmer.

22. Weather : Short-Term :: Climate : **Trends**

The answer is **c.** Climate is defined as trends in weather (which is short-term).

23. High Pressure : Calm :: Low Pressure : **Stormy**

The answer is **c.** A high pressure system brings calm weather; a low pressure system brings stormy weather.

24. Strong : Stubborn :: Ox : **Mule**

The answer is **d.** The common similes "strong as an ox" and "stubborn as a mule" can both be used to describe people.

25. Penguin : Book Publisher :: **Universal** : Film Production Company

The answer is **b.** Penguin is the name of a book publisher. Universal is the name of a film production company.

26. Zinc : **Immunity** :: Iron : Oxygen

The answer is **b.** Zinc is a mineral that promotes immunity; iron is a mineral that promotes oxygen transmission.

27. Privy : Secret :: Sympathetic : **Grief**

The answer is **b.** Privy is sharing in a secret, and sympathetic is sharing in grief.

28. Minotaur : Perseus :: **Monstrous** : Heroic

The answer is **a.** In Greek mythology, the Minotaur was a monstrous beast and Perseus was a heroic mortal.

29. 3 : 4 :: Earth : Mars

The answer is **b.** Earth is the third planet from the sun in our solar system; Mars is the fourth planet from the sun.

30. Neck : **Waist** :: Shirt : Pants

The answer is **c.** The neck is part of a shirt. The waist is part of a pair of pants.

31. Light : Windy :: **Paris** : Chicago

The answer is **a.** Paris is known as the City of Light just as Chicago is known as the Windy City.

32. Mulholland : **Bourbon** :: California : Louisiana

The answer is **c.** Mulholland Drive is a famous street in Los Angeles, California; Bourbon Street is a famous street in New Orleans, Louisiana.

33. Holster : Pistol :: **Sheath** : Knife

The answer is **c.** A holster holds a pistol, and a sheath holds a knife.

34. Red : Black :: Herring : **Sheep**

The answer is **d.** "Red herring" is a common expression meaning "a misleading or irrelevant matter." "Black sheep" is a common expression meaning "an outsider or misfit."

35. Quart : Gallon :: 1 : **4**

The answer is **b.** There are four quarts in one gallon—the ratio is 1 to 4.

36. Diagonal : Rectangle :: **Diameter** : Circle

The answer is **b.** The diagonal of a rectangle is the distance from one corner to the opposite corner. The diameter of a circle is the distance across a circle through its center.

37. Cellar : House :: **Hold** : Ship

The answer is **b.** A cellar is a lower storage area in a house, and a hold is a lower storage area on a ship.

38. Annex : **Building** :: Insert : Book

The answer is **b.** An annex is a structure added to a building, and an insert is something added to a book.

39. Charlotte : Emily :: **George** : Ira

The answer is **d.** Writers Charlotte and Emily Brontë were sisters. Composer George and lyricist Ira Gershwin were brothers.

40. Night and Day : **Stardust** :: I Got You Under My Skin : Heart and Soul

The answer is **a.** "Night and Day " and "I Got You Under My Skin" are songs by composer Cole Porter. "Stardust" and "Heart and Soul" are songs by composer Hoagy Carmichael.

41. Haste : Waste :: **Three** : Crowd

The answer is **b.** According to well-known proverbs, haste makes waste, and three is a crowd.

42. Purse : Super :: Plea : **Leap**

The answer is **d.** Purse is an anagram for super, and plea is an anagram for leap.

43. The Call of the Wild : Yukon :: The Long Winter : **Midwest**

The answer is **a.** Jack London's novel *The Call of the Wild* is set in the Yukon territory of Canada. Laura Ingalls Wilder's novel *The Long Winter* is set in the Midwest region of the United States.

44. In limbo : Forgotten :: In the doghouse : **Trouble**

The answer is **d.** "In limbo" is a common expression referring to a state of being forgotten. "In the doghouse" is a common expression referring to a state of being in trouble.

45. Lesotho : **South Africa** :: San Marino : Italy

The answer is **a.** Lesotho is an independent country that is entirely surrounded by South Africa. San Marino is an independent country entirely surrounded by Italy.

46. Nietzsche : **Nihilism** :: Petrarch : Humanism

The answer is **b.** German philosopher Friedrich Nietzsche is associated with the philosophical doctrine of nihilism. Francesco Petrarch was associated with the philosophical doctrine of humanism.

47. To : Too :: Loot : **Lute**

The answer is **d.** Too is a homophone for to, and loot is a homophone for lute.

48. G : Treble :: **F** : Bass

The answer is **d.** In music, G clef is another name for the treble clef and F clef is another name for the bass clef.

49. Stem : Heartbeat :: Cerebrum : **Memory**

The answer is **d.** The brain's stem controls heartbeat; the cerebrum facilitates memory.

50. A Raisin in the Sun : **Illinois** :: Bus Stop : Kansas

The answer is **b.** Lorraine Hansberry's play A Raisin in the Sun is set in the state of Illinois. William Inge's play Bus Stop is set in the state of Kansas.

51. Saudi Arabia : **Riyadh** :: Egypt : Cairo

The answer is **c.** Riyadh is the capital of Saudi Arabia. Cairo is the capital of Egypt.

52. Sheep : Ruminant :: Pluto : **Dwarf Planet**

The answer is **c.** A sheep is an example of a ruminant; Pluto is an example of a dwarf planet.

53. Cerebrum : Cerebellum :: Learning : **Balance**

The answer is **a.** In the human brain, the cerebrum is responsible for learning, and the cerebellum is responsible for coordinating movement and balance.

54. Congress : Parliament :: Senate : **Lords**

The answer is **b.** The House of Lords is the upper chamber of Parliament; the Senate is the upper chamber of Congress.

55. **Erosion** : Rainfall :: Condensation : Humidity

The answer is **a.** Erosion is a result of rainfall, and condensation is a result of humidity.

56. Democracy : Ochlocracy :: People : **Mob**

The answer is **c.** Democracy is rule by the people; ocholocracy is rule by a mob.

57. Moot : Kangaroo :: Hypothetical : **Irregular Procedures**

The answer is **a.** A kangaroo court uses irregular procedures. A moot court tries hypothetical cases.

58. Data Entry : Excavation :: **Computer** : Backhoe

The answer is **b.** A computer is a machine used for data entry. A backhoe is a machine used for excavation.

59. Christianity : **Paganism** :: Crucifix : Pentacle

The answer is **c.** The crucifix is a symbol of Christianity. The pentacle, a five pointed star, is a symbol of Paganism.

60. Rodents : Mammals :: Red Giants : **Stars**

The answer is **c.** Rodents are a kind of mammal; red giants are a kind of star.

61. Durkheim : *Suicide* :: McLuhan : *Understanding Media*

The answer is **a.** Sociologist Durkheim is the author of *Suicide*. McLuhan is the author of *Understanding Media*.

62. Talons : **Osprey** :: Pouch : Pelican

The answer is **a.** The talons of an osprey allow it to catch food; the pouch of a pelican allows it to catch food.

63. Ginsburg : **Breyer** :: Sotomayor : Kagan

The answer is **c.** Justices Ginsburg and Breyer were appointed to the US Supreme Court by President Clinton. Justices Sotomayor and Kagan were appointed by President Obama.

64. Echidna : Monotreme :: Koala : **Marsupial**

The answer is **b.** Echidnas and koalas are both examples of mammals; an echidna is a monotreme, while a koala is a marsupial.

65. Hood Ornament : Car :: **Figurehead** : Ship

The answer is **d.** A hood ornament is a decorative model that sits on the front of a car; a figurehead is a decorative sculpture that sits at the head of a sea ship.

66. Seamstress : Stylist :: Sew : **Coordinate**

The answer is **c.** In fashion, a seamstress sews clothing and a stylist coordinates clothing.

67. Binge : Begin :: Tea : **Eat**

The answer is **c.** Binge is an anagram for begin, and tea is an anagram for eat.

68. Scent : Echolocation :: Dog : **Bat**

The answer is **c.** Dogs have a keen sense of scent that they use to sense their location; bats use echolocation to locate objects.

69. Kidneys : Regulating water balance :: **Pancreas** : Secreting hormones

The answer is **a.** The kidneys' function is regulation of water balance; the pancreas' function is the secretion of hormones.

70. No : Know :: Steal : **Steel**

The answer is **c.** No is a homophone for know, and steal is a homophone for steel.

71. Napa : **Milwaukee** :: Wine : Beer

The answer is **a.** Napa is an area of California known for wine production. Milwaukee is a city in Wisconsin known for beer production.

72. Urologist : Bladder :: Oncologist : **Cancer**

The answer is **a.** A urologist is a doctor who treats the bladder. An oncologist is a doctor who treats cancer.

73. Cruiseliner : Passengers :: **Library** : Books

The answer is **d.** A cruiseliner houses passengers, and a library houses books.

74. **Sun Tzu** : Niccolò Machiavelli :: China : Italy

The answer is **a.** Chinese military strategist Sun Tzu wrote a book about military strategy called *The Art of War*, as did Niccolò Machiavelli of Italy.

75. x-axis : y-axis :: $(x, 0)$: **$(0, y)$**

The answer is **c.** $(x, 0)$ is a point on the x-axis $(0, y)$ is a point on the y-axis.

76. Compass : Circle :: **Protractor** : Angle

The answer is **c.** A compass is a device used for constructing circles. A protractor is a device used for constructing or measuring angles.

77. Schopenhauer : Bizet :: **Nietzsche** : Debussy

The answer is **c.** Arthur Schopenhauer and Friedrich Nietzsche were both German philosophers. Georges Bizet and Claude Debussy were French composers.

78. $\frac{3}{4}$: .75 :: $\frac{1}{8}$: **.125**

The answer is **a.** .75 is the decimal equivalent of $\frac{3}{4}$, and .125 is the decimal equivalent of $\frac{1}{8}$.

79. Son : Sun :: **So** : Sew

The answer is **a.** Son is a homophone for sun, and so is a homophone for sew.

80. Bolshoi : Moscow :: Joffrey : Chicago

The answer is **b.** Bolshoi ballet is a dance company from Moscow. Joffrey Ballet is a dance company from Chicago.

81. *The Divine Comedy* : **Pilgrim's Progress** :: *An American Tragedy* : *Thérèse*

The answer is **a.** Dante's *The Divine Comedy* and John Bunyan's *Pilgrim's Progress* can both be classified as allegorical literature. Theodore Dreiser's *An American Tragedy* and Émile Zola's *Thérèse* can both be classified as naturalistic literature.

82. January 3 : **July 4** :: Perihelion : Aphelion

The answer is **c.** On approximately January 3, our planet is closer to the Sun than during any other time; this position is called perihelion. On approximately July 4, Earth is farther from the Sun than during any other time; this position is called aphelion.

83. Plato : Nomanalism :: **Locke** : Empiricism

The answer is **c.** The philosopher Plato founded the theory of nomanalism, which emphasizes a belief in abstract terms rather than abstract objects. John Locke founded empiricism, which theorizes that the human mind is shaped by experiences.

84. Loie Fuller : Katherine Dunham :: Isadora Duncan : Gus Giordano

The answer is **c.** Loie Fuller and Isadora Duncan are modern dancers. Katherine Dunham and Gus Giordano are jazz dancers.

85. Odin : Frigga :: Zeus : **Hera**

The answer is **a.** In mythology, Odin is the Norse king of the gods and Frigga is his wife. Zeus is the Greek counterpart of Odin and Hera is his wife.

86. Butterfly : Utility :: **Gavel** : Splitting maul

The answer is **a.** Butterfly and utility are two types of knives. A gavel and a splitting maul are two types of hammers.

87. Tull : Seed drill :: Dewar : Thermos

The answer is **a.** Jethro Tull is the inventor of the seed drill. James Dewar is the inventor of the thermos.

88. Clastres : Paraguay :: **Levi-Strauss** : Brazil

The answer is **a.** The anthropologist Pierre Clastres studied the Guayaki tribe in Paraguay. Claude Levi-Strauss performed his fieldwork in Brazil.

89. Epistemology : Nature of Knowledge :: Logic : Arguments

The answer is **b.** Epistemology is a branch of philosophy that deals with the nature of knowledge. Logic is a branch that deals with the study of arguments.

90. Mollusk : Arthropod :: **Clam** : House Fly

The answer is **a.** A clam is a mollusk; a lobster is an arthropod.

91. 78 : 21 :: Nitrogen : **Oxygen**

The answer is **a.** Clean, dry air is 78 percent nitrogen and 21 percent oxygen.

92. Degas : **Cassatt** :: de Kooning : Beauchamp

The answer is **b.** Edgar Degas and Mary Cassatt were both painters of the impressionist movement. Elaine de Kooning and Robert Beauchamp were both expressionist painters.

93. Maodun : China :: Bagutta : **Italy**

The answer is **a.** The Maodun is a prestigious literary prize in China, while the Bagutta Prize is an Italian literary award.

94. **Cirrus** : 20,000 Feet :: Stratus : 6,000 Feet

The answer is **d.** Cirrus clouds are the high clouds, found at above 20,000 feet; Stratus clouds are low clouds, found beneath 6,500 feet.

95. Nictitate : **Wink** :: Expectorate : Spit

The answer is **a.** To nictitate means to wink, and to expectorate means to spit.

96. Paramecium : Moss :: **Protista** : Plantae

The answer is **b.** Mosses belong to the kingdom Plantae; Paramecium belongs to the kingdom Protista.

97. 21 : Down Syndrome :: 15 : **Tay-Sachs**

The answer is **c.** Down Syndrome is caused by an abnormality involving the 21st chromosome; Tay Sachs disease is caused by an abnormality involving the 15th chromosome.

98. 30 : 150 :: **110** : 70

The answer is **b.** Two supplementary angles equal 180 degrees. 30 plus 150 equals 180. 70 plus 110 equals 180.

99. Fecund : Infertile :: **Slow** : Fleet

The answer is **b.** Fecund is an antonym for infertile, and slow is an antonym for fleet.

100. First : Third :: Autotrophs : **Carnivores**

The answer is **d.** Autotrophs are at the first trophic level; carnivores are at the third (and fourth) trophic levels.

101. **Dashiki** : Men :: Kaftan : Women

The answer is **d.** A dashiki is a colorful West African garment worn by men traditionally. A kaftan is a colorful West African garment worn by women traditionally.

102. Egregious : Bad :: **Minuscule** : Small

The answer is **a.** Egregious means very bad, and minuscule means very small.

103. Crosshatching : Repoussé :: **Illustration** : Metalworking

The answer is **c.** Crosshatching is an illustration technique. Repoussé is a metalworking technique.

104. "Twilight Zone" : **"Alfred Hitchcock Presents"** :: "Eye of the Beholder" : "Lamb to the Slaughter"

The answer is **b.** "Eye of the Beholder" is a famous episode of the classic television program "The Twilight Zone." "Lamb to the Slaughter" is a classic episode of the television program "Alfred Hitchcock Presents."

105. Ouzo : Mediterranean :: **Aquavit** : Scandinavia

The answer is **c.** Ouzo is a liquor from the Mediterranean. Aquavit is a liquor from Scandinavia.

106. Screw : Lever :: Spring : **Axle**

The answer is **c.** A screw and a lever are two types of simple machines. A spring and an axle are two kinds of mechanical components.

107. Trot : **Canter** :: Jog : Sprint

The answer is **b.** A trot is slower than a canter, and a jog is slower than a sprint.

108. Caliper : **Planimeter** :: Length : Area

The answer is **b.** A caliper is an instrument used to measure length. A planimeter is an instrument used to measure area.

109. 18 : 80 :: 41 : $(\frac{1}{4})$-1

The answer is **c.** 1^8 equals 1 and 8^0 equals 1. 4^1 equals 4 and $(\frac{1}{4})^{-1}$ equals 4.

110. Gambol : **Skip** :: Gamble : Bet

The answer is **a.** To gambol means to skip, and to gamble means to bet.

111. Yard : Meter :: **Mile** : Kilometer

The answer is **d.** In the metric system, 1 yard equals .9144 meters. One mile equals 1.6093 kilometers.

112. Dolorous : **Weepy** :: Sonorous : Loud

The answer is **b.** Dolorous is a synonym for weepy, and sonorous is a synonym for loud.

113. Penurious : **Stingy** :: Deep : Significant

The answer is **b.** Penurious is a synonym for stingy, and deep is a synonym for significant.

114. Kohler : Chimps :: Thorndike : **Cats**

The answer is **c.** The psychologist Kohler worked with chimps while Thorndike worked with cats.

115. Friedman : Keynes :: Keynes : **Marx**

The answer is **c.** The American economist Milton Friedman opposed the British economist John Maynard Keynes. Keynes opposed Marx.

116. Somnolent : Nap :: Truculent : **War**

The answer is **c.** Being somnolent can lead to a nap, and being truculent can lead to war.

117. Quiet : Plangent :: Contemptible : Estimable

The answer is **b.** Quiet is an antonym for plangent, and contemptible is an antonym for estimable.

118. Backlighting : Scumbling :: Chiaroscuro : Glazing

The answer is **b.** In art, backlighting and chiaroscuro are lighting styles; scumbling and glazing are types of painting brush strokes.

119. Real : Imaginary :: $\sqrt{5}$: $\sqrt{-1}$

The answer is **c.** $\sqrt{5}$ is a real number. $\sqrt{-1}$ is an imaginary number.

120. Amiens : **French Revolution** :: Versailles : World War I

The answer is **d.** The French Revolution ended in 1802 with the treaty of Amiens. World War I ended in 1918 with the treaty of Versailles.

Scoring Your MAT Practice Test

As mentioned in Chapter 1, when you receive your personal score report for the official MAT, you'll be provided with a scaled score and two percentile ranks, all of which are derived from the number of items you answered correctly—known as your raw score.

Because there are different forms and formats of the official MAT, and typically 20 of the 120 questions on the official MAT are experimental and do not count toward your official scaled score and percentile ranks, it is impossible to create an accurate raw score to scaled score or raw score to percentile chart for this and the other practice tests found in this book. In the end, you are striving to correctly answer the highest number of questions as possible and familiarize yourself with the MAT format so you're fully prepared to do your best on test day. For now, what's much more important than your overall score is how you did on each of the content areas tested by the exam. You need to diagnose your strengths and weaknesses so that you can concentrate your efforts as you prepare. The question types are mixed in the practice exam, so in order to tell where your strengths and weaknesses lie, you'll need to compare your answer sheet with the following **MAT Practice Test 7 Review**, which shows which of the content areas each question falls into.

Use your performance here in conjunction with the LearningExpress Test Preparation System in Chapter 2 to help you devise a study plan. You should plan to spend more time studying areas that correspond to the questions you found hardest and less time on the content areas in which you did well. Once you have spent some time reviewing, take the next MAT Practice Test to see if you've improved.

MAT PRACTICE TEST 7 REVIEW	
CONTENT AREA	**QUESTION NUMBERS**
Language and Vocabulary	2, 7, 13, 14, 27, 33, 37, 38, 41, 42, 47, 55, 67, 70, 73, 79, 95, 99, 102, 107, 110, 112, 113, 116, 117
Humanities	1, 4, 6, 8, 10, 28, 39, 40, 43, 46, 48, 50, 77, 80, 81, 83, 84, 92, 93, 103, 118
Social Science	9, 11, 15, 18, 19, 21, 31, 45, 51, 54, 56, 57, 61, 63, 85, 88, 89, 114, 115, 120
Natural Science	3, 16, 17, 22, 23, 26, 29, 49, 52, 53, 60, 62, 64, 68, 69, 82, 90, 91, 94, 96, 97, 100
General	5, 12, 24, 25, 30, 32, 34, 44, 58, 59, 65, 66, 71, 72, 74, 86, 87, 101, 104, 105, 106, 108
Mathematics	20, 35, 36, 75, 76, 78, 98, 109, 111, 119

10 ▶ MAT Practice Test 8

CHAPTER SUMMARY

Here's another sample MAT test for you to practice with.

For this practice test, simulate the actual test-taking experience as closely as you can. Find a quiet place to work where you won't be disturbed. If you own this book, use the answer sheet on the following pages and find some #2 pencils to fill in the circles. Use a timer or stopwatch to time yourself— you'll have 60 minutes to complete the official MAT. After you take the test, use the detailed answer explanations that follow to review any questions you missed.

MAT Practice Test 8

1.	(a)	(b)	(c)	(d)
2.	(a)	(b)	(c)	(d)
3.	(a)	(b)	(c)	(d)
4.	(a)	(b)	(c)	(d)
5.	(a)	(b)	(c)	(d)
6.	(a)	(b)	(c)	(d)
7.	(a)	(b)	(c)	(d)
8.	(a)	(b)	(c)	(d)
9.	(a)	(b)	(c)	(d)
10.	(a)	(b)	(c)	(d)
11.	(a)	(b)	(c)	(d)
12.	(a)	(b)	(c)	(d)
13.	(a)	(b)	(c)	(d)
14.	(a)	(b)	(c)	(d)
15.	(a)	(b)	(c)	(d)
16.	(a)	(b)	(c)	(d)
17.	(a)	(b)	(c)	(d)
18.	(a)	(b)	(c)	(d)
19.	(a)	(b)	(c)	(d)
20.	(a)	(b)	(c)	(d)
21.	(a)	(b)	(c)	(d)
22.	(a)	(b)	(c)	(d)
23.	(a)	(b)	(c)	(d)
24.	(a)	(b)	(c)	(d)
25.	(a)	(b)	(c)	(d)
26.	(a)	(b)	(c)	(d)
27.	(a)	(b)	(c)	(d)
28.	(a)	(b)	(c)	(d)
29.	(a)	(b)	(c)	(d)
30.	(a)	(b)	(c)	(d)
31.	(a)	(b)	(c)	(d)
32.	(a)	(b)	(c)	(d)
33.	(a)	(b)	(c)	(d)
34.	(a)	(b)	(c)	(d)
35.	(a)	(b)	(c)	(d)
36.	(a)	(b)	(c)	(d)
37.	(a)	(b)	(c)	(d)
38.	(a)	(b)	(c)	(d)
39.	(a)	(b)	(c)	(d)
40.	(a)	(b)	(c)	(d)
41.	(a)	(b)	(c)	(d)
42.	(a)	(b)	(c)	(d)
43.	(a)	(b)	(c)	(d)
44.	(a)	(b)	(c)	(d)
45.	(a)	(b)	(c)	(d)

46.	(a)	(b)	(c)	(d)
47.	(a)	(b)	(c)	(d)
48.	(a)	(b)	(c)	(d)
49.	(a)	(b)	(c)	(d)
50.	(a)	(b)	(c)	(d)
51.	(a)	(b)	(c)	(d)
52.	(a)	(b)	(c)	(d)
53.	(a)	(b)	(c)	(d)
54.	(a)	(b)	(c)	(d)
55.	(a)	(b)	(c)	(d)
56.	(a)	(b)	(c)	(d)
57.	(a)	(b)	(c)	(d)
58.	(a)	(b)	(c)	(d)
59.	(a)	(b)	(c)	(d)
60.	(a)	(b)	(c)	(d)
61.	(a)	(b)	(c)	(d)
62.	(a)	(b)	(c)	(d)
63.	(a)	(b)	(c)	(d)
64.	(a)	(b)	(c)	(d)
65.	(a)	(b)	(c)	(d)
66.	(a)	(b)	(c)	(d)
67.	(a)	(b)	(c)	(d)
68.	(a)	(b)	(c)	(d)
69.	(a)	(b)	(c)	(d)
70.	(a)	(b)	(c)	(d)
71.	(a)	(b)	(c)	(d)
72.	(a)	(b)	(c)	(d)
73.	(a)	(b)	(c)	(d)
74.	(a)	(b)	(c)	(d)
75.	(a)	(b)	(c)	(d)
76.	(a)	(b)	(c)	(d)
77.	(a)	(b)	(c)	(d)
78.	(a)	(b)	(c)	(d)
79.	(a)	(b)	(c)	(d)
80.	(a)	(b)	(c)	(d)
81.	(a)	(b)	(c)	(d)
82.	(a)	(b)	(c)	(d)
83.	(a)	(b)	(c)	(d)
84.	(a)	(b)	(c)	(d)
85.	(a)	(b)	(c)	(d)
86.	(a)	(b)	(c)	(d)
87.	(a)	(b)	(c)	(d)
88.	(a)	(b)	(c)	(d)
89.	(a)	(b)	(c)	(d)
90.	(a)	(b)	(c)	(d)

91.	(a)	(b)	(c)	(d)
92.	(a)	(b)	(c)	(d)
93.	(a)	(b)	(c)	(d)
94.	(a)	(b)	(c)	(d)
95.	(a)	(b)	(c)	(d)
96.	(a)	(b)	(c)	(d)
97.	(a)	(b)	(c)	(d)
98.	(a)	(b)	(c)	(d)
99.	(a)	(b)	(c)	(d)
100.	(a)	(b)	(c)	(d)
101.	(a)	(b)	(c)	(d)
102.	(a)	(b)	(c)	(d)
103.	(a)	(b)	(c)	(d)
104.	(a)	(b)	(c)	(d)
105.	(a)	(b)	(c)	(d)
106.	(a)	(b)	(c)	(d)
107.	(a)	(b)	(c)	(d)
108.	(a)	(b)	(c)	(d)
109.	(a)	(b)	(c)	(d)
110.	(a)	(b)	(c)	(d)
111.	(a)	(b)	(c)	(d)
112.	(a)	(b)	(c)	(d)
113.	(a)	(b)	(c)	(d)
114.	(a)	(b)	(c)	(d)
115.	(a)	(b)	(c)	(d)
116.	(a)	(b)	(c)	(d)
117.	(a)	(b)	(c)	(d)
118.	(a)	(b)	(c)	(d)
119.	(a)	(b)	(c)	(d)
120.	(a)	(b)	(c)	(d)

Directions: For each question, select the answer choice in the parentheses that best completes the analogy.

1. Rock & Roll : 50s :: (**a.** Country & Western **b.** Blues **c.** Jazz **d.** Hip Hop) : 80s

2. Éire : (**a.** Czech **b.** Slovenjia **c.** Slovensko **d.** Serbia) :: Ireland : Slovakia

3. McKinley : Rainier :: Alaska : (**a.** Rocky **b.** Cascade **c.** Sierra Nevada **d.** Sawatch)

4. Pegasus : Unicorn :: (**a.** Scales **b.** Hoof **c.** Mane **d.** Wings) : Horn

5. Hydrology : (**a.** Water **b.** Hydrogen **c.** Cycles **d.** Surface) :: Biology : Life

6. Jane Austen : Christopher Marlowe :: (**a.** Novelist **b.** Poet **c.** Illustrator **d.** Sculptor) : Dramatist

7. Stratus : Cloud :: (**a.** Murmur **b.** Lightning **c.** Thunderous **d.** Night) : Sound

8. Shell : (**a.** Key **b.** Barrel joint **c.** Head **d.** String) :: Mouthpiece : Bell

9. Nourish : (**a.** Feed **b.** Sleep **c.** Growth **d.** Wheat) :: Coddle : Comfort

10. Multiple of 5 : 75 :: Multiple of 6 : (**a.** 45 **b.** 52 **c.** 68 **d.** 114)

11. Ransom : Captive :: (**a.** Prisoner **b.** Gratuity **c.** Military **d.** Restaurant) : Service

12. Tureen : (**a.** Napkin **b.** Soup **c.** Spoon **d.** Pilsner) :: Goblet : Wine

13. (**a.** Welt **b.** Wind **c.** Blotch **d.** Rug) : Blow :: Stain : Spill

14. Lexington and Concord : Bull Run :: Revolutionary War : (**a.** World War I **b.** Spanish-American War **c.** Civil War **d.** French and Indian War)

15. (**a.** Drowned **b.** Coast Guard **c.** River **d.** Levee) : Flood :: Helmet : Injury

16. (**a.** Foot **b.** Doctor **c.** Charges **d.** Bond) : Bill :: Reimburse : Expenses

17. Dutch : (**a.** Netherlands **b.** Denmark **c.** Norway **d.** Sweden) :: Spaniard : Spain

18. Cerebellum : Balance :: (**a.** Cerebrum **b.** Stem **c.** Olfactory Bulb **d.** Brain) : Breathing

19. (**a.** Washington **b.** Franklin **c.** Whitney **d.** Bell) : Lightning Rod :: Gutenberg : Movable Type

20. Herbivore : Plants :: (**a.** Scavenger **b.** Decomposer **c.** Pescavore **d.** Carnivore) : Meat

21. Motor City : The Windy City :: (**a.** New York **b.** Detroit **c.** Sioux City **d.** Fresno) : Chicago

22. LSAT : MCAT :: Law : (**a.** Music **b.** Masters **c.** Medical **d.** Military)

23. Photosynthesis : Burning Fossil Fuels :: Oxygen : (**a.** Water **b.** Carbon Dioxide **c.** Hydrogen **d.** Oil)

24. White : Seventh-Day Adventist :: Hubbard : (**a.** Mormonism **b.** Wicca **c.** Theosophy **d.** Scientology)

25. Tibia : Fibula :: Radius : (**a.** Carpal **b.** Ulna **c.** Sternum **d.** Arm)

26. Amber : Resin :: (**a.** Sediment **b.** Fossils **c.** Cast **d.** Organism) : Mineral Deposits

27. (**a.** Crossword **b.** Poach **c.** Sports **d.** Willing) : Game :: Plagiarize : Words

28. Herbert : Hoover :: Franklin : (**a.** Madison **b.** Pierce **c.** Monroe **d.** Adams)

29. Sick : Dog :: (**a.** Kind **b.** Hungry **c.** Funny **d.** Beautiful) : Horse

30. Steering Wheel : Bus :: Handlebar : (**a.** Motor-cycle **b.** Yacht **c.** Spoke **d.** Helmet)

31. Vinyl Record : Compact Disc :: (**a.** Sonic **b.** Electronic **c.** Musical **d.** Analog) : Digital

32. (**a.** Golf **b.** Lawyer **c.** Hospital **d.** Pension) : Retirement :: Settlement : Injury

33. Apple : (**a.** Coconut **b.** Orange **c.** Potato **d.** Water) :: Tree : Ground

34. Lederhosen : (**a.** Ireland **b.** Russia **c.** Germany **d.** Poland) :: Kilt : Scotland

35. Glade : (**a.** Woods **b.** Greenish **c.** Royalty **d.** Water) :: Castle : Moat

36. Trellis : Garden :: Fireplace : (**a.** Smoke **b.** House **c.** Log **d.** Ash)

37. Pilot : (**a.** Airplane **b.** Guide **c.** Driver **d.** License) :: Doctor : Repair

38. Sari : India :: (**a.** Sarong **b.** Serape **c.** Kilt **d.** Kimono) : Mexico

39. Girders : Skeleton :: Building : (**a.** Cranium **b.** Shape **c.** Body **d.** Bones)

40. (**a.** 0 **b.** 1 **c.** -1 **d.** $\frac{1}{2}$) : Addition :: 1 : Multiplication

41. Timbre : (**a.** Rising action **b.** Rhythm **c.** Falling action **d.** Vocal) :: Exposition : Climax

42. 7.5% : .075 :: 125% : (**a.** .0125 **b.** .125 **c.** 1.25 **d.** 12.5)

43. Pavarotti : Callas :: (**a.** Bass **b.** Alto **c.** Tenor **d.** Baritone) : Soprano

44. Colossus : (**a.** Greece **b.** Rhodes **c.** Egypt **d.** Island) :: Lion : Belfort

45. Moon : Tides :: (**a.** Fission **b.** Supernova **c.** Fusion **d.** Hydrogen) : Starshine

46. 63 : Jupiter :: 0 : (**a.** Venus **b.** Earth **c.** Neptune **d.** Saturn)

47. Chloroplasts : Ribosomes :: Photosynthesis : (**a.** Immunity **b.** Protein Production **c.** Transport **d.** Energy)

48. (**a.** Copperfield **b.** Scrooge **c.** Magwich **d.** Pip) : Twist :: Murdstone : Fagin

49. Gorgon : Cerberus :: (**a.** Skin **b.** Eyes **c.** Hair **d.** Fangs) : Tail

50. Peck : Quart :: (**a.** Kiss **b.** Gallon **c.** Glass **d.** Pound) : Pint

51. M : L :: C : (**a.** V **b.** X **c.** M **d.** VI)

52. Canticle : Piousness :: Dirge : (**a.** Excitement **b.** Desire **c.** Religion **d.** Mournfulness)

53. Cyclops : 1 :: Argus : (**a.** 2 **b.** 5 **c.** 10 **d.** 100)

54. Dalí : Surrealism :: Braque : (**a.** Realism **b.** Pop **c.** Cubism **d.** Portraits)

55. Nike : Victory :: (**a.** Ares **b.** Artemis **c.** Hades **d.** Hermes) : Hunt

56. Hawaii : 1959 :: (**a.** New York **b.** South Carolina **c.** Arizona **d.** Maine) : 1912

57. Acrylic : Oil :: Ebony : (**a.** Ivory **b.** Mahogany **c.** Black **d.** Water)

58. Sophocles : B.C. :: (**a.** Euripedes **b.** Pindar **c.** Dante **d.** Virgil) : A.D.

59. (**a.** Drawing **b.** Ward **c.** Sludge **d.** Lean) : Draw :: List : Silt

60. Cabal : (**a.** Plot **b.** Plant **c.** Cable **d.** Stop) :: Output : Yield

61. Reveille : (**a.** Dance **b.** Sunrise **c.** Night **d.** Awaken) :: Taps : Lights Out

62. 1 : Washington :: (**a.** 5 **b.** 12 **c.** 50 **d.** 100) : Franklin

63. 45 : 30 :: 300 : (**a.** 100 **b.** 150 **c.** 200 **d.** 250)

64. Dozen : Score :: 12 : (**a.** 10 **b.** 20 **c.** 50 **d.** 100)

65. Badger : Annoy :: (**a.** Fox **b.** Quarrel **c.** Point **d.** Reconcile) : Dispute

66. (**a.** Thyme **b.** Rice **c.** Tofu **d.** Spelt) : Wheat :: Lentil : Legume

67. Wed : (**a.** Engagement **b.** Match **c.** Rain **d.** Dew) :: Teem : Meet

68. Bossa Nova : Brazil :: Chanson : (**a.** Portugal **b.** France **c.** Paris **d.** Croatia)

69. (**a.** Flexible **b.** Tap **c.** Arena **d.** End) : Proscenium :: Ballroom : Thrust

70. Reykjavik : Helsinki :: Iceland : (**a.** Sweden **b.** Greenland **c.** Finland **d.** Norway)

71. Euphrates : (**a.** Asia **b.** Greece **c.** Africa **d.** Australia) :: St. Lawrence : North America

72. Time : Mad :: News : (**a.** Fashion **b.** Humor **c.** Anger **d.** Culture)

73. (**a.** Attica **b.** Alcatraz **c.** Sing Sing **d.** Eastern State) : New York :: Leavenworth : Kansas

74. (**a.** Sudan **b.** Chad **c.** Yemen **d.** Ethiopia) : Djibouti :: Argentina : Uruguay

75. Missouri : (**a.** Mississippi **b.** Indiana **c.** St. Louis **d.** Lake Huron) :: Indian : Arctic

76. Iran : Persia :: Myanmar : (**a.** Burma **b.** Mongolia **c.** Laos **d.** Rhodesia)

77. Endocrine : Hormones :: (**a.** Respiratory **b.** Reproductive **c.** Integumentary **d.** Nervous) : Barrier

78. Muscular : Skeletal :: Movement : (**a.** Reproduction **b.** Protection **c.** Immunity **d.** Regulation)

79. Sternum : Breast Plate :: Patella : (**a.** Elbow **b.** Skull **c.** Rib **d.** Knee Cap)

80. Skew : Gloomy :: Slant : (**a.** Glee **b.** Foible **c.** Desperate **d.** Gloaming)

81. Dresdenite : (**a.** Switzerland **b.** Germany **c.** Lithuania **d.** Sweden) :: Muscovite : Russia

82. Freud : Stages of Development :: Allport : (**a.** Personality **b.** Operant Conditioning **c.** IQ Theory **d.** Phrenology)

83. DNA : Fossils :: Genetic Code : (**a.** Evolution **b.** RNA **c.** Paleontologist **d.** Epoch)

84. (**a.** Song **b.** Valve **c.** Trombone **d.** Band) : Trumpet :: Fret : Guitar

85. (**a.** Film **b.** Engraving **c.** Bathroom **d.** Decoration) : Frame :: Mosaic : Tile

86. Homburg : (**a.** Belt **b.** Jacket **c.** Scarf. **d.** Hat) :: Winkle picker : Shoe

87. Basil : (**a.** Bay **b.** Mint **c.** Cloves **d.** Garlic) :: Rosemary : Mace

88. Lysosome : (**a.** Reproduction **b.** Energy **c.** Digestion **d.** Transport) :: Vacuoule : Storage

89. Tricycle : Wheel :: (**a.** August **b.** Day **c.** Perennial **d.** Trimester) : Month

90. Resin : (**a.** Raisin **b.** Cream **c.** Varnish **d.** Pudding) :: Gelatin : Preserves

91. $\frac{1}{5} : \frac{3}{10} ::$ 2 : (**a.** 4 **b.** 3 **c.** 4 **d.** 8)

92. 2nd : Ordinal :: (**a.** Fraction **b.** 3rd **c.** 2 **d.** 1st) : Cardinal

93. Chomsky : Transformational grammar :: (**a.** Skinner **b.** Pavlov **c.** Humboldt **d.** Whitehead) : Radical Behaviorism

94. Light : (**a.** Heat **b.** Sound **c.** Waves **d.** Particles) :: 671,000,000 : 768

95. (**a.** Machine heads **b.** Frets **c.** Saddle **d.** Pickguard) : Sound hole :: Headstock : Body

96. Foreshortening : (**a.** Hue **b.** Perspective **c.** Clarity **d.** Opacity) :: Stippling : Shade

97. Wheat : Chaff :: Quality : (**a.** Thresh **b.** Whole **c.** Inadequacy **d.** Worth)

98. Swing : Ax :: (**a.** Honor **b.** Dull **c.** Parry **d.** Knife) : Sword

99. Skinner : Galton :: Environment : (**a.** Punishment **b.** Heredity **c.** Stimulus **d.** Race)

100. Inner Core : Outer Core :: Solid : (**a.** Gas **b.** Liquid **c.** Plasma **d.** Mantle)

101. Decrescendo : (**a.** Crescendo **b.** Finance **c.** Boom **d.** Volume) :: Recession : Economy

102. Chagrin : Criticism :: Sag : (**a.** Cringe **b.** Pressure **c.** Nag **d.** Redress)

103. Mumbai : Ahmadabad :: Tianjin : (**a.** Bangkok **b.** Hyderabad **c.** Nagoya **d.** Qingdao)

104. Rationalism : (**a.** Empiricism **b.** Logic **c.** Sociology **d.** Aesthetics) :: Reason : Experience

105. Folderol : (**a.** Cash **b.** Greed **c.** Nonsense **d.** Event) :: Benevolence : Charity

106. Risible : (**a.** Liquid **b.** Clean **c.** Funny **d.** Above) :: Unseen : Invisible

107. (**a.** Government **b.** Status **c.** Population **d.** Residence) : Units :: Society : Individual

108. Syria : (**a.** Damascus **b.** Amman **c.** Lataka **d.** Tripoli) :: Lebanon : Beirut

109. Melting : Boiling :: Liquid : (**a.** Gas **b.** Crystallization **c.** Freezing **d.** Solid)

110. 100 : Mass On Earth :: (**a.** 0 **b.** 85 **c.** 100 **d.** 115) : Mass on the Moon

111. Margaret Mead : Anthropology :: Bertrand Russell : (**a.** Psychology **b.** Philosophy **c.** Literature **d.** Chemistry)

112. Radio : Gamma :: (**a.** Red **b.** Orange **c.** Indigo **d.** Blue) : Violet

113. Fonio : (**a.** Sorghum **b.** Triticale **c.** Quinoa **d.** Shiitake) :: Millet : Truffle

114. Protist : Monera :: (**a.** Mildew **b.** Algea **c.** Ameba **d.** Fern) : Fungi

115. Gymnosperm : Conifer :: Angiosperm : (**a.** Ginkgo **b.** Fern **c.** Orchid **d.** Liverwort)

116. (**a.** Blue spruce **b.** Sitka spruce **c.** Pecan **d.** Northern red oak) : Cottonwood :: Colorado : Wyoming

117. Fisheye : (**a.** Telephoto **b.** Digital **c.** Workstation **d.** Reflex) :: Teleconverter : Mainframe

118. Economy : Parsimony :: (**a.** Disagreement **b.** Fissure **c.** Bounty **d.** River) : Rift

119. Logorrhea : Words :: (**a.** Cash **b.** Wealth **c.** Mint **d.** Pesos) : Money

120. $.75 : \frac{3}{4} :: .125 :$ (**a.** $\frac{1}{3}$ **b.** $\frac{1}{4}$ **c.** $\frac{1}{5}$ **d.** $\frac{1}{8}$)

Answers

1. Rock & Roll : 50s :: **Hip Hop** : 80s

The answer is **d.** Rock & Roll first became an important and popular form of music during the 1950s. Hip Hop first became an important and popular form of music during the 1980s.

2. Éire : **Slovensko** :: Ireland : Slovakia

The answer is **c.** Éire is the domestic name of Ireland. Slovensko is the domestic name of Slovakia.

3. McKinley : Rainier :: Alaska : **Cascade**

The answer is **b.** Mount McKinley is in the Alaska mountain range. Mount Rainier is in the Cascade mountain range.

4. Pegasus : Unicorn :: **Wings** : Horn

The answer is **d.** Pegasus, according to mythology, was a horse with wings; the unicorn was a horned horse.

5. Hydrology : **Water** :: Biology : Life

The answer is **a.** Hydrology is the study of water; biology is the study of life.

6. Jane Austen : Christopher Marlowe :: **Novelist** : Dramatist

The answer is **a.** Jane Austen was a famous novelist. Christopher Marlowe was a famous dramatist.

7. Stratus : Cloud :: **Murmur** : Sound

The answer is **a.** Stratus is a type of low cloud formation, and a murmur is a low sound.

8. Shell : **Head** :: Mouthpiece : Bell

The answer is **c.** The shell and the head are both parts of drums. The mouthpiece and the bell are both parts of horns.

9. Nourish : **Growth** :: Coddle : Comfort

The answer is **c.** To nourish is to encourage growth, and to coddle is to encourage comfort.

10. Multiple of 5 : 75 :: Multiple of 6 : **114**

The answer is **d.** 75 is a multiple of 5. 114 is a multiple of 6.

11. Ransom : Captive :: **Gratuity** : Service

The answer is **b.** Ransom is money paid for a captive, and gratuity is money paid for a service.

12. Tureen : **Soup** :: Goblet : Wine

The answer is **b.** A tureen is used to hold soup, and a goblet is used to hold wine.

13. Welt : Blow :: Stain : Spill

The answer is **a.** A welt is the result of a blow, and a stain is the result of a spill.

14. Lexington and Concord : Bull Run :: Revolutionary War : **Civil War**

The answer is **c.** Both the battles of Lexington and Concord and the battle of Bull Run were the first main battles in their respective wars: the Revolutionary War and the Civil War.

15. **Levee** : Flood :: Helmet : Injury

The answer is **d.** A levee prevents a flood, and a helmet prevents injury.

16. **Foot** : Bill :: Reimburse : Expenses

The answer is **a.** To foot means to pay a bill, and to reimburse means to pay for expenses.

17. Dutch : **Netherlands** :: Spaniard : Spain

The answer is **a.** Residents of the Netherlands are Dutch, residents of Spain are Spaniards.

18. Cerebellum : Balance :: **Stem** : Breathing

The answer is **b.** The brain's cerebellum controls balance; the brain stem controls respiration.

19. **Franklin** : Lightning Rod :: Gutenberg : Movable Type

The answer is **b.** Benjamin Franklin invented the lightning rod and Johannes Gutenberg invented movable type.

20. Herbivore : Plants :: **Carnivore** : Meat

The answer is **d.** Herbivores consume plants; carnivores consume meat.

21. Motor City : The Windy City :: **Detroit** : Chicago

The answer is **b.** Motor City is the nickname of Detroit and the Windy City is the nickname of Chicago.

22. LSAT : MCAT :: Law : **Medical**

The answer is **c.** The LSAT, or Law School Admission Test, is the test one takes in order to gain admission into law school. The MCAT, or Medical College Admission Test, is the test one takes in order to gain admission into medical school.

23. Photosynthesis : Burning Fossil Fuels :: Oxygen : **Water**

The answer is **a.** Water is a byproduct of photosynthesis; carbon dioxide is a byproduct of burning fossil fuels.

24. White : Seventh-Day Adventist :: Hubbard : **Scientology**

The answer is **d.** White founded the Seventh-Day Adventist church and Hubbard founded the Church of Scientology.

25. Tibia : Fibula :: Radius : **Ulna**

The answer is **b.** The tibia and fibula are the lower leg bones; the radius and ulna are the lower arm bones.

26. Amber : Resin :: **Sediment** : Mineral Deposits

The answer is **a.** Amber is made of resin; sediment is made of mineral deposits.

27. **Poach** : Game :: Plagiarize : Words

The answer is **b.** To poach means to take some-one else's property and call it your own, and to plagiarize is to take someone else's words and call them your own.

28. Herbert : Hoover :: Franklin : Pierce

The answer is **b.** Herbert Hoover and Franklin Pierce were both presidents of the United States.

29. Sick : Dog :: **Hungry** : Horse

The answer is **b.** "Sick as a dog" is a figurative phrase, as is "hungry as a horse."

30. Steering Wheel : Bus :: Handlebar : **Motorcycle**

The answer is **a.** A driver steers a bus using its steering wheel. A motorcyclist steers a motor-cycle using its handlebar.

31. Vinyl Record : Compact Disc :: **Analog** : Digital

The answer is **d.** Analog recording is used to capture sound on a vinyl record. Digital record-ing is used to capture sound on a compact disc.

32. **Pension** : Retirement :: Settlement : Injury

The answer is **d.** A pension is money awarded after retirement, and a settlement is money awarded after an injury.

33. Apple : **Potato** :: Tree : Ground

The answer is **c.** An apple grows on a tree. A potato grows in the ground.

34. Lederhosen : **Germany** :: Kilt : Scotland

The answer is **c.** Lederhosen are German breeches. A kilt is a Scottish skirt.

35. Glade : **Woods** :: Castle : Moat

The answer is **a.** A glade is surrounded by woods, and a castle is surrounded by a moat.

36. Trellis : Garden :: Fireplace : **House**

The answer is **b.** A trellis is found in a garden, and a fireplace is found in a house.

37. Pilot : **Guide** :: Doctor : Repair

The answer is **b.** To pilot means to guide, and to doctor means to repair.

38. Sari : India :: **Serape** : Mexico

The answer is **b.** A sari is traditional clothing worn in India, and a serape is traditional cloth-ing worn in Mexico.

39. Girders : Skeleton :: Building : **Body**

The answer is **c.** Girders form the framework of a building; the skeleton detemines the shape of the body.

40. **0** : Addition :: 1 : Multiplication

The answer is **a.** 0 is the additive iden-tity. 0 added to any number leaves the number unchanged. 1 is the multiplicative identity. 1 multiplied by any number leaves the number unchanged.

41. Timbre : **Rhythm** :: Exposition : Climax

The answer is **b.** Timbre and rhythm are two characteristics of music. Exposition and climax are two characteristics of drama.

42. 7.5% : .075 :: 125% : **1.25**

The answer is **c.** .075 is the decimal equivalent of 7.5%. 1.25 is the decimal equivalent of 125%.

43. Pavarotti : Callas :: **Tenor** : Soprano

The answer is **c.** Luciano Pavarotti was an opera singer who sang in the tenor range. Maria Callas was an opera singer who sings in the soprano range.

44. Colossus : **Rhodes** :: Lion : Belfort

The answer is **b.** The Colossus of Rhodes is a gigantic statue on the island of Rhodes, sculpted by Charles of Lindos. The Lion of Belfort is a gigantic statue in Belfort, France, sculpted by Frédéric Bartholdi.

45. Moon : Tides :: **Fusion** : Starshine

The answer is **c.** The moon creates the tides; fusion creates stars' glow.

46. 63 : Jupiter :: 0 : **Venus**

The answer is **a.** Jupiter has 63 moons. Venus has no moons.

47. Chloroplasts : Ribosomes :: Photosynthesis : **Protein Production**

The answer is **b.** Chloroplasts engage in photosynthesis; ribosomes engage in protein production.

48. **Copperfield** : Twist :: Murdstone : Fagin

The answer is **a.** In Charles Dickens's novel *David Copperfield*, David Copperfield is the hero and Mr. Murdstone is the villain. In his novel *Oliver Twist*, Oliver Twist is the hero and Fagin is the villain.

49. Gorgon : Cerberus :: **Hair** : Tail

The answer is **c.** In Greek mythology, a gorgon is a mythical creature that has snakes in place of hair. Cerberus is a mythical creature with a snake in place of a tail.

50. Peck : Quart :: **Gallon** : Pint

The answer is **b.** A peck is a unit of measure equal to 8 quarts, and a gallon is a unit of measurement equal to 8 pints.

51. M : L :: C : **V**

The answer is **a.** M (1000) divided by L (50) is 20, as is C (100) divided by V (5).

52. Canticle : Piousness :: Dirge : **Mournfulness**

The answer is **d.** A canticle is a kind of hymn intended to instill a feeling of piousness in the listener. A dirge is a slow, lamenting song intended to instill mournfulness in the listener.

53. Cyclops : 1 :: Argus : **100**

The answer is **d.** Cyclops was the mythical creature with one eye, and Argus was a creature with 100 eyes.

54. Dalí : Surrealism :: Braque : **Cubism**

The answer is **c.** Salvador Dalí is known as a surrealist painter, and Georges Braque is known as a cubist.

55. Nike : Victory :: **Artemis** : Hunt

The answer is **b.** Nike is the goddess of victory, and Artemis is the goddess of the hunt.

56. Hawaii : 1959 :: **Arizona** : 1912

The answer is **c.** Hawaii became a state in 1959, and Arizona became a state in 1912.

57. Acrylic : Oil :: Ebony : **Mahogany**

The answer is **b.** Acrylic and oil are two types of paint. Ebony and mahogany are two types of wood.

58. Sophocles : B.C. :: **Dante** : A.D.

The answer is **c.** Sophocles was born in B.C., and Dante was born and lived A.D.

59. **Ward** : Draw :: List : Silt

The answer is **b.** Ward is an anagram for draw, and list is an anagram for silt.

60. Cabal : **Plot** :: Output : Yield

The answer is **a.** Cabal is a synonym for plot, and output is a synonym for yield.

61. Reveille : **Awaken** :: Taps : Lights Out

The answer is **d.** Reveille is a musical signal to awaken, and taps is a musical signal for lights out.

62. 1 : Washington :: **100** : Franklin

The answer is **d.** George Washington's portrait is on the one-dollar bill, and Benjamin Franklin's is on the 100 dollar bill.

63. 45 : 30 :: 300 : **200**

The answer is **c.** $\frac{2}{3}$ times 45 equals 30. $\frac{2}{3}$ times 300 equals 200.

64. Dozen : Score :: 12 : **20**

The answer is **b.** A dozen is a set of 12 objects. A score is a set of 20 objects.

65. Badger : Annoy :: **Quarrel** : Dispute

The answer is **b.** To badger is to annoy persistently, and to quarrel is to dispute actively.

66. **Spelt** : Wheat :: Lentil : Legume

The answer is **d.** Spelt is a wheat, and a lentil is a legume.

67. Wed : **Dew** :: Teem : Meet

The answer is **d.** Wed is a palindrome for dew, and teem is a palindrome for meet.

68. Bossa Nova : Brazil :: Chanson : **France**

The answer is **b.** A bossa nova is a type of song from Brazil. A chanson is a type of song from France.

69. **Tap** : Proscenium :: Ballroom : Thrust

The answer is **b.** Tap and ballroom are two types of dance shoes. Proscenium and thrust are two types of stages.

70. Reykjavik : Helsinki :: Iceland : **Finland**

The answer is **c.** Reykjavik is the capital of Iceland and Helsinki is the capital of Finland.

71. Euphrates : **Asia** :: St. Lawrence : North America

The answer is **a.** The Euphrates River is in Asia. The St. Lawrence River is in North America.

72. Time : Mad :: News : **Humor**

The answer is **b.** *Time* is a news magazine. *Mad* is a humor magazine.

73. **Attica** : New York :: Leavenworth : Kansas

The answer is **a.** Attica is a prison in New York and Leavenworth is a prison in Kansas.

74. **Ethiopia** : Djibouti :: Argentina : Uruguay

The answer is **d.** Ethiopia borders Djibouti to the west. Argentina borders Uruguay to the west.

75. Missouri : **Mississippi** :: Indian : Arctic

The answer is **a.** The Missouri and the Mississippi are both rivers; the Indian and the Arctic are both oceans.

76. Iran : Persia :: Myanmar : **Burma**

The answer is **a.** Persia is the former name of Iran and Burma is the former name of Myanmar.

77. Endocrine : Hormones :: **Integumentary** : Barrier

The answer is **c.** The endocrine system provides hormones for the body; the integumentary system provides a waterproof barrier for the body.

78. Muscular : Skeletal :: Movement : **Protection**

The answer is **b.** The muscular system aids in movement; the skeletal system aids in protection.

79. Sternum : Breast Plate :: Patella : **Knee Cap**

The answer is **d.** The common name for the sternum is the breast plate. The common name for the patella is the knee cap.

80. Skew : Gloomy :: Slant : **Desperate**

The answer is **c.** Skew is a synonym of slant, and gloomy is a synonym for desperate.

81. Dresdenite : **Germany** :: Muscovite : Russia

The answer is **b.** A Dresdenite resides in Dresden, Germany. A Muscovite resides in Moscow, Russia.

82. Freud : Stages of Development :: Allport : **Personality**

The answer is **a.** Freud is known for his psychological work related to stages of development. Allport is known for his work related to personality psychology.

83. DNA : Fossils :: Genetic Code : **Evolution**

The answer is **a.** DNA helps scientists map the genetic code; fossils help scientists map evolution.

84. **Valve** : Trumpet :: Fret : Guitar

The answer is **b.** A valve is part of a trumpet, and a fret is part of a guitar.

85. **Film** : Frame :: Mosaic : Tile

The answer is **a.** A film is composed of individual frames, and a mosaic is composed of individual tiles.

86. Homburg : **Hat** :: Winkle picker : Shoe

The answer is **d.** A homburg is a type of hat and a winkle picker is a type of shoe.

87. Basil : **Cloves** :: Rosemary : Mace

The answer is **c.** Basil and rosemary are both herbs. Cloves and mace are spices.

88. Lysosome : **Digestion** :: Vacuole : Storage

The answer is **c.** The primary role of a cell's lysosome is digestion; the primary role of a cell's vacuole is storage for food, water, or waste.

89. Tricycle : Wheel :: **Trimester** : Month

The answer is **d.** A tricycle has three wheels, and a trimester has three months.

90. Resin : **Varnish** :: Gelatin : Preserves

The answer is **c.** Resin is used in making varnishes, and gelatin is used in making preserves.

91. $\frac{1}{5} : \frac{3}{10} :: 2 : 3$

The answer is **b.** The fraction $\frac{1}{5}$ is equal to $\frac{2}{10}$. The ratio of $\frac{1}{5}$ to $\frac{3}{10}$ is 2 to 3.

92. 2nd : Ordinal :: **2** : Cardinal

The answer is. **c.** 2nd is an example of an ordinal number, and 2 is an example of a cardinal number.

93. Chomsky : Transformational grammar :: **Skinner** : Radical Behaviorism

The answer is **a.** Transformational grammar is a concept originated by philosopher Noam Chomsky. Radical behaviorism is a concept originated by philosopher B.F. Skinner.

94. Light : **Sound** :: 671,000,000 : 768

The answer is **b.** Sound waves travel at sea level at about 768 miles per hour; light travels at about 671 million miles per hour.

95. **Machine heads** : Sound hole :: Headstock : Body

The answer is **a.** On a guitar, the machine heads, which are used to tune the instrument, are located on its headstock. The sound hole, which helps the guitar resonate, are located on its body.

96. Foreshortening : **Perspective** :: Stippling : Shade

The answer is **b.** Foreshortening is an artistic technique that affects the perspective of an image. Stippling is an artistic technique that affects the shade of an image.

97. Wheat : Chaff :: Quality : **Inadequacy**

The answer is **c.** Wheat is an antonym of chaff, and quality is an antonym of inadequacy.

98. Swing : Ax :: **Parry** : Sword

The answer is **c.** Swing is an action taken with an ax, and parry is an action taken with a sword.

99. Skinner : Galton :: Environment : **Heredity**

The answer is **b.** Skinner was a psychologist who believed that one's environment shaped behavior, while Galton believed that heredity shaped behavior.

100. Inner Core : Outer Core :: Solid : **Plasma**

The answer is **c.** The first law of thermodynamics says that energy cannot be created or destroyed, but it can be transformed. The second law of thermodynamics relates to entropy.

101. Decrescendo : **Volume** :: Recession : Economy

The answer is **d.** A decrescendo is a reduction in volume, and a recession is a reduction in the economy.

102. Chagrin : Criticism :: Sag : **Pressure**

The answer is **b.** Chagrin can be the result of criticism, and sag is the result of pressure.

103. Mumbai : Ahmadabad :: Tianjin : **Qingdao**

The answer is **d.** Both Mumbai and Ahmadabad are large cities in India. Tianjin and Qingdao are large cities in China.

104. Rationalism : **Empiricism** :: Reason : Experience

The answer is **a.** In philosophy, rationalism stresses that reason is the basis for knowledge. Empiricism stresses that experience is.

105. Folderol : **Nonsense** :: Benevolence : Charity

The answer is **c.** Folderol is a synonym for nonsense, and benevolence is a synonym for charity.

106. Risible : **Funny** :: Unseen : Invisible

The answer is **c.** Risible is a synonym for funny, and unseen is a synonym for invisible.

107. **Population** : Units :: Society : Individual

The answer is **c.** In sociology, a population is comprised of units and a society is comprised of individuals.

108. Syria : **Damascus** :: Lebanon : Beirut

The answer is **a.** Damascus is the capital of Syria just as Beirut is the capital of Lebanon.

109. Melting : Boiling :: Liquid : **Gas**

The answer is **a.** Melting is defined as moving from a solid state to a liquid state; boiling is defined as moving from a liquid state to a gaseous state.

110. 100 : Mass On Earth :: **100** : Mass on the Moon

The answer is **c.** Mass is the same on the moon or on the earth, regardless of gravity.

111. Margaret Mead : Anthropology :: Bertrand Russell : **Philosophy**

The answer is **b.** Margaret Mead was a renowned anthropologist of the 20th century. Bertrand Russell was a renowned philosopher of the 20th century.

112. Radio : Gamma :: **Red** : Violet

The answer is **a.** Radio sound waves are the longest, while gamma sound waves are the shortest. Red light waves are the longest light waves visible to humans; violet waves are the shortest.

113. Fonio : **Shiitake** :: Millet : Truffle

The answer is **d.** Fonio and millet are two types of grain. Shiitakes and truffles are two types of edible fungi.

114. Protist : Monera :: **Mildew** : Fungi

The answer is **a.** A protist belongs to the kingdom Monera; mildew belongs to the kingdom Fungi.

115. Gymnosperm : Conifer :: Angiosperm : **Orchid**

The answer is **c.** A conifer is a gymnosperm; an orchid is an angiosperm.

116. **Blue spruce** : Cottonwood :: Colorado : Wyoming

The answer is **a.** The blue spruce is the state tree of Colorado. The cottonwood is the state tree of Wyoming.

117. Fisheye : **Workstation** :: Teleconverter : Mainframe

The answer is **c.** Fisheye and teleconverter are two types of camera lenses. A workstation and a mainframe are two types of computers.

118. Economy : Parsimony :: **Fissure** : Rift

The answer is **b.** Economy is a synonym of parsimony, and fissure is a synonym of rift.

119. Logorrhea : Words :: **Wealth** : Money

The answer is **b.** Logorrhea is an excess of words, and wealth is an excess of money.

120. $.75 : \frac{3}{4} :: .125 : \frac{1}{8}$

The answer is **d.** $\frac{3}{4}$ is the decimal equivalent of .75. $\frac{1}{8}$ is the decimal equivalent of .125.

Scoring Your MAT Practice Test

As mentioned in Chapter 1, when you receive your personal score report for the official MAT, you'll be provided with a scaled score and two percentile ranks, all of which are derived from the number of items you answered correctly—known as your raw score.

Because there are different forms and formats of the official MAT, and typically 20 of the 120 questions on the official MAT are experimental and do not count toward your official scaled score and percentile ranks, it is impossible to create an accurate raw score to scaled score or raw score to percentile chart for this and the other practice tests found in this book. In the end, you are striving to correctly answer the highest number of questions as possible and familiarize yourself with the MAT format so you're fully prepared to do your best on test day. For now, what's much more important than your overall score is how you did on each of the content areas tested by the exam. You need to diagnose your strengths and weaknesses so that you can concentrate your efforts as you prepare. The question types are mixed in the practice exam, so in order to tell where your strengths and weaknesses lie, you'll need to compare your answer sheet with the **MAT Practice Test 8 Review** below, which shows which of the content areas each question falls into.

Use your performance here in conjunction with the LearningExpress Test Preparation System in Chapter 2 to help you devise a study plan. You should plan to spend more time studying areas that correspond to the questions you found hardest and less time on the content areas in which you did well. Once you have spent some time reviewing, take the next MAT Practice Test to see if you've improved.

CONTENT AREA	QUESTION NUMBERS
Language and Vocabulary	7, 9, 11, 13, 15, 16, 27, 32, 35, 59, 60, 65, 66, 67, 80, 84, 85, 97, 98, 101, 102, 105, 106, 118, 119
Humanities	1, 4, 6, 8, 31, 41, 43, 44, 48, 49, 52, 53, 54, 55, 56, 58, 68, 69, 93, 95, 96
Social Science	2, 3, 14, 17, 19, 24, 28, 70, 71, 74, 75, 76, 81, 82, 99, 103, 104, 107, 108, 111
Natural Science	5, 18, 20, 23, 25, 26, 39, 45, 46, 47, 77, 78, 79, 83, 88, 94, 100, 109, 110, 112, 114, 115
General	12, 21, 22, 29, 30, 33, 34, 36, 37, 38, 57, 61, 62, 72, 73, 86, 87, 89, 90, 113, 116, 117
Mathematics	10, 40, 42, 50, 51, 63, 64, 91, 92, 120

CHAPTER

11 ▶ MAT Practice Test 9

CHAPTER SUMMARY
Here's another sample MAT test for you to practice with.

For this practice test, simulate the actual test-taking experience as closely as you can. Find a quiet place to work where you won't be disturbed. If you own this book, use the answer sheet on the following pages and find some #2 pencils to fill in the circles with. Use a timer or stopwatch to time yourself—you'll have 60 minutes to complete the official MAT. After you take the test, use the detailed answer explanations that follow to review any questions you missed.

MAT Practice Test 9

1.	ⓐ	ⓑ	ⓒ	ⓓ
2.	ⓐ	ⓑ	ⓒ	ⓓ
3.	ⓐ	ⓑ	ⓒ	ⓓ
4.	ⓐ	ⓑ	ⓒ	ⓓ
5.	ⓐ	ⓑ	ⓒ	ⓓ
6.	ⓐ	ⓑ	ⓒ	ⓓ
7.	ⓐ	ⓑ	ⓒ	ⓓ
8.	ⓐ	ⓑ	ⓒ	ⓓ
9.	ⓐ	ⓑ	ⓒ	ⓓ
10.	ⓐ	ⓑ	ⓒ	ⓓ
11.	ⓐ	ⓑ	ⓒ	ⓓ
12.	ⓐ	ⓑ	ⓒ	ⓓ
13.	ⓐ	ⓑ	ⓒ	ⓓ
14.	ⓐ	ⓑ	ⓒ	ⓓ
15.	ⓐ	ⓑ	ⓒ	ⓓ
16.	ⓐ	ⓑ	ⓒ	ⓓ
17.	ⓐ	ⓑ	ⓒ	ⓓ
18.	ⓐ	ⓑ	ⓒ	ⓓ
19.	ⓐ	ⓑ	ⓒ	ⓓ
20.	ⓐ	ⓑ	ⓒ	ⓓ
21.	ⓐ	ⓑ	ⓒ	ⓓ
22.	ⓐ	ⓑ	ⓒ	ⓓ
23.	ⓐ	ⓑ	ⓒ	ⓓ
24.	ⓐ	ⓑ	ⓒ	ⓓ
25.	ⓐ	ⓑ	ⓒ	ⓓ
26.	ⓐ	ⓑ	ⓒ	ⓓ
27.	ⓐ	ⓑ	ⓒ	ⓓ
28.	ⓐ	ⓑ	ⓒ	ⓓ
29.	ⓐ	ⓑ	ⓒ	ⓓ
30.	ⓐ	ⓑ	ⓒ	ⓓ
31.	ⓐ	ⓑ	ⓒ	ⓓ
32.	ⓐ	ⓑ	ⓒ	ⓓ
33.	ⓐ	ⓑ	ⓒ	ⓓ
34.	ⓐ	ⓑ	ⓒ	ⓓ
35.	ⓐ	ⓑ	ⓒ	ⓓ
36.	ⓐ	ⓑ	ⓒ	ⓓ
37.	ⓐ	ⓑ	ⓒ	ⓓ
38.	ⓐ	ⓑ	ⓒ	ⓓ
39.	ⓐ	ⓑ	ⓒ	ⓓ
40.	ⓐ	ⓑ	ⓒ	ⓓ
41.	ⓐ	ⓑ	ⓒ	ⓓ
42.	ⓐ	ⓑ	ⓒ	ⓓ
43.	ⓐ	ⓑ	ⓒ	ⓓ
44.	ⓐ	ⓑ	ⓒ	ⓓ
45.	ⓐ	ⓑ	ⓒ	ⓓ

46.	ⓐ	ⓑ	ⓒ	ⓓ
47.	ⓐ	ⓑ	ⓒ	ⓓ
48.	ⓐ	ⓑ	ⓒ	ⓓ
49.	ⓐ	ⓑ	ⓒ	ⓓ
50.	ⓐ	ⓑ	ⓒ	ⓓ
51.	ⓐ	ⓑ	ⓒ	ⓓ
52.	ⓐ	ⓑ	ⓒ	ⓓ
53.	ⓐ	ⓑ	ⓒ	ⓓ
54.	ⓐ	ⓑ	ⓒ	ⓓ
55.	ⓐ	ⓑ	ⓒ	ⓓ
56.	ⓐ	ⓑ	ⓒ	ⓓ
57.	ⓐ	ⓑ	ⓒ	ⓓ
58.	ⓐ	ⓑ	ⓒ	ⓓ
59.	ⓐ	ⓑ	ⓒ	ⓓ
60.	ⓐ	ⓑ	ⓒ	ⓓ
61.	ⓐ	ⓑ	ⓒ	ⓓ
62.	ⓐ	ⓑ	ⓒ	ⓓ
63.	ⓐ	ⓑ	ⓒ	ⓓ
64.	ⓐ	ⓑ	ⓒ	ⓓ
65.	ⓐ	ⓑ	ⓒ	ⓓ
66.	ⓐ	ⓑ	ⓒ	ⓓ
67.	ⓐ	ⓑ	ⓒ	ⓓ
68.	ⓐ	ⓑ	ⓒ	ⓓ
69.	ⓐ	ⓑ	ⓒ	ⓓ
70.	ⓐ	ⓑ	ⓒ	ⓓ
71.	ⓐ	ⓑ	ⓒ	ⓓ
72.	ⓐ	ⓑ	ⓒ	ⓓ
73.	ⓐ	ⓑ	ⓒ	ⓓ
74.	ⓐ	ⓑ	ⓒ	ⓓ
75.	ⓐ	ⓑ	ⓒ	ⓓ
76.	ⓐ	ⓑ	ⓒ	ⓓ
77.	ⓐ	ⓑ	ⓒ	ⓓ
78.	ⓐ	ⓑ	ⓒ	ⓓ
79.	ⓐ	ⓑ	ⓒ	ⓓ
80.	ⓐ	ⓑ	ⓒ	ⓓ
81.	ⓐ	ⓑ	ⓒ	ⓓ
82.	ⓐ	ⓑ	ⓒ	ⓓ
83.	ⓐ	ⓑ	ⓒ	ⓓ
84.	ⓐ	ⓑ	ⓒ	ⓓ
85.	ⓐ	ⓑ	ⓒ	ⓓ
86.	ⓐ	ⓑ	ⓒ	ⓓ
87.	ⓐ	ⓑ	ⓒ	ⓓ
88.	ⓐ	ⓑ	ⓒ	ⓓ
89.	ⓐ	ⓑ	ⓒ	ⓓ
90.	ⓐ	ⓑ	ⓒ	ⓓ

91.	ⓐ	ⓑ	ⓒ	ⓓ
92.	ⓐ	ⓑ	ⓒ	ⓓ
93.	ⓐ	ⓑ	ⓒ	ⓓ
94.	ⓐ	ⓑ	ⓒ	ⓓ
95.	ⓐ	ⓑ	ⓒ	ⓓ
96.	ⓐ	ⓑ	ⓒ	ⓓ
97.	ⓐ	ⓑ	ⓒ	ⓓ
98.	ⓐ	ⓑ	ⓒ	ⓓ
99.	ⓐ	ⓑ	ⓒ	ⓓ
100.	ⓐ	ⓑ	ⓒ	ⓓ
101.	ⓐ	ⓑ	ⓒ	ⓓ
102.	ⓐ	ⓑ	ⓒ	ⓓ
103.	ⓐ	ⓑ	ⓒ	ⓓ
104.	ⓐ	ⓑ	ⓒ	ⓓ
105.	ⓐ	ⓑ	ⓒ	ⓓ
106.	ⓐ	ⓑ	ⓒ	ⓓ
107.	ⓐ	ⓑ	ⓒ	ⓓ
108.	ⓐ	ⓑ	ⓒ	ⓓ
109.	ⓐ	ⓑ	ⓒ	ⓓ
110.	ⓐ	ⓑ	ⓒ	ⓓ
111.	ⓐ	ⓑ	ⓒ	ⓓ
112.	ⓐ	ⓑ	ⓒ	ⓓ
113.	ⓐ	ⓑ	ⓒ	ⓓ
114.	ⓐ	ⓑ	ⓒ	ⓓ
115.	ⓐ	ⓑ	ⓒ	ⓓ
116.	ⓐ	ⓑ	ⓒ	ⓓ
117.	ⓐ	ⓑ	ⓒ	ⓓ
118.	ⓐ	ⓑ	ⓒ	ⓓ
119.	ⓐ	ⓑ	ⓒ	ⓓ
120.	ⓐ	ⓑ	ⓒ	ⓓ

Directions: For each question, select the answer choice in the parentheses that best completes the analogy.

1. (**a.** Allegro **b.** Organ **c.** Forte **d.** Accordion) : Loud :: Piano : Quiet

2. (**a.** Drama **b.** Literature **c.** Story **d.** Biography) : Documentary :: Book : Film

3. Mythical : Historical :: General : (**a.** Participatory **b.** Particular **c.** Colonel **d.** Orderly)

4. Son : Nuclear :: (**a.** Father **b.** Mother **c.** Cousin **d.** Daughters) : Extended

5. Gilbert : Lerner :: (**a.** Team **b.** Sullivan **c.** Composer **d.** Rice) : Loewe

6. 6 : 66 :: (**a.** 4 **b.** 6 **c.** 11 **d.** 12) : 132

7. Jalopy : Car :: (**a.** Driveway **b.** Dump **c.** Castle **d.** Luxury) : House

8. Denim : Cotton :: (**a.** Sheep **b.** Uniform **c.** Sweater **d.** Linen) : Flax

9. Cabana : Pool :: Chalet : (**a.** Billiards **b.** Swiss **c.** Ocean **d.** Mountain)

10. Iran : (**a.** Syria **b.** Russia **c.** Iraq **d.** Persia) :: Germany : Prussia

11. Earth : 365 :: Mercury : (**a.** 20 **b.** 88 **c.** 365 **d.** 429)

12. Des Moines : Iowa :: (**a.** Dallas **b.** Fort Worth **c.** Austin **d.** Cedar Rapids) : Texas

13. Alcohol : (**a.** Heart **b.** Liver **c.** Kidneys **d.** Pancreas) :: Tobacco : Lungs

14. Comedy : (**a.** Drama **b.** Kabuki **c.** Pantomime **d.** Musical) :: Greece : Japan

15. Rumba : Ragtime :: (**a.** Cool **b.** Samba **c.** Brazil **d.** Modal) : Bebop

16. Circular : Elongated :: Red Blood Cell : (**a.** Egg **b.** Neuron **c.** White Blood Cell **d.** Skin Cell)

17. Power Plant : Storage Area :: (**a.** Mitochondria **b.** Golgi Complex **c.** Lysosomes **d.** Chlorophyll) : Vacuole

18. Perimeter : Area :: $4x$: (**a.** x **b.** $8x$ **c.** $x2$ **d.** $4x2$)

19. Coif : Hair :: (**a.** Shower **b.** Close **c.** Praise **d.** Score) : Musical

20. Red : White :: (**a.** Blood **b.** Clot **c.** Oxygen **d.** Platelets) : Protection

21. Duvet : (**a.** Ceiling **b.** Legs **c.** Bed **d.** Neck) :: Beret : Head

22. Stage : Play :: (**a.** Shoot **b.** Edit **c.** Reel **d.** Script) : Film

23. Moccasin : Snake :: (**a.** Alligator **b.** Waders **c.** Asp **d.** Loafer) : Shoe

24. Monarch : (**a.** Queen **b.** Butterfly **c.** Royal **d.** Venom) :: King : Cobra

25. Junket : (**a.** Trounce **b.** Trip **c.** Refuse **d.** Trinket) :: Junk : Trash

26. Inner : Outer :: Mercury : (**a.** Venus **b.** Earth **c.** Mars **d.** Uranus)

27. Tuscan : Italy :: Provençal : (**a.** Switzerland **b.** Spain **c.** France **d.** England)

28. Ragtime : United States :: Raga : (**a.** Cloth **b.** Country **c.** Piano **d.** India)

29. Diamond : Baseball :: Court : (**a.** Poker **b.** Jury **c.** Grass **d.** Squash)

30. (**a.** Toast **b.** Coffee **c.** Brownies **d.** Pizza) : Cocoa :: Omelet : Egg

31. 15 : 14 :: 5 : (**a.** 3 **b.** 7 **c.** 11 **d.** 13)

32. (**a.** Spoon **b.** Spill **c.** Heat **d.** Stock) : Soup :: Latex : Paint

33. (**a.** Date **b.** Seer **c.** Book **d.** General) : Future :: Historian : Past

34. Protractor : Angle :: Ruler : (**a.** Rectangle **b.** Length **c.** Classroom **d.** King)

35. Myopic : Farsighted :: (**a.** Benevolent **b.** Famous **c.** Turgid **d.** Wasted) : Obscure

36. La Bohème : (**a.** Puccini **b.** Verdi **c.** Mussorgsky **d.** Strauss) :: Pagliacci : Leoncavallo

37. Tacit : Implied :: (**a.** Shoddy **b.** Taciturn **c.** Forthright **d.** Superior) : Inferior

38. (**a.** Biographer **b.** Novelist **c.** Essayist **d.** Poet) : Cinquain :: Composer : Fugue

39. Zeus : Jupiter :: Hermes : (**a.** Mars **b.** Apollo **c.** Mercury **d.** Atlas)

40. (**a.** Glockenspiel **b.** Marimba **c.** Hammond **d.** Mallet) : Xylophone :: Metal : Wood

41. (**a.** Hera **b.** Aphrodite **c.** Minerva **d.** Juno) : Venus :: Poseidon : Neptune

42. Midas : (**a.** Gold **b.** King **c.** Cybele **d.** Food) :: Circe : Pig

43. (**a.** Ligeia **b.** Usher **c.** Prospero **d.** King Pest) : Masque of the Red Death :: Fortunato : Cask of Amontillado

44. Vaunt : Boast :: Skewer : (**a.** Flaunt **b.** Criticize **c.** Prepare **d.** Avoid)

45. Mosaics : Tile :: (**a.** Quilting **b.** Calligraphy **c.** Fretwork **d.** Macramé) : Yarn

46. Bunker Hill : Revolutionary War :: (**a.** Concord **b.** Alamo **c.** Boston Massacre **d.** Bull Run) : Civil War

47. (**a.** Melville **b.** Faulkner **c.** Kerouac **d.** Hemingway) : Southern :: Hawthorne : Northern

48. Alveoli : Respiratory :: (**a.** Ventricles **b.** Villae **c.** Capillaries **d.** Lungs) : Circulatory

49. Van Buren : 8th :: (**a.** Lincoln **b.** Jackson **c.** Adams **d.** Pierce) : 16th

50. Xerxes : Persia :: Nebuchadnezzar : (**a.** Mesopotamia **b.** Egypt **c.** Babylon **d.** Peru)

51. Le Corbusier : Architecture :: Rodin : (**a.** Symphony **b.** Sculpture **c.** Novel **d.** Automobile)

52. Vein : Artery :: Thin : (**a.** Oxygen **b.** Venule **c.** Thick **d.** Pressure)

53. Menshevik : (**a.** Trotskyite **b.** Bolshevik **c.** Tsarist **d.** Marxism) :: Kerensky : Lenin

54. Gall : Vex :: Hex : (**a.** Fix **b.** Jinx **c.** Index **d.** Vixen)

55. (**a.** Field **b.** Fodder **c.** Farm **d.** Windmill) : Silo :: Art : Museum

56. Iota : Jot :: (**a.** One **b.** Ilk **c.** Tab **d.** Jet) : Type

57. (**a.** Belief **b.** Death **c.** Cohesion **d.** Fear) : Unity :: Dearth : Scarcity

58. 18th : Prohibition of Alcohol :: (**a.** 19th **b.** 21st **c.** 22nd **d.** 25th) : Repeal of 18th

59. Bivouac : (**a.** Diplomacy **b.** Sergeant **c.** Soldier **d.** Camp) :: Axis : Alliance

60. Chronograph : Time :: Pipette : (**a.** Mass **b.** Energy **c.** Space **d.** Volume)

61. Secret : Furtive :: Audible : (**a.** Resonant **b.** Nap **c.** Sack **d.** Ring)

62. Pummel : Hit :: (**a.** Disbelief **b.** Poem **c.** Chant **d.** Question) : Recite

63. Retton : (**a.** Triathlon **b.** Gymnastics **c.** Vault **d.** Balance beam) :: Hamill : Figure Skating

64. (**a.** Hormones **b.** Adrenaline **c.** Lungs **d.** Spleen) : Immunological :: Thyroid : Endocrine

65. Bile : Liver :: (**a.** Enzymes **b.** Digestion **c.** Nutrients **d.** Gall Bladder) : Pancreas

66. (**a.** Quarrel **b.** Lie **c.** Apology **d.** Perjury) : Forgiveness :: Bribe : Influence

67. (**a.** Purist **b.** Eden **c.** Displeasure **d.** Agnostic) : Tradition :: Hedonist : Pleasure

68. United Kingdom : Barbados :: Australia : (**a.** Haiti **b.** Aruba **c.** Hong Kong **d.** Jamaica)

69. (**a.** Magellan **b.** Cortes **c.** de Vaca **d.** Orellana) : Aztecs :: Pizarro : Incas

70. Seemly : (**a.** Burnt **b.** Invisible **c.** Attractive **d.** Horrid) :: Torrid : Scorching

71. Mount Rainier : Mount Shasta :: Washington : (**a.** California **b.** Colorado **c.** Alaska **d.** Oregon)

72. Iran : Iraq :: Tehran : (**a.** Kuwait **b.** Baghdad **c.** Mosul **d.** Karbala)

73. Pepsin : (**a.** Esophagus **b.** Acid **c.** Stomach **d.** Intestine) :: Saliva : Mouth

74. McGill : Oxford :: (**a.** Australia **b.** Canada **c.** Scotland **d.** Massachusetts) : England

75. Nosegay : Flowers :: (**a.** Tickle **b.** Fruit **c.** Team **d.** Ball) : Players

76. .03 : .0009 :: (**a.** .2 **b.** .02 **c.** .002 **d.** .0002) : .000004

77. Isocracy : (**a.** One **b.** All **c.** Few **d.** Power) :: Meritocracy : Merit

78. Mars : War :: (**a.** Jupiter **b.** Venus **c.** Saturn **d.** Hermes) : Agriculture

79. Ethiopia : Abyssinia :: Zaire : (**a.** Rhodesia **b.** Gold Coast **c.** Congo **d.** Zimbabwe)

80. $\frac{1}{2} : \frac{1}{4} :: \frac{2}{3} :$ (**a.** $\frac{1}{2}$ **b.** $\frac{1}{3}$ **c.** $\frac{1}{6}$ **d.** 1)

81. Tooth : (**a.** Molar **b.** Tongue **c.** Comb **d.** Spoon) :: Tine : Fork

82. Autotroph : (**a.** Photosynthesis **b.** Heterotroph **c.** Glucose **d.** Atp) :: Producer : Consumer

83. Ratchet : (**a.** Tools **b.** Shrink **c.** Yards **d.** Stages) :: Grow : Inches

84. 3.7 : 4 :: 7.3 : (**a.** 7 **b.** 7.5 **c.** 8 **d.** 7.4)

85. Blue Eyes : Recessive :: Brown Eyes : (**a.** Genotype **b.** Phenotype **c.** Dominant **d.** Heterozygous)

86. Proton : Neutron :: Positive : (**a.** Negative **b.** Nucleus **c.** Atom **d.** Neutral)

87. Oktoberfest : Mardi Gras :: (**a.** Berlin **b.** Pittsburgh **c.** Oslo **d.** Munich) : New Orleans

88. (**a.** Telegraph **b.** Autograph **c.** Phonautograph **d.** Telephone) : Phonograph :: Velocipede : Bicycle

89. $\frac{1}{3} : \frac{2}{3}$ :: (**a.** 20 **b.** 30 **c.** 10 **d.** 120) : 60

90. 20 : 240 :: (**a.** 18 **b.** 12 **c.** 15 **d.** 6) : 180

91. *My Bondage and My Freedom* : *I Know Why the Caged Bird Sings* :: (**a.** *Black Boy* **b.** *An American Life* **c.** *Desert Solitaire* **d.** *Invisible Man*) : *Their Eyes Were Watching God*

92. (**a.** Boris Godunov **b.** The Fire Bird **c.** Toccata and Fugue **d.** Ave Maria) : The Rites of Spring :: Night on Bald Mountain : Pictures at an Exhibition

93. Rivera : Murals :: (**a.** Degas **b.** Hopper **c.** Matisse **d.** Calder) : Mobiles

94. Fatuous : Sensible :: (**a.** Fat **b.** Lofty **c.** Specific **d.** Generous) : Generic

95. Baleful : Beneficent :: Sparse : (**a.** Woeful **b.** Belligerent **c.** Corrupt **d.** Dense)

96. First : (**a.** Australopithecus **b.** Africanus **c.** Most Complete **d.** Oldest) :: Dart : Johanson

97. Syntax : Phonology :: (**a.** Phonetics **b.** Morphology **c.** Grammar **d.** Applied) : Semantics

98. Extend : Abridge :: Establish : (**a.** Uproot **b.** Bridge **c.** Fix **d.** Make)

99. Surfeit : Excess :: Excuse : (**a.** Forfeit **b.** Disallow **c.** Explanation **d.** Surface)

100. Cordon : (**a.** Corduroy **b.** Troops **c.** Chicken **d.** Thread) :: Seam : Stitches

101. Religion : Speech :: Press : (**a.** Assembly **b.** Bear arms **c.** Militia **d.** Fair Trial)

102. Kuhn : Butenandt :: Domagk : (**a.** Curie **b.** Pasternak **c.** Pauling **d.** Gordimer)

103. (**a.** Fame **b.** Shame **c.** Inequality **d.** Balance) : Ignominy :: Equity : Fairness

104. Curry : King :: (**a.** Bush **b.** Oswald **c.** Hinckley **d.** Brady) : Reagan

105. Butterfly : (**a.** Moth **b.** Fly **c.** Grasshopper **d.** Beetle) :: Lepidoptera : Orthoptera

106. Log 10 : Log 100 :: 1 : (**a.** 2 **b.** 4 **c.** 10 **d.** 20)

107. Quicksilver : Mercury :: Goldbrick : (**a.** Worker **b.** Idler **c.** Money **d.** Idol)

108. 186 : 50 :: Hurricane : (**a.** Tropical Depression **b.** Tropical Storm **c.** Eye **d.** Surge)

109. Neanderthal : Germany :: Cro-Magnon : (**a.** Botswana **b.** Kenya **c.** France **d.** China)

110. (**a.** Jakarta **b.** Cubao **c.** Manila **d.** Quezon City) : Philippines :: Istanbul : Turkey

111. Spontaneous Generation : (**a.** Biogenesis **b.** Big Bang **c.** Maggots **d.** Hypothesis) :: Evolution : Creationism

112. Sputnik : Atlantis :: (**a.** Hubble **b.** Challenger **c.** Telstar **d.** Discovery) : Endeavour

113. (**a.** Obscure **b.** Whip **c.** Lie **d.** Explain) : Obfuscate :: Hinder : Help

114. Ammonia : 12 :: Vinegar : (**a.** 1 **b.** 3 **c.** 7 **d.** 14)

115. Invective : Abuse :: Imposture : (**a.** Sham **b.** Imposition **c.** Injection **d.** Insurrection)

116. Lapidary : (**a.** Cows **b.** Gems **c.** Rabbits **d.** Movies) :: Dramaturge : Plays

117. Tarpaulin : Rain :: (**a.** Stove **b.** Picnic **c.** Puddle **d.** Apron) : Stain

118. Sine x : Opposite :: Cosine x : (**a.** Hypotenuse **b.** Tangent x **c.** Adjacent **d.** Secant x)

119. Rotation : (**a.** Earth **b.** Sun **c.** Hemisphere **d.** Axis) :: Revolution : Point In Space

120. Place : Manner :: Alveolar : (**a.** Nasal **b.** Velar **c.** Tongue **d.** Length)

Answers

1. **Forte** : Loud :: Piano : Quiet

   The answer is **c.** In music, the Italian word forte means loud and the Italian word piano means quiet.

2. **Biography** : Documentary :: Book : Film

   The answer is **d.** A book about a nonfiction person is called a biography. A film about a nonfiction person is called a documentary.

3. Mythical : Historical :: General : **Particular**

   The answer is **b.** Mythical is an antonym for historical, and general is an antonym for particular.

4. Son : Nuclear :: **Cousin** : Extended

   The answer is **c.** A son is part of a nuclear family, and a cousin is part of an extended family.

5. Gilbert : Lerner :: **Sullivan** : Loewe

   The answer is **b.** W.S. Gilbert and Arthur Sullivan were a British team best known for writing comic operas. Alan Jay Lerner and Frederick Loewe were an American team who wrote songs for Broadway shows.

6. 6 : 66 :: **12** : 132

   The answer is **d.** 6 times 11 equals 66. 12 times 11 equals 132.

7. Jalopy : Car :: **Dump** : House

   The answer is **b.** A jalopy is an old, dilapidated car, and a dump is a term for a dilapidated house.

8. Denim : Cotton :: **Linen** : Flax

   The answer is **d.** Denim is a fabric made from cotton, and linen is a fabric made from flax.

9. Cabana : Pool :: Chalet : **Mountain**

   The answer is **d.** A cabana can be found near a pool, and a chalet is found near a mountain.

10. Iran : **Persia** :: Germany : Prussia

    The answer is **d.** Iran was formerly called Persia, and Germany was formerly called Prussia.

11. Earth : 365 :: Mercury : **88**

    The answer is **b.** An Earth year is 365 Earth days; a Mercury year is 88 Earth days.

12. Des Moines : Iowa :: **Austin** : Texas

    The answer is **c.** Des Moines is the capital of Iowa, and Austin is the capital of Texas.

13. Alcohol : **Liver** :: Tobacco : Lungs

    The answer is **b.** Long-term effects of alcohol abuse include liver damage; long-term effects of tobacco include lung disease.

14. Comedy : **Kabuki** :: Greece : Japan

The answer is **b.** Comedy is a kind of theater that originated in Greece. Kabuki is a kind of theater that originated in Japan.

15. Rumba : Ragtime :: **Samba** : Bebop

The answer is **b.** Rumba and samba are two types of Latin dances. Ragtime and bebop are two types of jazz music.

16. Circular : Elongated :: Red Blood Cell : **Neuron**

The answer is **b.** Red blood cells are circular; neurons are elongated.

17. Power Plant : Storage Area :: **Mitochondria** : Vacuole

The answer is **a.** Mitochondria are cells' power plants; vacuoles are cells' storage areas.

18. Perimeter : Area :: 4x : x^2

The answer is **c.** The perimeter of a square is the sum of the lengths of its sides. A square that has a side x has a perimeter of $4x$ and an area of x^2.

19. Coif : Hair :: **Score** : Musical

The answer is **d.** To coif means to arrange hair, and to score means to arrange a musical.

20. Red : White :: **Oxygen** : Protection

The answer is **c.** Red blood cells' primary function is to carry oxygen to cells; white blood cells' primary function is to provide immunity by fighting infectious diseases.

21. Duvet : **Bed** :: Beret : Head

The answer is **c.** A duvet goes on a bed, and a beret goes on a head.

22. Stage : Play :: **Shoot** : Film

The answer is **a.** To put on a play is to stage it and to make a film is to shoot it.

23. Moccasin : Snake :: **Loafer** : Shoe

The answer is **d.** A moccasin is a type of snake, and a loafer is a type of shoe.

24. Monarch : **Butterfly** :: King : Cobra

The answer is **b.** A monarch is a type of butterfly and a king is a type of cobra.

25. Junket : **Trip** :: Junk : Trash

The answer is **b.** A junket is a synonym for a trip, and junk is a synonym for trash.

26. Inner : Outer :: Mercury : **Uranus**

The answer is **d.** Mercury, Venus, Earth, and Mars are the inner planets. Uranus is an outer planet.

27. Tuscan : Italy :: Provençal : **France**

The answer is **c.** Tuscan relates to a region of Italy, and Provençal relates to a region of France.

28. Ragtime : United States :: Raga : **India**

The answer is **d.** Ragtime is a type of music from the United States, and raga is a type of music from India.

29. Diamond : Baseball :: Court : **Squash**

The answer is **d.** Baseball is played on a diamond, and squash is played on a court.

30. Brownies : Cocoa :: Omelet : Egg

The answer is **c.** Brownies have cocoa as an ingredient, and an omelet has eggs as an ingredient.

31. 15 : 14 :: 5 : **7**

The answer is **b.** 5 is a factor of 15, it divides evenly into 15. 7 is a factor of 14; it divides evenly into 14.

32. Stock : Soup :: Latex : Paint

The answer is **d.** Stock is the base of soup, and latex is the base of paint.

33. Seer : Future :: Historian : Past

The answer is **b.** A seer looks into the future, and a historian looks into the past.

34. Protractor : Angle :: Ruler : **Length**

The answer is **b.** A protractor is used to measure an angle, and a ruler is used to measure length.

35. Myopic : Farsighted :: **Famous** : Obscure

The answer is **b.** Myopic is an antonym for far-sighted, and famous is an antonym of obscure.

36. La Bohème : **Puccini** :: Pagliacci : Leoncavallo

The answer is **a.** La Bohème is an opera by Giacomo Puccini, and Pagliacci is an opera by Ruggero Leoncavallo.

37. Tacit : Implied :: **Shoddy** : Inferior

The answer is **a.** Tacit is another word for implied, and shoddy is another word for inferior.

38. Poet : Cinquain :: Composer : Fugue

The answer is **d.** A poet would write a cinquain, which is a type of a poem. A composer would write a fugue, which is a type of musical composition.

39. Zeus : Jupiter :: Hermes : **Mercury**

The answer is **c.** In Greek and Roman mythology, Zeus is the name for the Greek god and Jupiter is the Roman equivalent. Similarly, Hermes is the Greek god and Mercury is the Roman equivalent.

40. Glockenspiel : Xylophone :: Metal : Wood

The answer is **a.** The bars of a glockenspiel are made of metal. The bars of a xylophone are made of wood.

41. Aphrodite : Venus :: Poseidon : Neptune

The answer is **b.** Aphrodite is the Greek name for the Roman goddess Venus; Poseidon is the Greek name for the Roman god Neptune.

42. Midas : **Gold** :: Circe : Pig

The answer is **a.** In Greek mythology, Midas was a king who turned everything he touched into gold. Circe was a goddess who turned humans into pigs.

43. Prospero : Masque of the Red Death :: Fortunato : Cask of Amontillado

The answer is **c.** Prospero is a character in Edgar Allan Poe's short story "The Masque of the Red Death." Fortunato is a character in Poe's "The Cask of Amontillado."

44. Vaunt : Boast :: Skewer : **Criticize**

The answer is **b.** To vaunt means to boast, and to skewer means to criticize.

45. Mosaics : Tile :: **Macramé** : Yarn

The answer is **d.** Tile is the material used in the art of mosaics. Yarn is the material used in the art of macramé.

46. Bunker Hill : Revolutionary War :: **Bull Run** : Civil War

The answer is **d.** Bunker Hill was a battle site in the Revolutionary War, and Bull Run was a battle site in the Civil War.

47. Faulkner : Southern :: Hawthorne : Northern

The answer is **b.** William Faulkner is known as a Southern writer, and Nathaniel Hawthorne is known as a Northern writer.

48. Alveoli : Respiratory :: **Capillaries** : Circulatory

The answer is **c.** Alveoli exchange oxygen and carbon dioxide with the respiratory system; capillaries are the site of exchange of gases and nutrients in the circulatory system.

49. Van Buren : 8th :: **Lincoln** : 16th

The answer is **a.** Martin Van Buren was the 8th president, and Abraham Lincoln was the 16th.

50. Xerxes : Persia :: Nebuchadnezzar : **Babylon**

The answer is **c.** Xerxes was the ancient king of Persia, and Nebuchadnezzar was the ancient king of Babylon.

51. Le Corbusier : Architecture :: Rodin : **Sculpture**

The answer is **b.** Le Corbusier was a French architect, and Rodin was a French sculptor.

52. Vein : Artery :: Thin : **Thick**

The answer is **c.** Veins are thin-walled; arteries are thick-walled.

53. Menshevik : **Bolshevik** :: Kerensky : Lenin

The answer is **b.** Kerensky led the Mensheviks and Lenin led the Bolsheviks after the Russian Revolution.

54. Gall : Vex :: Hex : **Jinx**

The answer is **b.** To gall is to vex, and to hex is to jinx.

55. Fodder : Silo :: Art : Museum

The answer is **b.** Fodder is kept in a silo, and art is kept in a museum.

56. Iota : Jot :: **Ilk** : Type

The answer is **b.** Iota and jot are synonyms, as are ilk and type.

57. Cohesion : Unity :: Dearth : Scarcity

The answer is **c.** Cohesion and unity are synonyms, as are dearth and scarcity.

58. 18th : Prohibition of Alcohol :: **21st** : Repeal of 18th

The answer is **b.** The 18th amendment of the U.S. Constitution outlined the prohibition of alcohol and the 21st amendment repealed the 18th amendment.

59. Bivouac : **Camp** :: Axis : Alliance

The answer is **d.** A bivouac is another word for a camp, and an axis is another word for an alliance.

60. Chronograph : Time :: Pipette : **Volume**

The answer is **d.** A chronograph is an instrument used to measure time. A pipette is an instrument used to measure liquid volume.

61. Secret : Furtive :: Audible : **Resonant**

The answer is **a.** Furtive is more intensely secret, and resonant is more intensely audible.

62. Pummel : Hit :: **Chant** : Recite

The answer is **c.** To pummel is to hit repeatedly, and to chant is to recite repeatedly.

63. Retton : **Gymnastics** :: Hamill : Figure Skating

The answer is **b.** In 1984, gymnast Mary Lou Retton won a gold Olympic medal. In 1976, Dorothy Hamill won a gold Olympic medal for figure skating.

64. Spleen : Immunological :: Thyroid : Endocrine

The answer is **d.** The spleen is an organ in the immunological system; the thyroid is a gland in the endocrine system.

65. Bile : Liver :: **Enzymes** : Pancreas

The answer is **a.** Bile is produced by the liver; enzymes are produced by the pancreas.

66. Apology : Forgiveness :: Bribe : Influence

The answer is **c.** An apology is used to attain forgiveness, and a bribe is used to attain influence.

67. Purist : Tradition :: Hedonist : Pleasure

The answer is **a.** A purist is fixated on tradition, and a hedonist is fixated on pleasure.

68. United Kingdom : Barbados :: Australia : **Jamaica**

The answer is **d.** The United Kingdom, Barbados, Australia and Jamaica are all countries within the Commonwealth of Nations that have Elizabeth II as their queen.

69. **Cortes** : Aztecs :: Pizarro : Incas

The answer is **b.** Cortes conquered the Aztec Empire just as Pizarro conquered the Incan Empire.

70. Seemly : **Attractive** :: Torrid : Scorching

The answer is **c.** Seemly is a synonym for attractive, and torrid is a synonym for scorching.

71. Mount Rainier : Mount Shasta :: Washington : **California**

The answer is **a.** Mount Rainier is in Washington and Mount Shasta is in California.

72. Iran : Iraq :: Tehran : **Baghdad**

The answer is **b.** Tehran is the capital of Iran and Baghdad is the capital of Iraq.

73. Pepsin : **Stomach** :: Saliva : Mouth

The answer is **c.** Saliva begins digestion in the mouth; pepsin continues digestion in the stomach.

74. McGill : Oxford :: **Canada** : England

The answer is **b.** McGill University is located in Canada, and Oxford University is located in England.

75. Nosegay : Flowers :: **Team** : Players

The answer is **c.** A nosegay is a group of flowers, and a team is a group of players.

76. .03 : .0009 :: **.002** : .000004

The answer is **c.** .03 squared is equal to .0009 and .002 squared is equal to .000004.

77. Isocracy : **All** :: Meritocracy : Merit

The answer is **b.** An isocracy is rule by all and a meritocracy is rule by merit.

78. Mars : War :: **Saturn** : Agriculture

The answer is **c.** In Roman mythology, Mars was the god of war and Saturn was the god of agriculture.

79. Ethiopia : Abyssinia :: Zaire : **Congo**

The answer is **c.** Ethiopia was formerly named Abyssinia and Zaire was formerly named Congo.

80. $\frac{1}{2} : \frac{1}{4} :: \frac{2}{3} : \frac{1}{3}$

The answer is **b.** $\frac{1}{4}$ is half of $\frac{1}{2}$. $\frac{1}{3}$ is half of $\frac{2}{3}$.

81. Tooth : **Comb** :: Tine : Fork

The answer is **c.** A tooth is part of a comb, and a tine is part of a fork.

82. Autotroph : **Heterotroph** :: Producer : Consumer

The answer is **b.** Autotrophs produce their own energy through photosynthesis; heterotrophs consume energy produced by others.

83. Ratchet : **Stages** :: Grow : Inches

The answer is **d.** To ratchet means to increase by stages, and to grow is to increase by inches.

84. 3.7 : 4 :: 7.3 : 7

The answer is **a.** 3.7 rounded to the nearest whole number is 4. 7.3 rounded to the nearest whole number is 7.

85. Blue Eyes : Recessive :: Brown Eyes : **Dominant**

The answer is **c.** Blue eyes are a recessive trait; brown eyes are a dominant trait.

86. Proton : Neutron :: Positive : **Neutral**

The answer is **d.** Protons are positively charged; neutrons are neutral.

87. Oktoberfest : Mardi Gras :: **Munich** : New Orleans

The answer is **d.** Oktoberfest is a festival that takes place every year in Munich, Bavaria. Mardi Gras is a festival that takes place every year in New Orleans, Louisiana.

88. Phonautograph : Phonograph :: Velocipede : Bicycle

The answer is **c.** The phonautograph is an early version of the phonograph; the velocipede is an early version of the bicycle.

89. $\frac{1}{3} : \frac{2}{3}$ :: **30** : 60

The answer is **b.** 30 is half of 60, and $\frac{1}{3}$ is half of $\frac{2}{3}$.

90. 20 : 240 :: **15** : 180

The answer is **c.** 20 times 12 is 240, and 15 times 12 is 180.

91. *My Bondage and My Freedom* : *I Know Why the Caged Bird Sings* :: **Invisible Man** : *Their Eyes Were Watching God*

The answer is **d.** *My Bondage and My Freedom* by Frederick Douglass and *I Know Why the Caged Bird Sings* by Maya Angelou are both autobiographies. *Invisible Man* by Ralph Ellison and *Their Eyes Were Watching God* by Zora Neale Hurston are both fictional novels.

92. The Fire Bird : The Rite of Spring :: Night on Bald Mountain : Pictures at an Exhibition

The answer is **b.** "The Fire Bird" and "The Rites of Spring" were both written by composer Igor Stravinsky. "Night on Bald Mountain" and "Pictures at an Exhibition" were both written by composer Modest Mussorgsky.

93. Rivera : Murals :: **Calder** : Mobiles

The answer is **d.** Diego Rivera was an artist known for his murals, and Alexander Calder was known for his mobiles.

94. Fatuous : Sensible :: **Specific** : Generic

The answer is **c.** Fatuous is an antonym for sensible, and specific is an antonym for generic.

95. Baleful : Beneficent :: Sparse : **Dense**

The answer is **d.** Baleful is an antonym for beneficent, and sparse is an antonym for dense.

96. First : **Most complete** :: Dart : Johanson

The answer is **c.** Donald Johanson identified the oldest of all known Australopithecus species in 1974. Raymond Dart made the first discovery of an Australopithecus species in 1924.

97. Syntax : Phonology :: **Morphology** : Semantics

The answer is **b.** The four main areas of theoretical linguistics are syntax, phonology, morphology, and semantics.

98. Extend : Abridge :: Establish : **Uproot**

The answer is **a.** To extend is an antonym of to abridge, and to establish is an antonym of to uproot.

99. Surfeit : Excess :: Excuse : **Explanation**

The answer is **c.** Surfeit is another word for excess, and excuse is another word for explanation.

100. Cordon : **Troops** :: Seam : Stitches

The answer is **b.** A cordon is a line of troops; a seam is a line of stitches.

101. Religion : Speech :: Press : **Assembly**

The answer is **a.** The first amendment of the U.S. Constitution deals with the freedom of religion, speech, press, and assembly.

102. Kuhn : Butenandt :: Domagk : **Pasternak**

The answer is **b.** Kuhn, Butenandt, Domagk and Pasternak are the only four Nobel Prize award winners who were forced by authorities to decline their prizes.

103. **Shame** : Ignominy :: Equity : Fairness

The answer is **b.** Shame is a synonym for ignominy, and equity is a synonym for fairness.

104. Curry : King :: **Hinckley** : Reagan

The answer is **c.** Izola Curry attempted to assassinate Martin Luther King Jr. and John Hinckley attempted to assassinate President Reagan.

105. Butterfly : **Grasshopper** :: Lepidoptera : Orthoptera

The answer is **c.** A butterfly is of the order Lepidoptera; a grasshopper is of the order Orthoptera.

106. Log 10 : Log 100 :: 1 : **2**

The answer is **a.** The log of 10 is 1 and the log of 100 is 2.

107. Quicksilver : Mercury :: Goldbrick : **Idler**

The answer is **b.** Quicksilver is a synonym for mercury, and goldbrick is a synonym for an idler.

108. 186 : 50 :: Hurricane : **Tropical Storm**

The answer is **b.** A hurricane has sustained winds of up to 186 miles per hour; a tropical storm has sustained winds of between 38 and 74 miles per hour.

109. Neanderthal : Germany :: Cro-Magnon : **France**

The answer is **c.** The first Neanderthal fossils were found in Germany; the first Cro-Magnon fossils were found in France.

110. Quezon City : Philippines :: Istanbul : Turkey

The answer is **d.** Quezon City is the largest city in the Philippines. Istanbul is the largest city in Turkey.

111. Spontaneous generation : **Biogenesis** :: Evolution : Creationism

The answer is **a.** Spontaneous generation is the belief that life could come from nonliving matter; this is the opposite of biogenesis, which is the belief that life can only come from life. Evolution and creationism are likewise competing hypotheses for how life came to be present on Earth.

112. Sputnik : Atlantis :: **Telstar** : Endeavour

The answer is **c.** Sputnik and Telstar are both names of satellites. Atlantis and Endeavour are both names of space shuttles.

113. Explain : Obfuscate :: Hinder : Help

The answer is **d.** To explain is an antonym of to obfuscate, and to hinder is an antonym of to help.

114. Ammonia : 12 :: Vinegar : **3**

The answer is **b.** Vinegar has a pH of around 3, which is relatively acidic; ammonia has a pH of about 12, which is relatively alkaline.

115. Invective : Abuse :: Imposture : **Sham**

The answer is **a.** Invective is a synonym for abuse, and imposture is a synonym for sham.

116. Lapidary : **Gems** :: Dramaturge : Plays

The answer is **b.** A lapidary is one who works with gems, and a dramaturge works with plays.

117. Tarpaulin : Rain :: **Apron** : Stain

The answer is **d.** A tarpaulin is used to protect from rain, and an apron is used to protect from stains.

118. Sine x : Opposite :: Cosine x : **Adjacent**

The answer is **c.** In a right triangle, sine x equals the ratio of the opposite side/hypotenuse. The cosine x equals the ratio of the adjacent side/hypotenuse.

119. Rotation : **Axis** :: Revolution : Point in space

The answer is **d.** Rotation is the turning of a body on its axis, and revolution is the motion of a body around a given point in space.

120. Place : Manner :: Alveolar : **Nasal**

The answer is **a.** Alveolar is a place of articulation, where the obstruction of the consonant occurs in the vocal tract. Nasal is a manner of articulation, how air escapes from the vocal tract when a consonant sound is made.

Scoring Your MAT Practice Test

As mentioned in Chapter 1, when you receive your personal score report for the official MAT, you'll be provided with a scaled score and two percentile ranks, all of which are derived from the number of items you answered correctly—known as your raw score.

Because there are different forms and formats of the official MAT, and typically 20 of the 120 questions on the official MAT are experimental and do not count toward your official scaled score and percentile ranks, it is impossible to create an accurate raw score to scaled score or raw score to percentile chart for this and the other practice tests found in this book. In the end, you are striving to correctly answer the highest number of questions as possible and familiarize yourself with the MAT format so you're fully prepared to do your best on test day. For now, what's much more important than your overall score is how you did on each of the content areas tested by the exam. You need to diagnose your strengths and weaknesses so that you can concentrate your efforts as you prepare. The question types are mixed in the practice exam, so in order to tell where your strengths and weaknesses lie, you'll need to compare your answer sheet with the following **MAT Practice Test 9 Review,** which shows which of the content areas each question falls into.

Use your performance here in conjunction with the LearningExpress Test Preparation System in Chapter 2 to help you devise a study plan. You should plan to spend more time studying areas that correspond to the questions you found hardest and less time on the content areas in which you did well. Once you have spent some time reviewing, take the next MAT practice test to see if you've improved.

MAT PRACTICE TEST 9 REVIEW	
CONTENT AREA	**QUESTION NUMBERS**
Language and Vocabulary	3, 7, 9, 21, 35, 37, 44, 54, 56, 57, 59, 61, 62, 66, 67, 70, 81, 94, 95, 98, 99, 100, 103, 113, 115
Humanities	1, 2, 5, 14, 15, 22, 36, 38, 40, 41, 42, 43, 45, 46, 47, 49, 50, 51, 91, 92, 93
Social Science	10, 12, 27, 39, 53, 58, 68, 69, 71, 72, 74, 77, 78, 79, 97, 101, 102, 104, 110, 120
Natural Science	11, 13, 16, 17, 20, 24, 26, 48, 52, 64, 65, 73, 82, 85, 86, 96, 105, 108, 109, 111, 114, 119
General	4, 8, 19, 23, 25, 28, 29, 30, 32, 33, 34, 55, 60, 63, 75, 83, 87, 88, 107, 112, 116, 117
Mathematics	6, 18, 31, 76, 80, 84, 89, 90, 106, 118

12 ▶ MAT Practice Test 10

CHAPTER SUMMARY

Here's another sample MAT test for you to practice with.

For this practice test, simulate the actual test-taking experience as closely as you can. Find a quiet place to work where you won't be disturbed. If you own this book, use the answer sheet on the following pages and find some #2 pencils to fill in the circles. Use a timer or stopwatch to time yourself— you'll have 60 minutes to complete the official MAT. After you take the test, use the detailed answer explanations that follow to review any questions you missed.

MAT Practice Test 10

1.	ⓐ	ⓑ	ⓒ	ⓓ	46.	ⓐ	ⓑ	ⓒ	ⓓ	91.	ⓐ	ⓑ	ⓒ	ⓓ
2.	ⓐ	ⓑ	ⓒ	ⓓ	47.	ⓐ	ⓑ	ⓒ	ⓓ	92.	ⓐ	ⓑ	ⓒ	ⓓ
3.	ⓐ	ⓑ	ⓒ	ⓓ	48.	ⓐ	ⓑ	ⓒ	ⓓ	93.	ⓐ	ⓑ	ⓒ	ⓓ
4.	ⓐ	ⓑ	ⓒ	ⓓ	49.	ⓐ	ⓑ	ⓒ	ⓓ	94.	ⓐ	ⓑ	ⓒ	ⓓ
5.	ⓐ	ⓑ	ⓒ	ⓓ	50.	ⓐ	ⓑ	ⓒ	ⓓ	95.	ⓐ	ⓑ	ⓒ	ⓓ
6.	ⓐ	ⓑ	ⓒ	ⓓ	51.	ⓐ	ⓑ	ⓒ	ⓓ	96.	ⓐ	ⓑ	ⓒ	ⓓ
7.	ⓐ	ⓑ	ⓒ	ⓓ	52.	ⓐ	ⓑ	ⓒ	ⓓ	97.	ⓐ	ⓑ	ⓒ	ⓓ
8.	ⓐ	ⓑ	ⓒ	ⓓ	53.	ⓐ	ⓑ	ⓒ	ⓓ	98.	ⓐ	ⓑ	ⓒ	ⓓ
9.	ⓐ	ⓑ	ⓒ	ⓓ	54.	ⓐ	ⓑ	ⓒ	ⓓ	99.	ⓐ	ⓑ	ⓒ	ⓓ
10.	ⓐ	ⓑ	ⓒ	ⓓ	55.	ⓐ	ⓑ	ⓒ	ⓓ	100.	ⓐ	ⓑ	ⓒ	ⓓ
11.	ⓐ	ⓑ	ⓒ	ⓓ	56.	ⓐ	ⓑ	ⓒ	ⓓ	101.	ⓐ	ⓑ	ⓒ	ⓓ
12.	ⓐ	ⓑ	ⓒ	ⓓ	57.	ⓐ	ⓑ	ⓒ	ⓓ	102.	ⓐ	ⓑ	ⓒ	ⓓ
13.	ⓐ	ⓑ	ⓒ	ⓓ	58.	ⓐ	ⓑ	ⓒ	ⓓ	103.	ⓐ	ⓑ	ⓒ	ⓓ
14.	ⓐ	ⓑ	ⓒ	ⓓ	59.	ⓐ	ⓑ	ⓒ	ⓓ	104.	ⓐ	ⓑ	ⓒ	ⓓ
15.	ⓐ	ⓑ	ⓒ	ⓓ	60.	ⓐ	ⓑ	ⓒ	ⓓ	105.	ⓐ	ⓑ	ⓒ	ⓓ
16.	ⓐ	ⓑ	ⓒ	ⓓ	61.	ⓐ	ⓑ	ⓒ	ⓓ	106.	ⓐ	ⓑ	ⓒ	ⓓ
17.	ⓐ	ⓑ	ⓒ	ⓓ	62.	ⓐ	ⓑ	ⓒ	ⓓ	107.	ⓐ	ⓑ	ⓒ	ⓓ
18.	ⓐ	ⓑ	ⓒ	ⓓ	63.	ⓐ	ⓑ	ⓒ	ⓓ	108.	ⓐ	ⓑ	ⓒ	ⓓ
19.	ⓐ	ⓑ	ⓒ	ⓓ	64.	ⓐ	ⓑ	ⓒ	ⓓ	109.	ⓐ	ⓑ	ⓒ	ⓓ
20.	ⓐ	ⓑ	ⓒ	ⓓ	65.	ⓐ	ⓑ	ⓒ	ⓓ	110.	ⓐ	ⓑ	ⓒ	ⓓ
21.	ⓐ	ⓑ	ⓒ	ⓓ	66.	ⓐ	ⓑ	ⓒ	ⓓ	111.	ⓐ	ⓑ	ⓒ	ⓓ
22.	ⓐ	ⓑ	ⓒ	ⓓ	67.	ⓐ	ⓑ	ⓒ	ⓓ	112.	ⓐ	ⓑ	ⓒ	ⓓ
23.	ⓐ	ⓑ	ⓒ	ⓓ	68.	ⓐ	ⓑ	ⓒ	ⓓ	113.	ⓐ	ⓑ	ⓒ	ⓓ
24.	ⓐ	ⓑ	ⓒ	ⓓ	69.	ⓐ	ⓑ	ⓒ	ⓓ	114.	ⓐ	ⓑ	ⓒ	ⓓ
25.	ⓐ	ⓑ	ⓒ	ⓓ	70.	ⓐ	ⓑ	ⓒ	ⓓ	115.	ⓐ	ⓑ	ⓒ	ⓓ
26.	ⓐ	ⓑ	ⓒ	ⓓ	71.	ⓐ	ⓑ	ⓒ	ⓓ	116.	ⓐ	ⓑ	ⓒ	ⓓ
27.	ⓐ	ⓑ	ⓒ	ⓓ	72.	ⓐ	ⓑ	ⓒ	ⓓ	117.	ⓐ	ⓑ	ⓒ	ⓓ
28.	ⓐ	ⓑ	ⓒ	ⓓ	73.	ⓐ	ⓑ	ⓒ	ⓓ	118.	ⓐ	ⓑ	ⓒ	ⓓ
29.	ⓐ	ⓑ	ⓒ	ⓓ	74.	ⓐ	ⓑ	ⓒ	ⓓ	119.	ⓐ	ⓑ	ⓒ	ⓓ
30.	ⓐ	ⓑ	ⓒ	ⓓ	75.	ⓐ	ⓑ	ⓒ	ⓓ	120.	ⓐ	ⓑ	ⓒ	ⓓ
31.	ⓐ	ⓑ	ⓒ	ⓓ	76.	ⓐ	ⓑ	ⓒ	ⓓ					
32.	ⓐ	ⓑ	ⓒ	ⓓ	77.	ⓐ	ⓑ	ⓒ	ⓓ					
33.	ⓐ	ⓑ	ⓒ	ⓓ	78.	ⓐ	ⓑ	ⓒ	ⓓ					
34.	ⓐ	ⓑ	ⓒ	ⓓ	79.	ⓐ	ⓑ	ⓒ	ⓓ					
35.	ⓐ	ⓑ	ⓒ	ⓓ	80.	ⓐ	ⓑ	ⓒ	ⓓ					
36.	ⓐ	ⓑ	ⓒ	ⓓ	81.	ⓐ	ⓑ	ⓒ	ⓓ					
37.	ⓐ	ⓑ	ⓒ	ⓓ	82.	ⓐ	ⓑ	ⓒ	ⓓ					
38.	ⓐ	ⓑ	ⓒ	ⓓ	83.	ⓐ	ⓑ	ⓒ	ⓓ					
39.	ⓐ	ⓑ	ⓒ	ⓓ	84.	ⓐ	ⓑ	ⓒ	ⓓ					
40.	ⓐ	ⓑ	ⓒ	ⓓ	85.	ⓐ	ⓑ	ⓒ	ⓓ					
41.	ⓐ	ⓑ	ⓒ	ⓓ	86.	ⓐ	ⓑ	ⓒ	ⓓ					
42.	ⓐ	ⓑ	ⓒ	ⓓ	87.	ⓐ	ⓑ	ⓒ	ⓓ					
43.	ⓐ	ⓑ	ⓒ	ⓓ	88.	ⓐ	ⓑ	ⓒ	ⓓ					
44.	ⓐ	ⓑ	ⓒ	ⓓ	89.	ⓐ	ⓑ	ⓒ	ⓓ					
45.	ⓐ	ⓑ	ⓒ	ⓓ	90.	ⓐ	ⓑ	ⓒ	ⓓ					

Directions: For each question, select the answer choice in the parentheses that best completes the analogy.

1. Presto : Tempo :: (**a.** Vivo **b.** Adagio **c.** Alto **d.** Bassoon) : Range

2. Yellow Submarine : Billie Jean :: Revolver : (**a.** Beatles **b.** Hit **c.** Michael Jackson **d.** Thriller)

3. Mend : Sewing :: Edit : (**a.** Darn **b.** Repair **c.** Manuscript **d.** Makeshift)

4. Alphabetical : (**a.** Sort **b.** Part **c.** List **d.** Order) :: Sequential : Files

5. Monteverdi : (**a.** Germany **b.** Venice **c.** Italy **d.** Greece) :: Haydn : Austria

6. 7 : < 9 :: 12 : (**a.** < 12 **b.** < 10 **c.** ≤ 10 **d.** > 10)

7. 4 : 6 :: (**a.** 2 **b.** 14 **c.** 8 **d.** 10) : 16

8. Brahms : Mahler :: Johannes : (**a.** Antonio **b.** William **c.** Richard **d.** Gustav)

9. Thicket : Shrubs :: (**a.** Sun **b.** Cluster **c.** Orbit **d.** Moon) : Stars

10. Baudelaire : (**a.** Dumas **b.** Fitzgerald **c.** Gilman **d.** Hawthorne) :: Cather : Faulkner

11. Pan : (**a.** Band **b.** Critic **c.** Author **d.** Lawyer) :: Ban : Judge

12. Platoon : Schindler's List :: Vietnam : (**a.** World War II **b.** Korea **c.** The American Revolution **d.** Operation Desert Storm)

13. Valise : (**a.** Bicycle **b.** Glass **c.** Vine **d.** Clothes) :: Cask : Wine

14. Neptune : Poseidon :: Jupiter : (**a.** Nike **b.** Mars **c.** Zeus **d.** Hera)

15. Huckster : (**a.** Corn **b.** Trucking **c.** Policeman **d.** Advertising) :: Gangster : Crime

16. Laconic : Words :: Parched : (**a.** Heat **b.** Moisture **c.** Desert **d.** Vapid)

17. Potable : (**a.** Drinking **b.** Potting **c.** Portable **d.** Navigable) :: Seaworthy : Sailing

18. Rook : Chess :: (**a.** Grass **b.** Tennis **c.** Shuttlecock **d.** Swing) : Badminton

19. (**a.** Chef **b.** Cafeteria **c.** Colleges **d.** Syllabus) : Course :: Menu : Meal

20. (**a.** Sinking **b.** Buoy **c.** Television **d.** River) : Channel :: Flare : Accident

21. Phoenix : Bird :: Pegasus : (**a.** Fish **b.** Horse **c.** Goat **d.** Snake)

22. Indifferent : (**a.** Stoic **b.** Altruist **c.** Cynic **d.** Zealous) :: Ardent : Zealot

23. Bulky : Streamlined :: (**a.** Blimp **b.** Aerodynamic **c.** Cluttered **d.** Obese) : Neat

24. (**a.** Indian **b.** Atlantic **c.** Arctic **d.** Pacific) : Mercury :: Ocean : Planet

25. Socialism : Capitalism :: (**a.** Cooperation **b.** Private property **c.** Duty **d.** Military) : Competition

26. (**a.** Aphrodisiac **b.** Mollusk **c.** Bed **d.** Sandwich) : Oyster :: Paddy : Rice

27. Slight : Hurt :: Lag : (**a.** Tardiness **b.** Braggart **c.** Heft **d.** Haste)

28. Fist : Hand :: (**a.** Wave **b.** Rings **c.** Circuit **d.** Foot) : Loop

29. Bunker Hill : (**a.** Fort Ticonderoga **b.** Salem **c.** Monticello **d.** Fishkill) :: Saratoga : Valley Forge

30. Einstein : Relativity :: (**a.** Galileo **b.** Copernicus **c.** Lamarck **d.** Darwin) : Evolution

31. (**a.** Hog **b.** Sheep **c.** Bear **d.** Chicken) : Lion :: Ursine : Leonine

32. Shortest : Longest :: December : (**a.** June **b.** May **c.** January **d.** March)

33. Cicada : (**a.** Fruit **b.** Mineral **c.** Cat **d.** Insect) :: Collie : Canine

34. Persimmon : (**a.** Cinnamon **b.** Oven **c.** Badger **d.** Berry) :: Cottontail : Rabbit

35. Fern : Plant :: (**a.** Catch **b.** Minnow **c.** Animal **d.** Sparrow) : Fish

36. Mallet : (**a.** Bowling **b.** Ball **c.** Croquet **d.** Net) :: Racket : Tennis

37. Seal : Wax :: (**a.** Stopper **b.** Bottle **c.** Dolphin **d.** Envelope) : Cork

38. $3 : \frac{1}{2}$ :: (**a.** Factor **b.** Integer **c.** Zero **d.** Product) : Fraction

39. Moray : Eel :: Morel : (**a.** Reel **b.** Slow **c.** Fungus **d.** Aquarium)

40. AC : Alternating current :: DC : (**a.** Diverse current **b.** Direct current **c.** Diode charge **d.** Dived cell)

41. Marshal : Prisoner :: Principal : (**a.** Teacher **b.** President **c.** Doctrine **d.** Student)

42. Moisten : (**a.** Water **b.** Soak **c.** Oven **d.** Grow) :: Cool : Freeze

43. Pylon : (**a.** Traffic **b.** Orange **c.** Safety **d.** Clarinet) :: Baton : Orchestra

44. Shankar : Liszt :: (**a.** Harp **b.** Sitar **c.** Tabla **d.** Lute) : Piano

45. Uffizi : (**a.** Rome **b.** Florence **c.** Berlin **d.** Madrid) :: Guggenheim : New York

46. American Revolution : Civil War :: Lexington and Concord : (**a.** Harper's Ferry **b.** Monticello **c.** Fredericksburg **d.** Gettysburg)

47. Wedge : Inclined plane :: Axe : (**a.** Screw **b.** Pulley **c.** Cat's paw **d.** Ramp)

48. Paris : (**a.** Manhattan **b.** Chicago **c.** London **d.** Madrid) :: Tate Modern : Louvre

49. (**a.** Cornwallis **b.** Sherman **c.** Ferdinand **d.** Jefferson) : Washington :: Lee : Grant

50. Physics : (**a.** Earthquakes **b.** Matter **c.** Poetry **d.** Sonatas) :: Eugenics : Heredity

51. Haiku : (**a.** One **b.** Three **c.** Five **d.** Seven) :: Villanelle : Nineteen

52. (**a.** Little Tramp **b.** Charlie **c.** Great Dictator **d.** Mustache) : Duke :: Chaplin : Wayne

53. Fop : (**a.** Appearance **b.** Movie **c.** Punishment **d.** Fairytale) :: Documentary : Reality

54. Allow : Resist :: Conductor : (**a.** Reducer **b.** Resistor **c.** Insulator **d.** Current)

55. Pastel : Chalk :: (**a.** Charcoal **b.** Grease **c.** Flour **d.** Dough) : Polymer

56. Oedipus : Jocasta :: (**a.** Agamemnon **b.** Aeschylus **c.** Electra **d.** Laius) : Clytemnestra

57. Gold : Au :: Silver : (**a.** Pb **b.** Ag **c.** Fe **d.** Sn)

58. Scythe : Shear :: Trowel : (**a.** Fasten **b.** Shape **c.** Slice **d.** Protect)

59. Dalí : (**a.** Surreal **b.** The Persistence of Memory **c.** Watch **d.** Ant) :: Magritte : The Son of Man

60. Vasquez de Coronado : Arizona :: Ponce de Leon : (**a.** Mississippi **b.** Missouri **c.** Florida **d.** Mexico)

61. 18th Amendment : Prohibition :: 19th Amendment : (**a.** Speech **b.** Suffrage **c.** Slavery **d.** Arms)

62. Dickinson : (**a.** Novella **b.** Poem **c.** Song **d.** Play) :: Dickens : Novel

63. Sniff : Inhale :: (**a.** Crush **b.** Snit **c.** Snip **d.** Adhere) : Lop

64. Chicken : Capon :: Horse : (**a.** Stallion **b.** Mare **c.** Filly **d.** Gelding)

65. Thrifty : (**a.** Virtue **b.** Vice **c.** Avarice **d.** Self-control) :: Hungry : Gluttonous

66. Pallid : Color :: Tactless : (**a.** Hue **b.** Tasteless **c.** Verve **d.** Diplomacy)

67. Coach : Rickshaw :: Sleigh : (**a.** Ferry **b.** Sled **c.** Ski **d.** Pedicab)

68. Admonish : (**a.** Administer **b.** Celebrate **c.** Negotiate **d.** Berate) :: Defeat : Conquer

69. Mercenary : Wages :: Dilettante : (**a.** Enjoyment **b.** Rifle **c.** Strife **d.** Market)

70. Obesity : Lack of vitamin C :: Diabetes : (**a.** High blood pressure **b.** Scurvy **c.** Exercise **d.** Malnutrition)

71. Scruff : Neck :: Stern : (**a.** Lecture **b.** Dirty **c.** Boat **d.** Warning)

72. Marquette : (**a.** Missouri **b.** Mississippi **c.** Lake Superior **d.** St. Lawrence) :: Hudson : Hudson

73. Outrage : Peeve :: Strive : (**a.** Attempt **b.** Curse **c.** Duel **d.** Shun)

74. Pavlov : Skinner :: Dogs : (**a.** Chimpanzees **b.** Snakes **c.** Light **d.** Rats)

75. (**a.** Blitzkrieg **b.** Atomic Bomb **c.** Trench **d.** Hand) : Tank :: World War I : World War II

76. Proton-Proton : Repel :: (**a.** Electron-Proton **b.** Electron-Neutron **c.** Electron-Electron **d.** Proton-Electron) : Attract

77. Potential : (**a.** Equilibrium **b.** Kinetic **c.** Activation **d.** Converted) :: Stored : Active

78. Ganymede : Jupiter :: (**a.** Hercules **b.** Titan **c.** Io **d.** Moon) : Saturn

79. Franny : Master :: (**a.** Alexander **b.** Rye **c.** Follower **d.** Zooey) : Margarita

80. (**a.** Lithography **b.** Calligraphy **c.** Choreography **d.** Cartography) : Dance :: Cinematography : Image

81. Pride : (**a.** Proud **b.** Forecast **c.** Sunny **d.** Fall) :: Calm : Storm

82. (**a.** Brief **b.** Judge **c.** Hypothesis **d.** Lawyer) : Court Case :: Abstract : Research Paper

83. 17 : 70 :: 21 : (**a.** 20 **b.** 27 **c.** $\sqrt{4}$ **d.** $\sqrt{1}$)

84. 212 : Fahrenheit :: (**a.** 0 **b.** 50 **c.** 100 **d.** 200) : Celsius

85. Dinosaurs : Mammals :: Mesozoic : (**a.** Precambrian **b.** Triassic **c.** Paleozoic **d.** Cenozoic)

86. Mandible : Jaw :: Metatarsal : (**a.** Chew **b.** Chest **c.** Foot **d.** Neck)

87. Femur : (**a.** Foot **b.** Thigh **c.** Phalange **d.** Muscle) :: Fibula : Calf

88. Flappers : 20s :: Mods : (**a.** 40s **b.** 50s **c.** 60s **d.** 70s)

89. Piston : Blade :: Sump : (**a.** Crankshaft **b.** Oil filter **c.** Head gasket **d.** Hub)

90. -5 : 25 :: .4 : (**a.** -4 **b.** .16 **c.** -.16 **d.** 4)

91. Plaid : Taupe :: (**a.** Amber **b.** Argyle **c.** Azure **d.** Aqua) : Auburn

92. (**a.** Cartography **b.** Husbandry **c.** Species **d.** Cryptography) : Codes :: Ornithology : Birds

93. Vamp : Shoe :: Hood : (**a.** Jacket **b.** Car **c.** Clean **d.** Crook)

94. 3^0 : 3^{-1} :: 3^2 : (**a.** 3^3 **b.** 3^1 **c.** 3^{-1} **d.** 3^{-2})

95. $\frac{6}{5}$: $\frac{2}{5}$ :: $\frac{2}{3}$: (**a.** $\frac{1}{3}$ **b.** $\frac{1}{6}$ **c.** $\frac{1}{9}$ **d.** $\frac{2}{9}$)

96. (**a.** Nonagon **b.** Hexagon **c.** Septum **d.** Octagon) : Nine :: Pentagon : Five

97. (**a.** Hoover **b.** Taft **c.** Mckinley **d.** Ford) : 1901 :: Lincoln : 1865

98. Wattle : (**a.** Waffle **b.** Griddle **c.** Gait **d.** Neck) :: Crust : Bread

99. (**a.** Spill **b.** Pitch **c.** Spool **d.** Sputter) : Spiel :: Snarl : Mess

100. El Cid : Spain :: Alexander : (**a.** Alexandria **b.** Britain **c.** Germany **d.** Macedonia)

101. (**a.** Logical **b.** Fortuitous **c.** Sartorial **d.** Homemade) : Tailored :: Gallant : Brave

102. Succor : (**a.** Aid **b.** Offense **c.** Flavor **d.** Sleep) :: Ire : Anger

103. (**a.** Confuse **b.** Disagree **c.** Exhort **d.** Enjoy) : Urge :: Enthrall : Interest

104. Kierkegaard : Nietzsche :: Peirce : (**a.** James **b.** Frege **c.** Wittgenstein **d.** Hegel)

105. Rack : (**a.** Billiards **b.** Scuba diving **c.** Railing **d.** Boating) :: Tack : Sailing

106. Paleocene : Tertiary :: Pleistocene : (**a.** Cenozoic **b.** Quaternary **c.** Triassic **d.** Miocene)

107. Epaulet : Shoulder :: Cravat : (**a.** Head **b.** Arm **c.** Neck **d.** Foot)

108. Cosine x : Secant x :: x : (**a.** x^2 **b.** $\frac{1}{x}$ **c.** $2x$ **d.** x^{-1})

109. Ankara : Turkey :: (**a.** Teheran **b.** Baghdad **c.** Istanbul **d.** Jordan) : Iraq

110. Tokyo : Edo :: (**a.** China **b.** Sri Lanka **c.** Mt. Fuji **d.** Vietnam) : Ceylon

111. Cytology : (**a.** Cyclones **b.** Psychology **c.** Pharmacology **d.** Cells) :: Geology : Rocks

112. Deference : Elder :: Indifference : (**a.** Defendant **b.** Child **c.** Stranger **d.** Judge)

113. Heliotrope : (**a.** Cake **b.** Angel **c.** Candle **d.** Shrub) :: Turnover : Pastry

114. (**a.** Tree **b.** Oak **c.** Forest **d.** Cone) : Deciduous :: Pine : Coniferous

115. (**a.** Bleat **b.** Wool **c.** Rot **d.** Fold) : Sheep :: Blight : Potato

116. Saluki : (**a.** London **b.** Egypt **c.** Chile **d.** Spain) :: Akita : Japan

117. (**a.** Senate **b.** Player **c.** Rookie **d.** Junior) : Team :: Freshman : Congress

118. 23 : 5 :: 34 : (**a.** 2 **b.** 5 **c.** 7 **d.** 10)

119. Reprove : (**a.** Policy **b.** Chide **c.** Testify **d.** Cancel) :: Approve : Sanction

120. Luanda : Angola :: (**a.** Addis Ababa **b.** Astana **c.** Amman **d.** Accra) : Jordan

Answers

1. Presto : Tempo :: **Alto** : Range

The answer is **c.** Presto is a very fast tempo. Alto is a mid-range instrument or voice.

2. Yellow Submarine : Billie Jean :: Revolver : **d. Thriller**

The answer is **d.** "Yellow Submarine" is a song from The Beatles' album Revolver; "Billie Jean" is a song from Michael Jackson's album Thriller.

3. Mend : Sewing :: Edit : **Manuscript**

The answer is **c.** One fixes sewing by mending; one fixes a manuscript by editing.

4. Alphabetical : **List** :: Sequential : Files

The answer is **c.** Alphabetical describes the ordering of a list and sequential describes the ordering of files.

5. Monteverdi : **Italy** :: Haydn : Austria

The answer **c.** Composer Claudio Monteverdi was born in Cremona, Italy. Composer Joseph Haydn was born in Rohrau, Austria.

6. 7 : ≤ 9 :: 12 : ≥ **10**

The answer is **d.** 7 is a number less than 9 (<). 12 is a number greater than 10 (>).

7. 4 : 6 :: **14** : 16

The answer is **b.** 4 plus 2 is 6, and 14 plus 2 is 16.

8. Brahms : Mahler :: Johannes : **Gustav**

The answer is **d.** Johannes was composer Brahms's first name. Gustav was composer Mahler's first name.

9. Thicket : Shrubs :: **Cluster** : Stars

The answer is **b.** A thicket is a group of shrubs, and a cluster is a group of stars.

10. Baudelaire : **Dumas** :: Cather : Faulkner

The answer is **a.** Charles Baudelaire and Alexandre Dumas were both French writers. Willa Cather and William Faulkner were both American writers.

11. Pan : **Critic** :: Ban : Judge

The answer is **b.** Pan is something a critic does, and ban is something a judge does.

12. Platoon : Schindler's List :: Vietnam : **World War II**

The answer is **a.** The 1986 film Platoon is set during the Vietnam War. The 1993 film Schindler's List is set during World War II.

13. Valise : **Clothes** :: Cask : Wine

The answer is **d.** A valise holds clothing and a cask holds wine.

14. Neptune : Poseidon :: Jupiter : **Zeus**

The answer is **c.** Neptune is the Roman name of the Greek god Poseidon, and Jupiter is the Roman name of the Greek god Zeus.

15. Huckster : **Advertising** :: Gangster : Crime

The answer is **d.** A huckster is one who deals in advertising, and a gangster is one who deals in crime.

16. Laconic : Words :: Parched : **Moisture**

The answer is **b.** Laconic is characterized by a lack of words, and parched is characterized by a lack of moisture.

17. Potable : **Drinking** :: Seaworthy : Sailing

The answer is **a.** Something potable is suitable for drinking, and something seaworthy is suitable for sailing.

18. Rook : Chess :: **Shuttlecock** : Badminton

The answer is **c.** A rook is a piece used in the game of chess, and a shuttlecock is used to play the game of badminton.

19. **Syllabus** : Course :: Menu : Meal

The answer is **d.** A syllabus is a description of a course, and a menu is a description of a meal.

20. **Buoy** : Channel :: Flare : Accident

The answer is **b.** A buoy is used to mark a channel, and a flare is used to mark an accident.

21. Phoenix : Bird :: Pegasus : **Horse**

The answer is **b.** Phoenix is a mythical bird, and Pegasus is a mythical horse.

22. Indifferent : **Stoic** :: Ardent : Zealot

The answer is **a.** Indifferent describes someone stoic, and ardent describes a zealot.

23. Bulky : Streamlined :: **Cluttered** : Neat

The answer is **c.** Bulky is an antonym of streamlined, and cluttered is an antonym of neat.

24. **Arctic** : Mercury :: Ocean : Planet

The answer is **c.** The Arctic Ocean is the smallest ocean, and Mercury is the smallest planet.

25. Socialism : Capitalism :: **Cooperation** : Competition

The answer is **a.** Socialism stresses cooperation and capitalism stresses competition.

26. **Bed** : Oyster :: Paddy : Rice

The answer is **c.** Oysters grow in a bed of the ocean, and rice grows in a paddy.

27. Slight : Hurt :: Lag : **Tardiness**

The answer is **a.** To slight causes hurt, and to lag causes tardiness.

28. Fist : Hand :: **Circuit** : Loop

The answer is **c.** A fist is a closed hand, and a circuit is a closed loop.

29. Bunker Hill : **Fort Ticonderoga** :: Saratoga : Valley Forge

The answer is **a.** Bunker Hill, Fort Ticonderoga, Saratoga, and Valley Forge were the major battles of the American Revolution.

30. Einstein : Relativity :: **Darwin** : Evolution

The answer is **d.** Einstein developed the theory of relativity while Darwin developed the theory of evolution.

31. Bear : Lion :: Ursine : Leonine

The answer is **c.** The adjective form of bear is ursine and the adjective form of lion is leonine.

32. Shortest : Longest :: December : **June**

The answer is **a.** The shortest day of the year is in December and the longest day of the year is in June.

33. Cicada : **Insect** :: Collie : Canine

The answer is **d.** A cicada is a type of insect, and a collie is a type of canine.

34. Persimmon : **Berry** :: Cottontail : Rabbit

The answer is **d.** A persimmon is a type of berry, and a cottontail is a type of rabbit.

35. Fern : Plant :: **Minnow** : Fish

The answer is **b.** A fern is a type of plant, and a minnow is a type of fish.

36. Mallet : **Croquet** :: Racket : Tennis

The answer is **c.** A mallet is used to play croquet, and a racket is used to play tennis.

37. Seal : Wax :: **Stopper** : Cork

The answer is **a.** A seal is made of wax, and a stopper is made of cork.

38. $3 : \frac{1}{2}$ :: **Integer** : Fractions

The answer is **b.** The set of integers include positive whole numbers, negative whole numbers, and zero. A fraction is a part of a whole number.

39. Moray : Eel :: Morel : **Fungus**

The answer is **c.** Moray is a type of eel, and morel is a type of fungus.

40. AC : Alternating Current :: DC : **Direct Current**

The answer is **b.** AC stands for alternating current, and DC stands for direct current.

41. Marshal : Prisoner :: Principal : **Student**

The answer is **d.** A marshal is a person in charge of a prisoner, and a principal is a person in charge of a student.

42. Moisten : **Soak** :: Cool : Freeze

The answer is **b.** To moisten is to wet less intensely than to soak, and to cool is to reduce the temperature less intensely than to freeze.

43. Pylon : **Traffic** :: Baton : Orchestra

The answer is **a.** A pylon is used to direct traffic, and a baton is used to direct an orchestra.

44. Shankar : Liszt :: **Sitar** : Piano

The answer is **b.** Ravi Shankar is a famous classical sitarist. Franz Liszt was a famous classical pianist.

45. Uffizi : **Florence** :: Guggenheim : New York

The answer is **b.** The Uffizi is a famous art museum in Florence and the Guggenheim is a famous art museum located in New York.

46. American Revolution : Civil War :: Lexington and Concord : **Harper's Ferry**

The answer is **a.** The American Revolution started with the battle of Lexington and Concord. The American Civil War started with the battle of Harper's Ferry.

47. Wedge : Inclined Plane :: Axe : **Cat's Paw**

The answer is **c.** An axe is an example of a wedge; a cat's paw is an example of an inclined plane.

48. Paris : **London** :: Tate Modern : Louvre

The answer is **c.** The Tate Modern Museum is located in London, England. The Louvre museum is located in Paris, France.

49. **Cornwallis** : Washington :: Lee : Grant

The answer is **a.** British General Cornwallis surrendered to George Washington to end the American Revolution. General Lee surrendered to General Grant to end the American Civil War.

50. Physics : **Matter** :: Eugenics : Heredity

The answer is **b.** Physics is a science that deals with matter, and eugenics is a science that deals with heredity.

51. Haiku : **Three** :: Villanelle : Nineteen

The answer is **b.** A haiku is a poem with three lines; a villanelle is a poem with nineteen lines.

52. **Little Tramp** : Duke :: Chaplin : Wayne

The answer is **a.** The Little Tramp was the nickname of comedian Charlie Chaplin. The Duke was the nickname of actor John Wayne.

53. Fop : **Appearance** :: Documentary : Reality

The answer is **a.** A fop is concerned with appearance, and a documentary is concerned with reality.

54. Allow : Resist :: Conductor : **Insulator**

The answer is **c.** A conductor allows the flow of electrical current; an insulator resists the flow of electrical current.

55. Pastel : Chalk :: **Dough** : Polymer

The answer is **d.** Pastel and chalk are two types of crayon. Dough and polymer are two types of modeling clay.

56. Oedipus : Jocasta :: **Electra** : Clytemnestra

The answer is **c.** In Greek mythology, Jocasta is the mother of Oedipus and Clytemnestra is the mother of Electra.

57. Gold : Au :: Silver : **Ag**

The answer is **b.** On the periodic table of elements, the symbol for gold is Au, and the symbol for silver is Ag.

58. Scythe : Shear :: Trowel : **Shape**

The answer is **b.** A scythe is a tool used for shearing. A trowel is a tool used for shaping.

59. Dalí : **The Persistence of Memory** :: Magritte : The Son of Man

The answer is **b.** The Persistence of Memory is a surreal painting by Salvador Dali; The Son of Man is a surreal painting by René Magritte.

60. Vasquez de Coronado : Arizona :: Ponce de Leon : **Florida**

The answer is **c.** Francisco Vasquez de Coronado was the first European to explore Arizona. Juan Ponce de Leon was the first European to explore Florida.

61. 18th Amendment : Prohibition :: 19th Amendment : **Suffrage**

The answer is **b.** The 18th Amendment dealt with prohibition, and the 19th dealt with suffrage.

62. Dickinson : **Poem** :: Dickens : Novel

The answer is **b.** Emily Dickinson was a poet, and Charles Dickens was a novelist.

63. Sniff : Inhale :: (**a.** Crush **b.** Snit **c.** Snip **d.** Adhere) : Lop

The answer is **c.** To sniff is less intense than to inhale, and to snip is less intense than to lop.

64. Chicken : Capon :: Horse : **Gelding**

The answer is **d.** A castrated chicken is called a capon and a castrated horse is a gelding.

65. Thrifty : **Avarice** :: Hungry : Gluttonous

The answer is **c.** Thrifty describes avarice, and hungry describes gluttonous.

66. Pallid : Color :: Tactless : **Diplomacy**

The answer is **d.** Pallid means lacking in color, and tactless means lacking diplomacy.

67. Coach : Rickshaw :: Sleigh : **Pedicab**

The answer is **d.** A coach and a sleigh are both horse-drawn conveyances. A rickshaw and a pedicab are human-drawn conveyances.

MAT PRACTICE TEST 10

68. Admonish : **Berate** :: Defeat : Conquer

The answer is **d.** To admonish is less intense than to berate, and to defeat is less intense than to conquer.

69. Mercenary : Wages :: Dilettante : **Enjoyment**

The answer is **a.** A mercenary performs a task for wages, and a dilettante does something for enjoyment.

70. Obesity : Lack Of Vitamin C :: Diabetes : **Scurvy**

The answer is **b.** Obesity can lead to diabetes; lack of vitamin C can lead to scurvy.

71. Scruff : Neck :: Stern : **Boat**

The answer is **c.** Scruff is the back of the neck, and stern is the back of a boat.

72. Marquette : **Mississippi** :: Hudson : Hudson

The answer is **b.** Jacques Marquette discovered the Mississippi River and Henry Hudson discovered the Hudson River.

73. Outrage : Peeve :: Strive : **Attempt**

The answer is **a.** To outrage is more intense than to peeve, and to strive is more intense than to attempt.

74. Pavlov : Skinner :: Dogs : **Rats**

The answer is **d.** The psychologist Pavlov worked with dogs and the psychologist Skinner worked with rats.

75. **Trench** : tank :: World War I : World War II

The answer is **c.** One of the characteristics of World War I was trench warfare. In World War II, it was tank warfare.

76. Proton-Proton : Repel :: **Electron-Proton** : Attract

The answer is **a.** Like charges repel; opposite charges attract. Neutrons have neutral charges.

77. Potential : **Kinetic** :: Stored : Active

The answer is **b.** Potential energy is stored energy; kinetic energy is active energy.

78. Ganymede : Jupiter :: **Titan** : Saturn

The answer is **b.** Ganymede is Jupiter's largest moon; Titan is Saturn's largest moon.

79. Franny : Master :: **Zooey** : Margarita

The answer is **d.** *Franny and Zooey* is a 1962 novel by J.D. Salinger. *The Master and Margarita* is a 1967 novel by Mikhail Bolgakov.

80. **Choreography** : Dance :: Cinematography : Image

The answer is **c.** In film, choreography is the art of arranging dance and cinematography is the art of arranging image.

81. Pride : **Fall** :: Calm : Storm

The answer is **d.** According to two well-known expressions, pride comes before a fall, and calm comes before the storm.

82. Brief : Court Case :: Abstract : Research Paper

The answer is **a.** A brief is a summary of a court case, and an abstract is a summary of a research paper.

83. $1^7 : 7^0 :: 2^1 : \sqrt{4}$

The answer is **c.** 1^7 equals 1 and 7^0 equals 1. 2^1 equals 2 and $\sqrt{4}$ equals 2.

84. 212 : Fahrenheit :: **100** : Celsius

The answer is **c.** 212 degrees Fahrenheit is the boiling point for water, as is 100 degrees Celsius.

85. Dinosaurs : Mammals :: Mesozoic : **Cenozoic**

The answer is **d.** Dinosaurs evolved in the Mesosoic Era; mammals evolved in the Cenozoic Era.

86. Mandible : Jaw :: Metatarsal : **Foot**

The answer is **c.** The mandible is part of the jaw, and the metatarsal is part of the foot.

87. Femur : **Thigh** :: Fibula : Calf

The answer is **b.** The femur is located in the thigh, and the fibula is located in the calf.

88. Flappers : 20s :: Mods : **60s**

The answer is **c.** Flappers are people associated with a cultural trend that originated in the 1920s. Mods are people associated with a cultural trend that originated in the 1960s.

89. Piston : Blade :: Sump : **Hub**

The answer is **d.** A piston and a sump are parts of an engine. A blade and a hub are parts of a propeller.

90. -5 : 25 :: .4 : **.16**

The answer is **b.** -5 squared equals 25. .4 squared equals .16.

91. Plaid : Taupe :: **Argyle** : Auburn

The answer is **b.** Plaid and argyle are two types of patterns. Taupe and auburn are two types of colors.

92. Cryptography : Codes :: Ornithology : Birds

The answer is **d.** Cryptography is the study of codes, and ornithology is the study of birds.

93. Vamp : Shoe :: Hood : **Car**

The answer is **b.** A vamp is part of a shoe, and a hood is part of a car.

94. $3^0 : 3^{-1} :: 3^2 : 3^1$

The answer is **b.** 3^0 equals 1 and 3^{-1} equals $\frac{1}{3}$. The ratio is 3 to 1. 3^2 equals 9 and 3^1 equals 3. The ratio is also 3 to 1.

95. $\frac{6}{5} : \frac{2}{5} :: \frac{2}{3} : \frac{2}{9}$

The answer is **d.** $\frac{6}{5}$ times $\frac{1}{3}$ equals $\frac{2}{5}$. $\frac{2}{3}$ times $\frac{1}{3}$ equals $\frac{2}{9}$.

96. Nonagon : Nine :: Pentagon : Five

The answer is **a.** A nonagon is a polygon with nine sides, and a pentagon is a polygon with five sides.

97. Mckinley : 1901 :: Lincoln : 1865

The answer is **c.** President McKinley was assassinated in 1901, and President Lincoln was assassinated in 1865.

98. Wattle : **Neck** :: Crust : Bread

The answer is **d.** The wattle is part of the neck, and crust is part of bread.

99. Pitch : Spiel :: Snarl : Mess

The answer is **b.** Pitch is a synonym for spiel, and snarl is a synonym for mess.

100. El Cid : Spain :: Alexander : **Macedonia**

The answer is **d.** El Cid was a military leader from Spain, and Alexander was a military leader of Macedonia.

101. Sartorial : Tailored :: Gallant : Brave

The answer is **c.** Sartorial is a synonym for tailored, and gallant is a synonym for brave.

102. Succor : **Aid** :: Ire : Anger

The answer is **a.** Succor means help or aid, and ire means anger.

103. Exhort : Urge :: Enthrall : Interest

The answer is **c.** To exhort is to urge strongly, and to enthrall is to interest strongly.

104. Kierkegaard : Nietzsche :: Peirce : **James**

The answer is **a.** The work of Kierkegaard and Nietzsche is the foundation for existentialism. The work of Peirce and James was the foundation for pragmatism.

105. Rack : **Billiards** :: Tack : Sailing

The answer is **a.** Rack is a term used in billiards, and tack is a term used in sailing.

106. Paleocene : Tertiary :: Pleistocene : **Quaternary**

The answer is **b.** The Paleocene epoch occurred during the Tertiary Period and the Pleistocene epoch occurred during the Quaternary Period.

107. Epaulet : Shoulder :: Cravat : **Neck**

The answer is **c.** An epaulet is worn on the shoulder, and a cravat is worn on the neck.

108. Cosine x : Secant x :: x : $\frac{1}{x}$

The answer is **b.** The secant is the reciprocal of the cosine ($\sec x = \frac{1}{\cos x}$). $\frac{1}{x}$ is the reciprocal of x.

109. Ankara : Turkey :: **Baghdad** : Iraq

The answer is **b.** Ankara is the capital of Turkey, and Baghdad is the capital of Iraq.

MAT PRACTICE TEST 10

110. Tokyo : Edo :: **Sri Lanka** : Ceylon

The answer is **b.** Tokyo was formerly known as Edo, and Sri Lanka was formerly known as Ceylon.

111. Cytology : **Cells** :: Geology : Rocks

The answer is **d.** Cytology is the study of cells, and geology is the study of rocks.

112. Deference : Elder :: Indifference : **Stranger**

The answer is **c.** Deference is shown to an elder, and indifference is shown to a stranger.

113. Heliotrope : **Shrub** :: Turnover : Pastry

The answer is **d.** A heliotrope is a type of shrub, and a turnover is a type of pastry.

114. **Oak** : Deciduous :: Pine : Coniferous

The answer is **b.** Oak is an example of a deciduous tree, and pine is an example of a coniferous tree.

115. **Rot** : Sheep :: Blight : Potato

The answer is **c.** Rot is a disease that strikes sheep, and blight is a disease that strikes potatoes.

116. Saluki : **Egypt** :: Akita : Japan

The answer is **b.** The Saluki is a breed of dog from Egypt, and the Akita is a breed of dog from Japan.

117. **Rookie** : Team :: Freshman : Congress

The answer is **c.** A rookie is a new member of a sports team; a freshman is a new representative in Congress.

118. 23 : 5 :: 34 : 7

The answer is **7.** The sum of the digits in the number 23 is 5 (2 + 3). The sum of the digits in the number 34 is 7 (3 + 4).

119. Reprove : **Chide** :: Approve : Sanction

The answer is **b.** Reprove is a synonym of chide, and approve is a synonym of sanction.

120. Luanda : Angola :: **Amman** : Jordan

The answer is **c.** Luanda is the capital of Angola and Amman is the capital of Jordan.

Scoring Your MAT Practice Test

As mentioned in Chapter 1, when you receive your personal score report for the official MAT, you'll be provided with a scaled score and two percentile ranks, all of which are derived from the number of items you answered correctly—known as your raw score.

Because there are different forms and formats of the official MAT, and typically 20 of the 120 questions on the official MAT are experimental and do not count toward your official scaled score and percentile ranks, it is impossible to create an accurate raw score to scaled score or raw score to percentile chart for this and the other practice tests found in this book. In the end, you are striving to correctly answer the highest number of questions as possible and familiarize yourself with the MAT format so you're fully prepared to do your best on test day. For now, what's much more important than your overall score is how you did on each of the content areas tested by the exam. You need to diagnose your strengths and weaknesses so that you can concentrate your efforts as you prepare. The question types are mixed in the practice exam, so in order to tell where your strengths and weaknesses lie, you'll need to compare your answer sheet with the following **MAT Practice Test 10 Review**, which shows which of the content areas each question falls into.

Use your performance here in conjunction with the LearningExpress Test Preparation System in Chapter 2 to help you devise a study plan. You should plan to spend more time studying areas that correspond to the questions you found hardest and less time on the content areas in which you did well. Once you have spent some time reviewing, take the next MAT Practice Test to see if you've improved.

CONTENT AREA	QUESTION NUMBERS
Language and Vocabulary	13, 16, 17, 19, 20, 22, 23, 27, 28, 53, 63, 65, 66, 68, 69, 71, 73, 98, 99, 101, 102, 103, 105, 112, 119
Humanities	1, 2, 5, 8, 10, 12, 14, 21, 44, 48, 51, 52, 55, 56, 59, 61, 62, 79, 80, 97, 100
Social Science	24, 25, 29, 30, 31, 32, 45, 46, 49, 60, 64, 72, 74, 75, 104, 106, 109, 110, 116, 120
Natural Science	9, 26, 33, 34, 35, 39, 40, 47, 50, 54, 57, 70, 76, 77, 78, 84, 85, 86, 87, 111, 113, 114
General	3, 4, 11, 15, 18, 36, 37, 41, 42, 43, 58, 67, 81, 82, 88, 89, 91, 92, 93, 107, 115, 117
Mathematics	6, 7, 38, 83, 90, 94, 95, 96, 108, 118

13 ▶ MAT Practice Test 11

CHAPTER SUMMARY
Here's the final sample MAT test for you to practice with.

For this last practice test, simulate the actual test-taking experience as closely as you can. Find a quiet place to work where you won't be disturbed. If you own this book, use the answer sheet on the following pages and find some #2 pencils to fill in the circles. Use a timer or stopwatch to time yourself—you'll have 60 minutes to complete the official MAT. After you take the test, use the detailed answer explanations that follow to review any questions you missed.

MAT Practice Test 11

1.	ⓐ	ⓑ	ⓒ	ⓓ
2.	ⓐ	ⓑ	ⓒ	ⓓ
3.	ⓐ	ⓑ	ⓒ	ⓓ
4.	ⓐ	ⓑ	ⓒ	ⓓ
5.	ⓐ	ⓑ	ⓒ	ⓓ
6.	ⓐ	ⓑ	ⓒ	ⓓ
7.	ⓐ	ⓑ	ⓒ	ⓓ
8.	ⓐ	ⓑ	ⓒ	ⓓ
9.	ⓐ	ⓑ	ⓒ	ⓓ
10.	ⓐ	ⓑ	ⓒ	ⓓ
11.	ⓐ	ⓑ	ⓒ	ⓓ
12.	ⓐ	ⓑ	ⓒ	ⓓ
13.	ⓐ	ⓑ	ⓒ	ⓓ
14.	ⓐ	ⓑ	ⓒ	ⓓ
15.	ⓐ	ⓑ	ⓒ	ⓓ
16.	ⓐ	ⓑ	ⓒ	ⓓ
17.	ⓐ	ⓑ	ⓒ	ⓓ
18.	ⓐ	ⓑ	ⓒ	ⓓ
19.	ⓐ	ⓑ	ⓒ	ⓓ
20.	ⓐ	ⓑ	ⓒ	ⓓ
21.	ⓐ	ⓑ	ⓒ	ⓓ
22.	ⓐ	ⓑ	ⓒ	ⓓ
23.	ⓐ	ⓑ	ⓒ	ⓓ
24.	ⓐ	ⓑ	ⓒ	ⓓ
25.	ⓐ	ⓑ	ⓒ	ⓓ
26.	ⓐ	ⓑ	ⓒ	ⓓ
27.	ⓐ	ⓑ	ⓒ	ⓓ
28.	ⓐ	ⓑ	ⓒ	ⓓ
29.	ⓐ	ⓑ	ⓒ	ⓓ
30.	ⓐ	ⓑ	ⓒ	ⓓ
31.	ⓐ	ⓑ	ⓒ	ⓓ
32.	ⓐ	ⓑ	ⓒ	ⓓ
33.	ⓐ	ⓑ	ⓒ	ⓓ
34.	ⓐ	ⓑ	ⓒ	ⓓ
35.	ⓐ	ⓑ	ⓒ	ⓓ
36.	ⓐ	ⓑ	ⓒ	ⓓ
37.	ⓐ	ⓑ	ⓒ	ⓓ
38.	ⓐ	ⓑ	ⓒ	ⓓ
39.	ⓐ	ⓑ	ⓒ	ⓓ
40.	ⓐ	ⓑ	ⓒ	ⓓ
41.	ⓐ	ⓑ	ⓒ	ⓓ
42.	ⓐ	ⓑ	ⓒ	ⓓ
43.	ⓐ	ⓑ	ⓒ	ⓓ
44.	ⓐ	ⓑ	ⓒ	ⓓ
45.	ⓐ	ⓑ	ⓒ	ⓓ

46.	ⓐ	ⓑ	ⓒ	ⓓ
47.	ⓐ	ⓑ	ⓒ	ⓓ
48.	ⓐ	ⓑ	ⓒ	ⓓ
49.	ⓐ	ⓑ	ⓒ	ⓓ
50.	ⓐ	ⓑ	ⓒ	ⓓ
51.	ⓐ	ⓑ	ⓒ	ⓓ
52.	ⓐ	ⓑ	ⓒ	ⓓ
53.	ⓐ	ⓑ	ⓒ	ⓓ
54.	ⓐ	ⓑ	ⓒ	ⓓ
55.	ⓐ	ⓑ	ⓒ	ⓓ
56.	ⓐ	ⓑ	ⓒ	ⓓ
57.	ⓐ	ⓑ	ⓒ	ⓓ
58.	ⓐ	ⓑ	ⓒ	ⓓ
59.	ⓐ	ⓑ	ⓒ	ⓓ
60.	ⓐ	ⓑ	ⓒ	ⓓ
61.	ⓐ	ⓑ	ⓒ	ⓓ
62.	ⓐ	ⓑ	ⓒ	ⓓ
63.	ⓐ	ⓑ	ⓒ	ⓓ
64.	ⓐ	ⓑ	ⓒ	ⓓ
65.	ⓐ	ⓑ	ⓒ	ⓓ
66.	ⓐ	ⓑ	ⓒ	ⓓ
67.	ⓐ	ⓑ	ⓒ	ⓓ
68.	ⓐ	ⓑ	ⓒ	ⓓ
69.	ⓐ	ⓑ	ⓒ	ⓓ
70.	ⓐ	ⓑ	ⓒ	ⓓ
71.	ⓐ	ⓑ	ⓒ	ⓓ
72.	ⓐ	ⓑ	ⓒ	ⓓ
73.	ⓐ	ⓑ	ⓒ	ⓓ
74.	ⓐ	ⓑ	ⓒ	ⓓ
75.	ⓐ	ⓑ	ⓒ	ⓓ
76.	ⓐ	ⓑ	ⓒ	ⓓ
77.	ⓐ	ⓑ	ⓒ	ⓓ
78.	ⓐ	ⓑ	ⓒ	ⓓ
79.	ⓐ	ⓑ	ⓒ	ⓓ
80.	ⓐ	ⓑ	ⓒ	ⓓ
81.	ⓐ	ⓑ	ⓒ	ⓓ
82.	ⓐ	ⓑ	ⓒ	ⓓ
83.	ⓐ	ⓑ	ⓒ	ⓓ
84.	ⓐ	ⓑ	ⓒ	ⓓ
85.	ⓐ	ⓑ	ⓒ	ⓓ
86.	ⓐ	ⓑ	ⓒ	ⓓ
87.	ⓐ	ⓑ	ⓒ	ⓓ
88.	ⓐ	ⓑ	ⓒ	ⓓ
89.	ⓐ	ⓑ	ⓒ	ⓓ
90.	ⓐ	ⓑ	ⓒ	ⓓ

91.	ⓐ	ⓑ	ⓒ	ⓓ
92.	ⓐ	ⓑ	ⓒ	ⓓ
93.	ⓐ	ⓑ	ⓒ	ⓓ
94.	ⓐ	ⓑ	ⓒ	ⓓ
95.	ⓐ	ⓑ	ⓒ	ⓓ
96.	ⓐ	ⓑ	ⓒ	ⓓ
97.	ⓐ	ⓑ	ⓒ	ⓓ
98.	ⓐ	ⓑ	ⓒ	ⓓ
99.	ⓐ	ⓑ	ⓒ	ⓓ
100.	ⓐ	ⓑ	ⓒ	ⓓ
101.	ⓐ	ⓑ	ⓒ	ⓓ
102.	ⓐ	ⓑ	ⓒ	ⓓ
103.	ⓐ	ⓑ	ⓒ	ⓓ
104.	ⓐ	ⓑ	ⓒ	ⓓ
105.	ⓐ	ⓑ	ⓒ	ⓓ
106.	ⓐ	ⓑ	ⓒ	ⓓ
107.	ⓐ	ⓑ	ⓒ	ⓓ
108.	ⓐ	ⓑ	ⓒ	ⓓ
109.	ⓐ	ⓑ	ⓒ	ⓓ
110.	ⓐ	ⓑ	ⓒ	ⓓ
111.	ⓐ	ⓑ	ⓒ	ⓓ
112.	ⓐ	ⓑ	ⓒ	ⓓ
113.	ⓐ	ⓑ	ⓒ	ⓓ
114.	ⓐ	ⓑ	ⓒ	ⓓ
115.	ⓐ	ⓑ	ⓒ	ⓓ
116.	ⓐ	ⓑ	ⓒ	ⓓ
117.	ⓐ	ⓑ	ⓒ	ⓓ
118.	ⓐ	ⓑ	ⓒ	ⓓ
119.	ⓐ	ⓑ	ⓒ	ⓓ
120.	ⓐ	ⓑ	ⓒ	ⓓ

Directions: For each question, select the answer choice in the parentheses that best completes the analogy.

1. Brethren : Sect :: Actors : (**a.** Company **b.** Church **c.** Liturgy **d.** Stagehand)

2. Poetry : Rhyme :: Philosophy : (**a.** Imagery **b.** Music **c.** Bylaw **d.** Theory)

3. Aesop : Fable :: Homer : (**a.** Temple **b.** Donkey **c.** Epic **d.** Greece)

4. Volume : (**a.** Measure **b.** Pint **c.** Encyclopedia **d.** Kitchen) :: Stanza : Poem

5. Company : Conglomerate :: Metal : (**a.** Alloy **b.** Aluminum **c.** Corporation **d.** Furnace)

6. (**a.** Epic **b.** Poet **c.** Haiku **d.** Rhyme) : Poem :: Fable : Story

7. De Soto : Spain :: Columbus : (**a.** West Indies **b.** Italy **c.** Portugal **d.** Santa Maria)

8. Quarry : Marble :: (**a.** Hive **b.** Bee **c.** Spread **d.** Reservoir) : Honey

9. Stiff : Supple :: Fierce : (**a.** Rigid **b.** Subtle **c.** Ferocious **d.** Tame)

10. Mustang : (**a.** Dog **b.** Horse **c.** Fish **d.** Bird) :: Jaguar : Cat

11. Olfactory : (**a.** Nose **b.** Ear **c.** Heart **d.** Vision) :: Optical : Eye

12. (**a.** Pancake **b.** Bullhorn **c.** Scalpel **d.** Truck) : Incising :: Spatula : Lifting

13. Break : Shift :: Minute : (**a.** Second **b.** Hour **c.** Spell **d.** Work)

14. Drudgery : Work :: Cacophony : (**a.** Noise **b.** Orchestra **c.** Telephone **d.** Dissonance)

15. Swaddle : (**a.** Delay **b.** Paddle **c.** Snake **d.** Envelop) :: Rattle : Shake

16. Rue : (**a.** Avenue **b.** Domino **c.** Regret **d.** Rules) :: Rule : Dominate

17. Felt : (**a.** Cloth **b.** Nose **c.** Sneeze **d.** Scale) :: Smelt : Fish

18. Bowler : (**a.** Hat **b.** Lane **c.** Trophy **d.** Ottoman) :: Satchel : Bag

19. (**a.** Hammer **b.** Cabinet **c.** Saw **d.** Plane) : Wood :: File : Nail

20. 80 : 40 :: 2 : (**a.** 8 **b.** 4 **c.** 1 **d.** 20)

21. John Coltrane : Saxophone :: Miles Davis : (**a.** Trumpet **b.** Piano **c.** Guitar **d.** Bass)

22. Pineapple : (**a.** Dole **b.** Hawaii **c.** Canada **d.** Mango) :: Orange : Florida

23. Swift : Satirical :: (**a.** Hemingway **b.** Fitzgerald **c.** Dos Passos **d.** Poe) : Macabre

24. Hilt : Sword :: Needle : (**a.** Tease **b.** Compass **c.** Dagger **d.** Kilt)

25. Griffin : Lion :: Satyr : (**a.** Owl **b.** Goat **c.** Wings **d.** Horse)

26. Crazy Horse : (**a.** Sioux **b.** Inuit **c.** Navajo **d.** Custer) :: Cochise : Apache

27. Ribbon : (**a.** Present **b.** Cut **c.** Bow **d.** Type-writer) :: Icing : Cake

28. Jetty : (**a.** Daffodils **b.** Beach **c.** Rocks **d.** Water) :: Bouquet : Flowers

29. (**a.** 5 **b.** $\frac{2}{1}$ **c.** 1 **d.** $\frac{3}{2}$) : 1.5 :: $\frac{1}{2}$: 0.5

30. Algebra : Calculus :: (**a.** Anatomy **b.** Knife **c.** Doctor **d.** Hospital) : Surgery

31. (**a.** Detective **b.** Hog **c.** Chocolate **d.** France) : Clue :: Pig : Truffle

32. Member : Club :: (**a.** Lion **b.** Win **c.** Medal **d.** Accept) : Pride

33. Epilogue : Novel :: (**a.** Dessert **b.** Repast **c.** Lunch **d.** Appetizer) : Meal

34. (**a.** Net **b.** Score **c.** Racket **d.** Serve) : Tennis :: Drive : Golf

35. $\sqrt{4}$: $\sqrt{9}$ :: $\sqrt{16}$: (**a.** $\sqrt{25}$ **b.** $\sqrt{36}$ **c.** $\sqrt{64}$ **d.** $\sqrt{100}$)

36. (**a.** War **b.** Brave **c.** Dove **d.** Cub) : Peace :: Lion : Courage

37. Lightweight : (**a.** Beam **b.** Boxer **c.** Heavyweight **d.** Traffic) :: Sedan : Automobile

38. Danse Macabre : (**a.** Easter **b.** Thanksgiving **c.** Independence Day **d.** Halloween) :: Carol of the Bells : Christmas

39. Sicily : Italy :: (**a.** Sardinia **b.** Syria **c.** Mesopotamia **d.** Crete) : Greece

40. Marx : Mussolini :: Communism : (**a.** Nationalism **b.** Fascism **c.** Socialism **d.** Communism)

41. (**a.** Kansas **b.** Middle Earth **c.** Emerald City **d.** Oz) : Mordor :: Dorothy : Frodo

42. (**a.** Jazz **b.** Country **c.** Bass **d.** Treble) : Classical :: 4 : 6

43. Magnesium : Chlorophyll :: (**a.** Silver **b.** Hydrogen **c.** Cobalt **d.** Iron) : Hemoglobin

44. (**a.** Opossum **b.** Ape **c.** Honeybee **d.** Moose) : Marsupial :: Monkey : Primate

45. Mississippi river : Gulf of Mexico :: Nile river : (**a.** Indian Ocean **b.** Mediterranean Sea **c.** Atlantic Ocean **d.** Persian Gulf)

46. Domain : Species :: Eon : (**a.** Epoch **b.** Era **c.** Period **d.** Stage)

47. (**a.** Atlas **b.** Zeus **c.** Athena **d.** Hercules) : Hera :: Titan : Goddess

48. William Tell : (**a.** Carmen **b.** Peer Gynt **c.** Don Giovanni **d.** Rigoletto) :: Rossini : Bizet

49. Guileless : Cunning :: Shameless : (**a.** Modesty **b.** Guile **c.** Winning **d.** Shameful)

50. Defer : Postpone :: Proffer : (**a.** Cause **b.** Tender **c.** Avoid **d.** Infer)

51. (**a.** Mica **b.** Water **c.** Lava **d.** Sand) : Bedrock :: Cement : Foundation

52. (**a.** Maslow **b.** Perls **c.** Piaget **d.** Freud) : Rogers :: Cognitive : Humanistic

53. Harrison : Tyler :: Grant : (**a.** Lee **b.** Hoover **c.** Johnson **d.** Hayes)

54. Jackson : (**a.** Grant **b.** Frida **c.** Georgia **d.** Maria) :: Pollock : Kahlo

55. Nosferatu : Caligari :: Vampire : (**a.** Mad Doctor **b.** Werewolf **c.** Somnambulist **d.** Zombie)

56. F.D. Roosevelt : (**a.** Senator **b.** Governor **c.** Mayor **d.** Vice President) :: G.W. Bush : Governor

57. Napoleonic : 1815 :: Korean : (**a.** 1945 **b.** 1953 **c.** 1958 **d.** 1960)

58. Fibula : Leg :: (**a.** Ulna **b.** Sternum **c.** Pelvis **d.** Tibia) : Arm

59. Declaration of Independence : Constitution :: 1776 : (**a.** 1774 **b.** 1789 **c.** 1776 **d.** 1782)

60. Freud : Oedipus :: (**a.** Rogers **b.** Maslow **c.** Adler **d.** Jung) : Inferiority

61. Cub : Bear :: Joey : (**a.** Cave **b.** Doll **c.** Kangaroo **d.** Truck)

62. (**a.** Barley **b.** Bread **c.** Soup **d.** Spelt) : Wheat :: Lentil : Legume

63. Pacific : (**a.** Saturn **b.** Jupiter **c.** Earth **d.** Uranus) :: Ocean : Planet

64. Gerrymander : Divide :: Filibuster : (**a.** Bend **b.** Punish **c.** Delay **d.** Rush)

65. Grant Wood : Jasper Johns :: American Gothic : (**a.** Whistler's Mother **b.** Three Flags **c.** A Starry Night **d.** Drowning Girl)

66. Bath : England :: (**a.** Lorca **b.** Lourdes **c.** Lucca **d.** Lucerne) : France

67. Fuji : Japan :: Kilimanjaro : (**a.** Africa **b.** China **c.** India **d.** Australia)

68. 11 : Binary :: (**a.** 2 **b.** 3 **c.** 5 **d.** 10) : Decimal

69. (**a.** Kill **b.** Hatchet **c.** Knife **d.** Noose) : Murder :: Bag : Collect

70. (**a.** Ghana **b.** California **c.** Sierra Leone **d.** Senegal) : Gold Coast :: Zimbabwe : Rhodesia

71. Om : (**a.** Spain **b.** Sweden **c.** Hindu **d.** Russia) :: Ganges : India

72. (**a.** Mt. Rainier **b.** Mauna Kea **c.** Lake Champlain **d.** Mt. Mckinley) : Highest :: Death Valley : Lowest

73. Inner Core : Outer Core :: Solid : (**a.** Gas **b.** Liquid **c.** Plasma **d.** Mantle)

74. Proboscis : (**a.** Prognosis **b.** Nose **c.** Ear **d.** Nausea) :: Abdomen : Gut

75. $\frac{0}{5}$: (**a.** $\frac{5}{0}$ **b.** $\frac{0}{1}$ **c.** $\frac{0}{-1}$ **d.** $\frac{5}{5}$) :: 0 : Undefined

76. Acute : Obtuse :: 50 : (**a.** 60 **b.** 75 **c.** 90 **d.** 150)

77. Carroll : Queen of Hearts :: Barrie : (**a.** Peter Pan **b.** Captain Hook **c.** Wendy **d.** Mermaid)

78. John Proctor : (**a.** Willy Loman **b.** Abigail Williams **c.** Lee Baum **d.** Arthur Miller) :: Biff Loman : Happy Loman

79. (**a.** Ocean **b.** Pod **c.** Porpoise **d.** Leap) : Dolphin :: Herd : Cow

80. Mynah : Bird :: Terrapin : (**a.** Hemisphere **b.** Beak **c.** Snake **d.** Turtle)

81. Mean : Average :: Kind : (**a.** Hurtful **b.** Meaning **c.** Variety **d.** Kindness)

82. Caliper : (**a.** Shape **b.** Temperature **c.** Distance **d.** Height) :: Scale : Weight

83. Bathysphere : (**a.** Sea **b.** Tub **c.** Oceanographer **d.** Universe) :: Telescope : Astronomer

84. Spelunker : (**a.** Spaceship **b.** Light **c.** Cave **d.** Wave) :: Astronomer : Space

85. Breach : (**a.** Seagull **b.** Beach **c.** Whale **d.** Foam) :: Fly : Bird

86. Beet : Turnip :: (**a.** Pumpkin **b.** Yam **c.** Lemon **d.** Almond) : Watermelon

87. Gondolier : Gondola :: Runner : (**a.** Rickshaw **b.** Track **c.** Unicycle **d.** Sneakers)

88. Eider : (**a.** Snow **b.** Plant **c.** Duck **d.** Pine) :: Cedar : Tree

89. $\frac{3}{4}$: 75% :: (**a.** $\frac{2}{3}$ **b.** $\frac{2}{5}$ **c.** $\frac{3}{5}$ **d.** $\frac{5}{6}$) : 60%

90. 80 : 120 :: (**a.** 100 **b.** 150 **c.** 200 **d.** 250) : 300

91. 360 : 2π :: Degree : (**a.** Circle **b.** Radian **c.** Circumference **d.** Angle)

92. Dryads : Tree :: Naiads : (**a.** Rock **b.** Fire **c.** Sky **d.** Water)

93. Festoon : Chain :: Creek : (**a.** Stream **b.** Inlay **c.** Crook **d.** Island)

94. Inchoate : (**a.** Incoherent **b.** Profitable **c.** Unfinished **d.** Choosy) :: Gainful : Worthwhile

95. Waterloo : Napoleon :: Appomattox : (**a.** Lincoln **b.** Grant **c.** Lee **d.** Sherman)

96. Scratch : Race :: (**a.** Draw **b.** King **c.** Card **d.** Fold) : Poker

97. Osier : (**a.** Artisan **b.** Basketry **c.** Ancient **d.** Needlepoint) :: Paper : Origami

98. Samuel Clemens : Mark Twain :: Mary Ann Evans : (**a.** Eudora Welty **b.** George Eliot **c.** George Sand **d.** Emily Brontë)

99. (**a.** Truckle **b.** Trickle **c.** Tickle **d.** Tuck) : Bow :: Stumble : Fall

100. (**a.** Red **b.** Morocco **c.** Guard **d.** Tassel) : Fez :: Pom-pom : Tam-o'-shanter

101. Thresher : (**a.** Robin **b.** Master **c.** Shark **d.** Policeman) :: Mastiff : Dog

102. Worth : Whort :: (**a.** Apex **b.** Arc **c.** Drain **d.** Sink) : Nadir

103. Theology : Religion :: Phenology : (**a.** Pheromones **b.** Psychology **c.** Climate **d.** Geology)

104. Whoop : Exuberance :: Keen : (**a.** Whoops **b.** Neat **c.** Mourning **d.** Diffidence)

105. Histrionic : (**a.** History **b.** Mechanic **c.** Actor **d.** Debate) :: Didactic : Teacher

106. Epistemology : Philosophy :: Rationalism : (**a.** Metaphysics **b.** Logic **c.** Epistemology **d.** Psychology)

107. Lock : Canal :: Dock : (**a.** Courtroom **b.** Locksmith **c.** Ear **d.** Duck)

108. Wildcat : (**a.** Bobcat **b.** Game **c.** Mountain **d.** Oil) :: Forage : Food

109. Scimitar : (**a.** Saber **b.** Bullet **c.** Vest **d.** Soldier) :: Revolver : Gun

110. Probity : (**a.** Honesty **b.** Prohibition **c.** Inquisition **d.** Eventuality) :: Probability : Likelihood

111. Perfidy : (**a.** Treachery **b.** Humor **c.** Forgiveness **d.** Performance) :: Satire : Parody

112. Ruth Benedict : Anthropology :: William James : (**a.** Philosophy **b.** Psychology **c.** Psychiatry **d.** Economics)

113. Freud : Psychoanalysis :: (**a.** Mendel **b.** Pavlov **c.** Newton **d.** Copernicus) : Genetics

114. Darwin : Mead :: Evolution : (**a.** Relativity **b.** Language **c.** Birth **d.** Culture)

115. Hector : (**a.** Bait **b.** Shun **c.** Embrace **d.** Trail) :: Foil : Thwart

116. Bow : Obeisance :: Objective : (**a.** Salute **b.** Worship **c.** Goal **d.** Subjective)

117. Ostrom : Economic Governance :: (**a.** Krugman **b.** Friedman **c.** Keynes **d.** Marx) : Trade Patterns

118. Mohs : (**a.** Intensity **b.** Damage **c.** Mineral **d.** Wind) :: Richter : Earthquake

119. Pound : United Kingdom :: (**a.** Franc **b.** Colon **c.** Peseta **d.** Dollar) : Costa Rica

120. V : X :: (**a.** I **b.** X **c.** L **d.** D) : C

Answers

1. Brethren : Sect :: Actors : **Company**

   The answer is **a.** Brethren are members of an order or sect, and actors are members of a company.

2. Poetry : Rhyme :: Philosophy : **Theory**

   The answer is **d.** Poetry is often comprised of rhyme; philosophy is often built on theory.

3. Aesop : Fable :: Homer : **Epic**

   The answer is **c.** Aesop is known for writing fables, and Homer is known for writing epics.

4. Volume : **Encyclopedia** :: Stanza : Poem

   The answer is **c.** A volume is part of an encyclopedia, and a stanza is part of a poem.

5. Company : Conglomerate :: Metal : **Alloy**

   The answer is **a.** A company is part of a conglomerate, and a metal is part of an alloy.

6. **Haiku** : Poem :: Fable : Story

   The answer is **c.** A haiku is a type of poem, and a fable is a type of story.

7. De Soto : Spain :: Columbus : **Italy**

   The answer is **b.** De Soto was a Spanish navigator, and Columbus was an Italian navigator.

8. Quarry : Marble :: **Hive** : Honey

   The answer is **a.** A quarry yields marble, and a hive yields honey.

9. Stiff : Supple :: Fierce : **Tame**

   The answer is **d.** Stiff is an antonym for supple, and fierce is an antonym for tame.

10. Mustang : **Horse** :: Jaguar : Cat

    The answer is **b.** A mustang is a type of horse, and a jaguar is a type of cat.

11. Olfactory : **Nose** :: Optical : Eye

    The answer is **a.** Olfactory relates to the sense of smell, or using the nose, and optical relates to vision, or using the eye.

12. **Scalpel** : Incising :: Spatula : Lifting

    The answer is **c.** A scalpel is used to make an incision, and a spatula is used for lifting.

13. Break : Shift :: Minute : **Hour**

    The answer is **b.** A break is part of a shift, and a minute is part of an hour.

14. Drudgery : Work :: Cacophony : **Noise**

    The answer is **a.** Drudgery is unpleasant work, and cacophony is unpleasant noise.

15. Swaddle : **Envelop** :: Rattle : Shake

    The answer is **d.** To swaddle means to envelop, and to rattle means to shake.

16. Rue : **Regret** :: Rule : Dominate

The answer is **c.** To rue means to regret, and to rule means to dominate.

17. Felt : **Cloth** :: Smelt : Fish

The answer is **a.** Felt is a type of cloth, and smelt is a type of fish.

18. Bowler : **Hat** :: Satchel : Bag

The answer is **a.** A bowler is a type of hat, and a satchel is a type of bag.

19. **Plane** : Wood :: File : Nail

The answer is **d.** A plane is a tool used to smooth and shape wood, and a file is a tool used to smooth and shape a nail.

20. 80 : 40 :: 2 : **1**

The answer is **c.** Half of 80 is 40, and half of 2 is 1.

21. John Coltrane : Saxophone :: Miles Davis : **Trumpet**

The answer is **a.** Jazz musician John Coltrane played the saxophone, and Miles Davis played the trumpet.

22. Pineapple : **Hawaii** :: Orange : Florida

The answer is **b.** Pineapples are grown in Hawaii, and oranges are grown in Florida.

23. Swift : Satirical :: **Poe** : Macabre

The answer is **d.** Jonathan Swift was known as a satirical writer, and Edgar Allan Poe was known for his macabre writing.

24. Hilt : Sword :: Needle : **Compass**

The answer is **b.** A hilt is part of a sword, and a needle is part of the compass.

25. Griffin : Lion :: Satyr : **Goat**

The answer is **b.** A Griffin is a mythical creature with the body of a lion, and a Satyr is a mythical creature with the body of a goat.

26. Crazy Horse : **Sioux** :: Cochise : Apache

The answer is **a.** Crazy Horse was the leader of the Sioux, and Cochise was the leader of the Apache.

27. Ribbon : **Present** :: Icing : Cake

The answer is **a.** A ribbon is used to decorate a present, and icing is used to decorate a cake.

28. Jetty : **Rocks** :: Bouquet : Flowers

The answer is **c.** A jetty is composed of rocks, and a bouquet is composed of flowers.

29. $\frac{3}{2}$: 1.5 :: $\frac{1}{2}$: 0.5

The answer is **d.** $\frac{3}{2}$ is the same as 1.5, and $\frac{1}{2}$ is the same as 0.5.

30. Algebra : Calculus :: **Anatomy** : Surgery

The answer is **a.** Algebra is a prerequisite for calculus, and anatomy is a prerequisite for surgery.

31. **Detective** : Clue :: Pig : Truffle

The answer is **a.** A detective hunts for clues, and a pig hunts for truffles.

32. Member : Club :: **Lion** : Pride

The answer is **a.** A member is part of a club, and a lion is part of a pride.

33. Epilogue : Novel :: **Dessert** : Meal

The answer is **a.** An epilogue comes at the end of a novel, and a dessert comes at the end of a meal.

34. **Serve** : Tennis :: Drive : Golf

The answer is **d.** A serve is an action in tennis, and a drive is an action in golf.

35. $\sqrt{4}$: $\sqrt{9}$ :: $\sqrt{16}$: $\sqrt{36}$

The answer is **b.** The $\sqrt{4}$ is equal to 2 and the $\sqrt{9}$ is equal to 3. The ratio is 2 to 3. The $\sqrt{16}$ is equal to 4 and the $\sqrt{36}$ is equal to 6. The ratio is 2 to 3.

36. **Dove** : Peace :: Lion : Courage

The answer is **c.** A dove is a symbol of peace, and a lion is a symbol of courage.

37. Lightweight : **Boxer** :: Sedan : Automobile

The answer is **b.** Lightweight is a classification for a boxer, and sedan is a classification for an automobile.

38. "Danse Macabre" : **Halloween** :: "Carol of the Bells" : Christmas

The answer is **d.** Camille Saint-Saëns's "Danse Macabre" is a musical composition associated with Halloween. Mykola Leontovych's "Carol of the Bells" is a composition associated with Christmas.

39. Sicily : Italy :: **Crete** : Greece

The answer is **d.** Sicily is a large Italian island and Crete is a large Greek island.

40. Marx : Mussolini :: Communism : **Fascism**

The answer is **b.** Marx founded what is considered modern communism and Mussolini founded modern fascism.

41. **Emerald City** : Mordor :: Dorothy : Frodo

The answer is **c.** In L. Frank Baum's *The Wonderful Wizard of Oz*, Dorothy goes on a quest to find the Emerald City. In J.R.R. Tolkein's *Lord of the Rings*, Frodo goes on a quest to find the land of Mordor.

42. **Bass** : Classical :: 4 : 6

The answer is **c.** A standard bass guitar has four strings. A standard classical guitar has six strings.

43. Magnesium : Chlorophyll :: **Iron** : Hemoglobin

The answer is **d.** Magnesium is in chlorophyll; iron is in hemoglobin.

44. Opossum : Marsupial :: Monkey : Primate

The answer is **a.** A monkey is an example of a primate, and an opossum is an example of a marsupial.

45. Mississippi river : Gulf of Mexico :: Nile river : **Mediterranean sea**

The answer is **b.** The Mississippi River flows into the Gulf of Mexico, and the Nile River flows into the Mediterranean Sea.

46. Domain : Species :: Eon : **Stage**

The answer is **d.** Domain is the largest classification of living things; species is the narrowest; Eon is the largest descriptor of Earth's geologic time scale; stage is the narrowest.

47. Atlas : Hera :: Titan : Goddess

The answer is **a.** According to Greek mythology, Atlas belonged to a race of deities known as the titans. Hera was a goddess.

48. William Tell : **Carmen** :: Rossini : Bizet

The answer is **a.** William Tell is an opera by Gioacchino Rossini. Carmen is an opera by Georges Bizet.

49. Guileless : Cunning :: Shameless : **Modesty**

The answer is **a.** To be guileless is to lack cunning, and to be shameless is to lack modesty.

50. Defer : Postpone :: Proffer : **Tender**

The answer is **b.** To defer is a synonym of to postpone, and to proffer is a synonym of to tender.

51. Mica : Bedrock :: Cement : Foundation

The answer is **a.** Mica makes up bedrock—on which skyscrapers are built; cement makes up a foundation—on which houses are built.

52. Piaget : Rogers :: Cognitive : Humanistic

The answer is **c.** Piaget was a proponent of cognitive psychology while Rogers was a proponent of humanistic psychology.

53. Harrison : Tyler :: Grant : **Hayes**

The answer is **d.** President Tyler succeeded President Harrison and President Hayes succeeded President Grant.

54. Jackson : **Frida** :: Pollock : Kahlo

The answer is **b.** Jackson Pollock and Frida Kahlo were both painters.

55. Nosferatu : Caligari :: Vampire : **Mad Doctor**

The answer is **a.** Nosferatu is a 1922 German film about a vampire. The Cabinet of Dr. Caligari is a 1920 German film about a mad doctor.

56. F.D. Roosevelt : **Governor** :: G.W. Bush : Governor

The answer is **b.** Roosevelt served as Governor of New York State prior to being elected President. Bush served as Governor of Texas before his election as President.

57. Napoleonic : 1815 :: Korean : **1953**

The answer is **b.** The Napoleonic Wars ended in 1815 and the Korean War ended in 1953.

58. Fibula : Leg :: **Ulna** : Arm

The answer is **a.** The fibula is a bone in the leg, and the ulna is a bone in the arm.

59. Declaration of Independence : Constitution :: 1776 : **1789**

The answer is **b.** The Declaration of Independence was signed in 1776 and the U.S. Constitution replaced the Articles of Confederation in 1789.

60. Freud : Oedipus :: **Adler** : Inferiority

The answer is **c.** Freud developed the theory of the Oedipus complex in psychology. Adler developed the theory of the inferiority complex.

61. Cub : Bear :: Joey : **Kangaroo**

The answer is **c.** A cub is a young bear, and a joey is a young kangaroo.

62. **Spelt** : Wheat :: Lentil : Legume

The answer is **d.** Spelt is a type of wheat, and lentil is a type of legume.

63. Pacific : **Jupiter** :: Ocean : Planet

The answer is **b.** The Pacific Ocean is the largest ocean and Jupiter is the largest planet.

64. Gerrymander : Divide :: Filibuster : **Delay**

The answer is **c.** To gerrymander is a political term meaning to divide land, and to filibuster is to delay legislature.

65. Grant Wood : Jasper Johns : American Gothic : **Three Flags**

The answer is **b.** American Gothic is a 1930 painting by Grant Wood. Three Flags is a 1958 painting by Jasper Johns.

66. Bath : England :: **Lourdes** : France

The answer is **b.** Restorative waters are found in Bath, England, as well as in Lourdes, France.

67. Fuji : Japan :: Kilimanjaro : **Africa**

The answer is **a.** Fuji is the highest mountain in Japan, and Kilimanjaro is Africa's highest mountain, located in Tanzania.

68. 11 : Binary :: **3** : Decimal

The answer is **b.** The number 11 in binary (base 2) is equal to the number 3 in decimal (base 10).

69. Hatchet : Murder :: Bag : Collect

The answer is **b.** "Hatchet man" is a slang nickname for a hired murderer; "bag man" is a slang nickname for a hired money collector.

70. Ghana : Gold Coast :: Zimbabwe : Rhodesia

The answer is **a.** Ghana was formerly called the Gold Coast, and Zimbabwe was formerly called Rhodesia.

71. Om : **Russia** :: Ganges : India

The answer is **d.** The Om is a river in Russia, and the Ganges is a river in India.

72. Mt. McKinley : Highest :: Death Valley : Lowest

The answer is **d.** Mt. McKinley is the highest point in the United States, and Death Valley is the lowest.

73. Inner Core : Outer Core :: Solid : **Liquid**

The answer is **b.** The Earth's inner core is solid and its outer core is liquid.

74. Proboscis : **Nose** :: Abdomen : Gut

The answer is **b.** Proboscis means nose, and abdomen means gut.

75. $\frac{0}{5} : \frac{5}{0} :: 0 :$ undefined

The answer is **a.** 0 divided by any number is equal to 0.

76. Acute : Obtuse :: 50 : 150

The answer is **d.** An acute angle measures less than 90 degrees (for example, 50 degrees). An obtuse angle is an angle that is more than 90 degrees (for example 150 degrees).

77. Carroll : Queen of Hearts :: Barrie : **Captain Hook**

The answer is **b.** The Queen of Hearts is the villain in Lewis Carroll's book *Alice's Adventures in Wonderland.* Captain Hook is the villain in J.M. Barrie's *Peter Pan.*

78. John Proctor : **Abigail Williams** :: Biff Loman : Happy Loman

The answer is **b.** John Proctor and Abigail Williams are characters in Arthur Miller's 1953 play The Crucible. Biff Loman and Happy Loman are characters in his 1949 play Death of a Salesman.

79. Pod : Dolphin :: Herd : Cow

The answer is **b.** A pod is a group of dolphins, and a herd is a group of cows.

80. Mynah : Bird :: Terrapin : **Turtle**

The answer is **d.** A mynah is a type of bird, and a terrapin is a type of turtle.

81. Mean : Average :: Kind : **Variety**

The answer is **c.** Mean is a synonym for average, and kind is a synonym for variety.

82. Caliper : **Distance** :: Scale : Weight

The answer is **c.** A caliper is an instrument that measures distance. A scale is an instrument that measures weight.

83. Bathysphere : **Oceanographer** :: Telescope : Astronomer

The answer is **c.** A bathyshere is used by an oceanographer, and a telescope is used by an astronomer.

84. Spelunker : **Cave** :: Astronomer : Space

The answer is **c.** A spelunker is someone explores caves, and an astronomer is someone who explores space.

85. Breach : **Whale** :: Fly : Bird

The answer is **c.** Breaching is a movement made by whales, and flying is a movement made by birds.

86. Beet : Turnip :: **Pumpkin** : Watermelon

The answer is **a.** The beet and the turnip are both root vegetables. The pumpkin and the watermelon are both pepos, which are hard-skinned fruits.

87. Gondolier : Gondola :: Runner : **Rickshaw**

The answer is **a.** A person who pilots a gondola is called a gondolier. A person who pilots a rick-shaw is called a runner.

88. Eider : **Duck** :: Cedar : Tree

The answer is **c.** An eider is a type of duck, and a cedar is a type of tree.

89. $\frac{3}{4}$: 75% :: $\frac{3}{5}$: 60%

The answer is **c.** $\frac{3}{4}$ written as a percentage is 75%. $\frac{3}{5}$ written as a percentage is 60%.

90. 80 : 120 :: **200** : 300

The answer is **c.** 120 is $1\frac{1}{2}$ times 80. 300 is $1\frac{1}{2}$ times 200.

91. 360 : 2π :: Degree : **Radian**

The answer is **b.** 360 degrees equals 2π radians.

92. Dryads : Tree :: Naiads : **Water**

The answer is **d.** The Dryads were mythical tree nymphs, and the Naiads were mythical water nymphs.

93. Festoon : Chain :: Creek : **Stream**

The answer is **a.** A festoon is another word for a decorative chain, and a creek is another word for a stream.

94. Inchoate : **Unfinished** :: Gainful : Worthwhile

The answer is **c.** Inchoate is a synonym for unfinished, and gainful is a synonym for worthwhile.

95. Waterloo : Napoleon :: Appomattox : **Lee**

The answer is **c.** Waterloo was the site of Napoleon's defeat, and Appomattox was the site of General Lee's defeat.

96. Scratch : Race :: **Fold** : Poker

The answer is **d.** To scratch is to withdraw from a race, and to fold is to withdraw from poker.

97. Osier : **Basketry** :: Paper : Origami

The answer is **b.** Osier is a willow used to make baskets, and paper is used to make origami.

98. Samuel Clemens : Mark Twain :: Mary Ann Evans : **George Eliot**

The answer is **b.** Samuel Clemens wrote under the name Mark Twain, and Mary Ann Evans wrote under the name George Eliot.

99. **Truckle** : Bow :: Stumble : Fall

The answer is **a.** To truckle means to bow, and to stumble means to fall.

100. **Tassel** : Fez :: Pom-pom : Tam-o'-shanter

The answer is **d.** A tassel is part of a fez, and a pom-pom is part of a tam-o'-shanter.

101. Thresher : **Shark** :: Mastiff : Dog

The answer is **c.** Thresher is a type of shark, and mastiff is a type of dog.

102. Worth : Whort :: **Drain** : Nadir

The answer is **c.** Worth is an anagram for whort, and drain is an anagram for nadir.

103. Theology : Religion :: Phenology : **Climate**

The answer is **c.** Theology is the study of religion, and phenology is the study of climate.

104. Whoop : Exuberance :: Keen : **Mourning**

The answer is **c.** A whoop is a sound of exuberance; a keen is a sound of mourning.

105. Histrionic : **Actor** :: Didactic : Teacher

The answer is **c.** Histrionic describes the a characteristic behavior of an actor, and didactic describes a characteristic behavior of a teacher.

106. Epistemology : Philosophy :: Rationalism : **Epistemology**

The answer is **c.** Epistemology is a branch, or division, of philosophy. Similarly, within philosophy, rationalism is a division of epistemology.

107. Lock : Canal :: Dock : **Courtroom**

The answer is **a.** A lock is found in a canal, and a dock is found in a courtroom.

108. Wildcat : **Oil** :: Forage : Food

The answer is **d.** To wildcat means to look for oil, and to forage means to look for food.

109. Scimitar : **Saber** :: Revolver : Gun

The answer is **a.** A scimitar is a saber, and a revolver is a gun.

110. Probity : **Honesty** :: Probability : Likelihood

The answer is **a.** Probity means honesty, and probability means likelihood.

111. Perfidy : **Treachery** :: Satire : Parody

The answer is **a.** Perfidy is a synonym for treachery, and satire is a synonym for parody.

112. Ruth Benedict : Anthropology :: William James : **Philosophy**

The answer is **a.** Benedict was a noted American anthropologist and James was a noted American philosopher.

113. Freud : Psychoanalysis :: **Mendel** : Genetics

The answer is **a.** Freud is considered the father of psychoanalysis, and Mendel is considered the father of genetics.

114. Darwin : Mead :: Evolution : **Culture**

The answer is **d.** Charles Darwin studied evolution and Margaret Mead studied culture.

115. Hector : **Bait** :: Foil : Thwart

The answer is **a.** Hector is a synonym of bait, and foil is a synonym for thwart.

116. Bow : Obeisance :: Objective : **Goal**

The answer is **c.** A bow is a synonym for an obeisance, and an objective is a synonym for a goal.

117. Ostrom : Economic Governance :: **Krugman** : Trade Patterns

The answer is **a.** Elinor Ostrom won the Nobel Prize in Economics for her work related to economic governance. Paul Krugman won the Nobel Prize for his work with trade patterns.

118. Mohs : **Mineral** :: Richter : Earthquake

The answer is **c.** The Mohs scale is used to measure the hardness of minerals, and the Richter scale is used to measure the intensity of earthquakes.

119. Pound : United Kingdom :: **Colon** : Costa Rica

The answer is **b.** The pound is the unit of currency of the United Kingdom, and the colón is the unit of currency in Costa Rica.

120. V : X :: **L** : C

The answer is **c.** In Roman numerals, V (5) is half of X (10), and L (50) is half of C (100).

Scoring Your MAT Practice Test

As mentioned in Chapter 1, when you receive your personal score report for the official MAT, you'll be provided with a scaled score and two percentile ranks, all of which are derived from the number of items you answered correctly—known as your raw score.

Because there are different forms and formats of the official MAT, and typically 20 of the 120 questions on the official MAT are experimental and do not count toward your official scaled score and percentile ranks, it is impossible to create an accurate raw score to scaled score or raw score to percentile chart for this and the other practice tests found in this book. In the end, you are striving to correctly answer the highest number of questions as possible and familiarize yourself with the MAT format so you're fully prepared to do your best on test day. For now, what's much more important than your overall score is how you did on each of the content areas tested by the exam. You need to diagnose your strengths and weaknesses so that you can concentrate your efforts as you prepare. The question types are mixed in the practice exam, so in order to tell where your strengths and weaknesses lie, you'll need to compare your answer sheet with the following **MAT Practice Test 11 Review**, which shows which of the content areas each question falls into.

Use your performance here in conjunction with the LearningExpress Test Preparation System in Chapter 2 to help you devise a study plan. You should plan to spend more time studying areas that correspond to the questions you found hardest and less time on the content areas in which you did well.

CONTENT AREA	QUESTION NUMBERS
Language and Vocabulary	1, 9, 11, 15, 16, 24, 49, 50, 81, 93, 94, 96, 97, 99, 100, 102, 104, 105, 107, 108, 110, 111, 115, 116
Humanities	2, 3, 4, 6, 7, 21, 23, 25, 26, 38, 41, 42, 47, 48, 54, 55, 65, 77, 78, 92, 95, 98
Social Science	39, 40, 45, 52, 53, 56, 57, 59, 60, 63, 64, 66, 67, 70, 71, 72, 106, 112, 114, 117
Natural Science	10, 14, 17, 32, 43, 44, 46, 51, 58, 61, 62, 73, 74, 79, 80, 83, 84, 85, 101, 103, 113, 118
General	5, 8, 12, 13, 18, 19, 22, 27, 28, 30, 31, 33, 34, 36, 37, 69, 82, 86, 87, 88, 109, 119
Mathematics	20, 29, 35, 68, 75, 76, 89, 90, 91, 120

ADDITIONAL ONLINE PRACTICE ▶

Whether you need help building basic skills or preparing for an exam, visit the LearningExpress Practice Center! On this site, you can access additional practice materials. Using the code below, you'll be able to log in and take an additional MAT practice exam. This online practice will also provide you with:

- **Immediate scoring**
- **Detailed answer explanations**
- **Personalized recommendations for further practice and study**

Log in to the LearningExpress Practice Center by using this URL: **www.learnatest.com/practice**

This is your Access Code: **7748**

Follow the steps online to redeem your access code. After you've used your access code to register with the site, you will be prompted to create a username and password. For easy reference, record them here:

Username: _____   Password: _____

With your username and password, you can log in and answer these practice questions as many times as you like.If you have any questions or problems, please contact LearningExpress customer service at 1-800-295-9556 ext. 2, or e-mail us at **customerservice@learningexpressllc.com**.